A Brave Man Stands Firm

A BRAVE MAN STANDS FIRM

THE HISTORIC BATTLES BETWEEN
CHIEF JUSTICE JOHN MARSHALL
AND PRESIDENT THOMAS JEFFERSON

Ronald C. Zellar

Algora Publishing
New York

Library of Congress Cataloging-in-Publication Data —

Zellar, Ronald C. (Ronald Craig), 1947-
  A brave man stands firm: the historic battles between Chief Justice John Marshall
and president Thomas Jefferson / Ronald C. Zellar.
     p. cm.
  Includes bibliographical references and index.
  ISBN 978-0-87586-882-0 (soft cover: alk. paper) — ISBN 978-0-87586-883-7 (hard
cover: alk. paper) — ISBN 978-0-87586-884-4 (ebook) 1. United States—Politics and
government—1801-1809. 2. Jefferson, Thomas, 1743-1826. 3. Marshall, John, 1755-1835. 4.
Burr, Aaron, 1756-1836—Trials, litigation, etc. I. Title.
  E331.Z45 2011
  973.4'6092—dc22
                        2011014489

Printed in the United States

To Mom and Dad, Conni and Ryan

When the sun mildly shines upon us, when the gentle zephyrs play around us, we can easily proceed forward in the straight path of our duty; but when black clouds enshroud the sky with darkness, when the tempest rages, the winds howl, and the waves break over us—when the thunders awfully roar over our heads, and the lightnings of heaven blaze around us—it is then that all the energies of the human soul are called into action. It is then that the truly brave man stands firm at this post. It is then that, by an unshaken performance of his duty, man approaches the nearest possible to the Divinity. Nor is there any object in the creation on which the Supreme Being can look down with more delight and approbation than on a human being in such a situation and thus acting. May that God who now looks down upon us, who has in his infinite wisdom called you into existence, and placed you in that seat to dispense justice to your fellow citizens, to preserve and protect innocence against persecution—may that god so illuminate your understanding that you may know what is right; and may he nerve your souls with the firmness and fortitude to act according to that knowledge.

   —Luther Martin
   Closing Argument, Aaron Burr Treason Trial

TABLE OF CONTENTS

PREFACE

I am not, by profession, an historian; but I do love history. The genesis of this book was a senior history thesis paper written by my son for an honor's history class at the University of Kentucky. I had recently retired from the practice of law when my son was researching and writing his paper. At that time, I was looking for a project to occupy my time. I am an avid reader, particularly in American history, and I hoped that learning more about Jefferson and Marshall would merge my love for the law with reading and researching history. I got lucky.

Before commencing my research, I knew far more about Jefferson than Marshall. My interest in history, particularly the early years of the American republic, was first triggered by a junior high school class trip to Philadelphia to see historical sites, led by my 7th-grade history teacher, Raymond Perry. Over the years, I visited Monticello and Colonial Williamsburg on numerous occasions. Both are tributes to Jefferson, as well they should be. I read numerous biographies about Jefferson that re-affirmed my opinion that he was a great man. However, I now realize that I had only studied Jefferson from afar. In fact, I had not actually studied Jefferson at all; I only digested the favorable opinions of the authors.

As for Marshall, I remember cursory mention of him in junior high and high school history classes, particularly in relation to the concept of judicial review. I learned somewhat more as an undergraduate student in various history and political science classes. While in law school, I read portions of

Marshall's great Constitutional law decisions: *Marbury v. Madison, McCulloch v. Maryland, Cohens v. Virginia,* and *Gibbons v. Ogden.* The historical context of the cases, however, was barely explored. After law school, I read little about Marshall. I skimmed Leonard Baker's *John Marshall: A Life in Law* when it was published in 1974. At that time, Marshall did not seem as interesting as Jefferson. My opinion has since changed.

I first became aware of certain Jefferson character flaws while reading Fawn Brodie's *Thomas Jefferson: An Intimate History,* also published in 1974. At the time, I hated her book. It was consistent with the "psycho-babble" of the 1960s and 1970s; I considered it one more attempt to tear down one of our icons. I was particularly incensed with Ms. Brodie's treatment of the "alleged" relationship of Jefferson with his slave, Sally Hemmings.

Now, after researching Thomas Jefferson, I realize that Ms. Brodie legitimately exposed many of his character flaws. Although Jefferson was an extraordinarily brilliant man, I see him now with more than his share of warts. Jefferson's opinions about slavery, his affairs with two married women (Betsey Walker and Maria Cosway) and with one of his slaves are troubling. (These topics are not the subject of this book, although I have been advised that to be "successful" a book needs sex). Even more disturbing are Jefferson's radical opinions (i.e., "the earth belongs to the living" and "a little rebellion now and then is a good thing"). Jefferson's reputation as the great protector of civil liberties was brilliantly challenged in Leonard Levy's *Jefferson and Civil Liberties: The Darker Side* and is most vividly portrayed throughout the prosecution of Aaron Burr. Perhaps of even greater concern to me, however, is the manner in which Jefferson treated people; particularly those with whom he disagreed. Jefferson had strong and bitter disagreements with George Washington, Alexander Hamilton, Aaron Burr, John and Abigail Adams, Patrick Henry, and John Marshall, among others. When Jefferson disagreed with someone, he exhibited a mean streak that bordered on hatred.

In contrast to Jefferson, I have found John Marshall to be a truly engaging, good, and brilliant man. He treated people with dignity and respect, even those with whom he disagreed. Thomas Jefferson and Judge Spencer Roane of Virginia appear to be the only persons Marshall disdained. During my research, I reread Chief Justice Marshall's great expositions on Constitutional law, as well as his letters and comments made about him by his contemporaries. I was particularly impressed with Marshall's court management of the Burr trial. It was a brilliant performance. Although Jefferson was always the smartest person in the room, Marshall (a brilliant man himself) was more down to earth. Future Supreme Court Associate Justice Story wrote, after meeting Marshall for the first time in 1808: "I love his laugh. It is too hearty for an intriguer."[1] Chief Justice John Roberts recently contrasted President Jefferson and Chief Justice Marshall: "Jefferson certainly did not have the common touch....[W]hen you look at him side by side with Marshall, Marshall comes across as more substantial, certainly more likeable. Yes, I think they'd both invite you to share their table and pour you a drink, but you kind of think you'd have a very academic discussion with Jefferson and you'd have a good time with Marshall."[2] Marshall, unfortunately, is not as well known as Jefferson.

This book will focus on the intersection between the two presidential terms of Thomas Jefferson and his relations with the judiciary, particularly Chief Justice John Marshall. In reality, there was no relationship; it was a war. During the Burr prosecution, Jefferson was not concerned with civil liberties; he was vindictive and at his worst. Marshall protected the civil liberties of the accused and preserved the rule of law.

I once read that "History is only 'the recorded part of the remembered part of the observed part of what happened."[3] Researching this book has been exciting and proved those words true. During my legal career, in preparation for trial, I interviewed witnesses and gathered relevant evidence. In researching this book, there were no live witnesses to interview. However, I was amazed at the treasure trove of contemporary information available. The papers of Thomas Jefferson, John Marshall, George Washington, and others provide extensive information. So, too, do the contemporaneous writings of two United States senators, John Quincy Adams and William Plumer. Information available online from the Library of Congress, particularly the Annals of Congress and the Thomas Jefferson Papers, proved useful. Multi-volume biographies written about John Marshall (Albert Beveridge) and Thomas Jefferson (Dumas Malone) were particularly helpful.

1 Joseph Story to Samuel P.F. Fay, February 25, 1808. Joseph Story. *Life and Letters of Joseph Story.* Edited by William W. Story. Volume I, pp. 166-168.
2 Jeffrey Rosen. *The Supreme Court: The Personalities and Rivalries That Defined America.* New York: Henry Holt and Company, LLC, 2006, pp. 223-224.
3 Willis P. Whichard. "A Place for Walter Clark in the American Judicial Tradition," *North Carolina Law Review*, Vol. 63 (January 1985), pp. 284, 287. From an address of Dr. George Taylor, Professor of History, University of North Carolina-Chapel Hill, February 8, 1960.

Actual quotations from Jefferson's letters, Marshall's opinions, and other original sources provide a more enlightening and accurate reflection of events than the usual paraphrasing. Thus, original sources are necessarily quoted at length.

Introduction

I considered America as my country, and Congress as my government.

—John Marshall

His lax lounging manners have made him popular with the bulk of the people in Richmond, and a profound hypocrisy with many thinking men in our country.

—Thomas Jefferson on John Marshall

After declaring independence from Great Britain and winning the Rev-olutionary War, the United States became a self-governing nation. The Constitution was drafted in 1787 and ratified by the states in 1788. Dur-ing George Washington's two-term presidency, commencing in 1789, he defined the office and paved the way for future chief executives. Washing-ton wrote famously that he "walked on untrodden soil."[4] James Madison, a primary actor in drafting, adopting and ratifying the Constitution, drafted the Bill of Rights during the first session of the first Congress and it became the first Ten Amendments to the Constitution. Madison was instrumental in defining the role of the Legislative Branch. However, for the first twelve

---

4 George Washington to Catharine Sawbridge Mccaulay Graham, January 9, 1790. The Papers of George Washington, Digital Edition, University of Virginia Press.

years of our newly-formed government, the third branch of government, the Judiciary, had yet to be defined.

Most believe the event that began to define the Judicial Branch occurred in 1801 when President John Adams nominated then Secretary of State John Marshall to become Chief Justice of the United States Supreme Court. A month after Marshall was sworn in as the fourth chief justice of the United States (John Jay, John Rutledge, and Oliver Ellsworth served previously), Thomas Jefferson was inaugurated as the third president. President Jefferson's election was historic; it marked the first time that the presidency changed political parties and the change was peaceful. Throughout history, such a peaceful transfer of power was unprecedented. Thomas Jefferson often referred to his election as "the Revolution of 1800" or the "second American Revolution."

Upon his assuming office on March 4, 1801, President Jefferson's Republican Party was in control of both the Executive and Legislative branches of the federal government. However, to President Jefferson's dismay, the Judicial Branch consisted exclusively of Federalist appointees, including Chief Justice John Marshall and all five associate justices on the United States Supreme Court. The relationship between President Jefferson, Chief Justice John Marshall and the judiciary during his presidency is the subject this book. Four major events will be discussed; events sometimes referred to as Jefferson's war on the judiciary. If it was a war, Chief Justice Marshall and his colleagues lost the early battles; however, at the conclusion of the Jefferson Administration, John Marshall and the judiciary prevailed. The role of the judiciary had been defined and was now a co-equal branch of government.

The trial of former vice president Aaron Burr for treason in 1807, the last great battle during the Jefferson presidency between President Jefferson and Chief Justice Marshall, is the primary focus of this book. The Burr case involved, by far, the most open and active role taken by President Jefferson in his battles with the judiciary. In earlier battles, although President Jefferson provided direction to supporters, his fingerprints cannot be directly identified. In contrast, President Jefferson publicly charged and denounced Aaron Burr as a traitor before Burr was ever charged with a crime, let alone convicted. Jefferson was extensively involved in Burr's prosecution, providing advice to the government's chief prosecutor on trial tactics and evidence. The presiding judge in the Burr trial was Chief Justice John Marshall, who sat as circuit judge. The trial became a monumental battle, surely the trial of the nineteenth century.

Three other conflicts between President Jefferson and Chief Justice Marshall during Jefferson's presidency will be described. The first involved repeal of the Judiciary Act of 1801 and adoption of the Judiciary Act of 1802. The second and, perhaps, most famous conflict involved the *Marbury v. Madison* case. Here, the Supreme Court asserted the principle of judicial review, a legal doctrine that insured that the judiciary would become a co-equal branch of government.[5] The third conflict involved impeachment of federal judges. The first impeachment involved a mentally ill Federal District Judge. The second effort was of far greater importance; the impeachment of Supreme Court Associate Justice Samuel Chase. Federalists not only were concerned that Republicans were attempting to remove a strong Federalist associate justice from the bench, but strongly believed that impeachment of Justice Chase was intended to send a message to other Federalist judges. Many thought that if the Chase impeachment was successful, Chief Justice Marshall would be next. Federalists believed that President Jefferson would not stop until the Court reflected his political views. Chase was acquitted and the politically charged atmosphere began to cool; the impeachment arrow in the quiver of Republicans was never used again by Jefferson and his supporters.[6]

Who were Thomas Jefferson and John Marshall and why did they become such great antagonists? Unquestionably, they were two of the most brilliant men of the founding generation. Both were from privileged backgrounds, Jefferson more so than Marshall. Both were close to their fathers and traced their ancestry to the powerful Randolph family of Virginia. In fact, Thomas Jefferson and John Marshall were third cousins, once removed.[7] Thomas Jefferson, twelve years older and historically better known, was the primary author of the Declaration of Independence, served as governor of Virginia, ambassador to France, secretary of state, vice president, and president for two terms. He was founder of the University of Virginia. His legacy extended through the presidential administrations of fellow Virginians James Madison and James Monroe. John Marshall, a practicing at-

---

5 James F. Simon, *What Kind of Nation*, pp. 173-190.
6 Melvin I. Urofsky, "Thomas Jefferson and John Marshall: What Kind of Constitution Shall We Have?" pp. 116-17; Simon, pp. 199-205.
7 Urofsky, p. 109.

torney, served in various governmental capacities, both state and federal, for almost sixty years, including service in the Revolutionary War, delegate to the Virginia Constitutional Ratification Convention, envoy and minister plenipotentiary to France, congressman, secretary of state, and for the final thirty-five years of his life, chief justice of the United States Supreme Court. Marshall's tenure as chief justice touched on the presidential administrations of John Adams, Thomas Jefferson, James Madison, James Monroe, John Quincy Adams, and Andrew Jackson. The conflicts between these two giants would become legendary.

There is one telling difference between Thomas Jefferson and John Marshall. Marshall, typical of most veterans of the Revolutionary War, believed that order and a strong central government was a necessity. John Marshall wrote in his *Autobiographical Sketch*, that from the time of his service in the Revolution, he "was confirmed in the habit of considering America as my country, and congress as my government."[8] In contrast, Jefferson, a true revolutionary, wrote to Abigail Adams in 1787 about Shay's Rebellion: "I like a little rebellion now and then." How different from Marshall, Washington, and other Federalists who deplored the anarchy of the 1780s that followed the War.[9] Marshall believed in an ordered society. Jefferson, more a philosopher and a romantic, was interested in ideas rather than order; John Marshall was interested in doing whatever it would take to make the United States successful. As a child, Marshall read and transcribed Alexander Pope's *Essay on Man*, a series of moral essays. Pope wrote: "Order is heaven's first law..."[10] and "An honest man is the noblest work of God."[11]

Historian Forrest McDonald opined, with some exaggeration, that Jefferson: "...was exposed to and felt himself lacking in the attributes of the Young Buck Virginian. His distant cousin John Marshall and Patrick Henry epitomized the type: neither of them ever seemed to study, both wore hunting clothes and chewed tobacco, both were surrounded by giggling girls who idolized them, both were men's men whom other men flocked around

8 *"The Events of My Life": An Autobiographical Sketch of John Marshall.* Ann Arbor and Washington, D.C: Clements Library, University of Michigan and Supreme Court Historical Society, 2001, p.17.

9 Thomas Jefferson to Abigail Adams, February 22, 1787. *PTJ*, Volume 11, pp. 174-175.

10   Alexander Pope. *Essay on Man*, Epistle IV, line 49.

11 Beveridge I, pp. 44-46; John Marshall. *The Autobiographical Sketch.*

enviously and attentively and in whose company others pretended to be comfortable. All his adult life Jefferson hated them."[12]

Prior to Thomas Jefferson becoming president in 1801, Jefferson and Marshall knew of one another, but had limited direct contact. During the controversy over relations with Great Britain, Marshall was a strong supporter of President George Washington and the Jay Treaty. In contrast, Jefferson opposed the Washington Administration and was far more supportive of France. Jefferson found time to criticize John Marshall's support for the Washington Administration in a letter to James Madison: "Though Marshall will be able to embarrass the Republican party in the assembly a good deal, yet upon the whole, his having gone into it will be of service. He has been hitherto able to do more mischief, acting under the mask of republicanism than he will be able to do after throwing it plainly off. His lax lounging manners have made him popular with the bulk of the people of Richmond, and a profound hypocrisy with many thinking men in our country."[13]

When Jefferson became president, he would have direct contact with recently appointed Chief Justice Marshall. Jefferson and Marshall had diametrically opposed views about the country and the judiciary. They clashed throughout Jefferson's eight years in office. Jefferson, who professed to be a man of the people, was an aristocrat, rarely coming into contact with the people; Marshall, although more aristocratic in his political thinking, was a man of the people. Jefferson was a staunch states-rights proponent; Marshall a nationalist, although he had great love for his home state of Virginia.

It has been often said that "an institution is lengthened by the shadow of one man."[14] This is certainly true of John Marshall, who established the Court, made the judiciary a co-equal branch of government, and served as Chief Justice of the United States Supreme Court from 1801–1835.

---

12   Forrest McDonald. *The Presidency of Thomas Jefferson.* Lawrence:University Press of Kansas, 1976, p.31.
13   Thomas Jefferson to James Madison, November 26, 1795. *PTJ* 28, pp. 539-540.
14   This phrase is usually attributed to Ralph Waldo Emerson in his *Self-Reliance Essays,* first published in 1841.

TRIAL OF THE CENTURY: THE TREASON PROSECUTION OF AARON BURR

Our president is a lawyer and a great one too. He certainly ought to know what it is that constitutes a war. Six months ago, he proclaimed that there was a civil war. And yet, for six months have they been hunting for it, and it still can not find one spot where it existed.

—Aaron Burr

This is a peculiar case, sir. The president has undertaken to prejudge my client by declaring, that 'Of his guilt there can be no doubt.' He has assumed to himself the knowledge of the Supreme Being himself, and pretended to search the heart of my highly respected friend (Burr). He has proclaimed him a traitor in the face of the country which has rewarded him. He has let slip the dogs of war, the hell-hounds of persecution, to hunt down my friend.

If I were to name this, I would call it the Will-o'-the wisp treason. For though it is said to be here and there and everywhere, yet it is no-where.

—Luther Martin

1. Background of the Burr Conspiracy

The Aaron Burr treason trial was one of the most publicized, controversial, and infamous trials in American legal history. It was unquestionably the trial of the nineteenth century. In addition to former vice president Aaron Burr standing trial for treason, the cast of trial characters has never been equaled. The protagonist and antagonist were, respectively, Chief Justice John Marshall and President Thomas Jefferson. Attorneys for the prosecution included United States Attorney George Hay and Special United States Attorney William Wirt, noted author and future United States Attorney General; defense attorneys included Luther Martin (long-time Maryland Attorney General), John Wickham (prominent Richmond attorney), and Edmund Randolph (former Governor and Attorney General of Virginia and Attorney General and Secretary State of the United States), with legal assistance provided by the accused, Aaron Burr, himself an accomplished attorney. Other key participants included the highest ranking military officer of the United States, General James Wilkinson; an Irish immigrant, Harmon Blennerhassett; and a then unknown writer, Washington Irving, who covered a portion of Burr's trial for a local New York newspaper. Cameo appearances were made by future president Andrew Jackson and future general of the army Winfield Scott.

The significance of this case cannot be overstated. Executive privilege was considered by an American court for the first time, personal clashes between President Thomas Jefferson and Chief Justice John Marshall became public, and an unfamiliar Thomas Jefferson was exposed.[15] Marshall was at his best, balancing judgment with incomparable legal ability and talent. Jefferson was at his worst, displaying meanness and little regard for civil liberties. Jefferson had been warned about Burr's activities for more than a year before he took action, ultimately choosing to believe a General who had conspired with Burr and was on the payroll of a foreign government (Spain). Jefferson made promises to a witness and later broke those promises, provided extraordinary advice and direction to the chief prosecutor throughout legal proceedings, and never accepted the judgment of the court or jury in this case.

AARON BURR

Understanding Aaron Burr is essential to understanding subsequent legal proceedings. Burr was truly an enigma. We know one thing for sure—after all investigations, indictments and trials, Aaron Burr was never convicted by a court or jury of a crime. Perhaps this explains why historians and legal scholars are unable to ascertain Burr's intent and whether Burr did, in fact, commit treason against the United States.

Aaron Burr was born in 1756 in New Jersey. The same age as John Marshall, he was 13 years Thomas Jefferson's junior. Unlike Jefferson and Marshall, who grew up in rural Virginia, Burr was raised in more populous areas (New Jersey and New York). Although Jefferson and Marshall shared a common heritage with the prominent Randolph family of Virginia, Burr's family was far more prestigious. Burr's grandfather was Jonathon Edwards, the famous New England preacher. Burr's father was the second president of the College of New Jersey, later Princeton University. He entered the College of New Jersey at age 13, graduating three years later. He distinguished himself during the American Revolution, particularly in the Battle of Quebec. General George Washington requested that Burr serve on his staff; the offer was declined. Washington later claimed that he never trusted Burr: "Colonel Burr is a brave and able officer but the question is, whether he has not equal talents at intrigue."[16]

---

15   Historian Leonard Levy referred to this as Jefferson's "dark side." Leonard W. Levy. *Jefferson and Civil Liberties: The Darker Side.*

16   General Washington quoted by John Adams in a letter to James Lloyd, February 17, 1815, Works of John Adams, 10:124; Edward J. Larson. *A Magnificent Catastrophe: The Tumultuous Election of 1800.* New York: Free Press, 2007, p.89.

After resigning from military service, Burr was admitted to the New York Bar in 1782 and became a prominent attorney. He married Theodosia Prevost and their marriage produced one child, daughter Theodosia. After his wife's death in 1792, Burr's daughter became the focal point in his life. Many historians refer to Burr as America's first feminist based upon his treatment of his daughter; not only for her formal education, but for Burr's insistence that she not be denied opportunities available solely to men.

Aaron Burr's political career began in 1784 when he was elected to the New York State Assembly. In 1791, Burr was selected United States Senator from New York, serving until 1797. After Burr defeated candidates supported by the powerful Clinton and Schuyler families, political forces were unleashed against him. These attacks, led by Alexander Hamilton, would ultimately result in Burr's political demise. In 1797, Burr unsuccessfully ran for vice president of the United States.

To enhance Thomas Jefferson's electoral prospects in the 1800 presidential election, Jefferson persuaded New Yorker Burr to become his vice presidential running mate. At that time, the Constitution provided that the candidate with the most electoral votes would be president and the runner-up vice president.[17] When Jefferson and Burr tied with 73 electoral votes, the contest was thrown into the House of Representatives for decision. After thirty-six contested ballots, Thomas Jefferson was declared president. Aaron Burr's failure to voluntarily withdraw from this contest severely strained future relations between Jefferson and Burr.

Following the electoral controversy, President Jefferson ignored Vice President Burr's patronage requests and isolated him. Their relationship was irretrievably damaged during debate over repeal of the Judiciary Act of 1801. When Vice President Burr, as President of the Senate, attempted to minimize partisanship, he was considered too even-handed to suit Jefferson. Burr later appeared at a Federalist sponsored celebration of George Washington's birthday and offered a toast to "the union of all honest men," further alienating him from Jefferson.[18] In addition to Jefferson, Burr had another prominent adversary: Alexander Hamilton. During the election of 1800, Hamilton urged his followers to support Jefferson over Burr (although Jefferson was hardly a Hamilton favorite). Hamilton wrote: "Burr will cer-

---

17 United States Constitution, Article II, Section 1.
18   Nancy Isenberg. *Fallen Founder: The Life of Aaron Burr*, pp. 245-246. This is a recent, well written and insightful biography about Aaron Burr.

tainly attempt to reform the government *à la Bonaparte*. He is as unprincipled and dangerous as any country can boast—as true a Cataline as ever met in midnight conclave."[19]

During his first term, President Jefferson made sure that the 1800 electoral vote controversy would never be repeated; a Constitutional Amendment was adopted clarifying the procedure for election of future presidential and vice presidential candidates.[20] By early 1804, it was apparent that Burr's days as vice president were numbered. Jefferson did not want Burr on the ticket during his re-election bid. Chief Justice Marshall observed to his brother: "There have been many caucuses lately among the democrats about which some curious stories are told. Burr is not only to be dropped but he has very narrowly as it is said escaped being denounced as a *traitor*. Some prudential considerations have induced the resolution to make the blow less open but not less deadly than was at first designed."[21] (Emphasis added.)

After Burr learned that he would not continue as vice president, he ran for Governor of New York. It was during the 1804 gubernatorial election that Burr's conflict with Alexander Hamilton reached its zenith; Burr believed that Hamilton was instrumental in his defeat by making statements defaming his character. Burr challenged Hamilton, requesting a retraction; when Hamilton refused, the famous duel ensued. On July 14, 1804, at the "interview," Burr killed Hamilton. Burr was indicted for Hamilton's death in New York and New Jersey. Burr's political career was already severely damaged by his estrangement from Jefferson and his gubernatorial defeat; the duel with Hamilton all but ended it. Perhaps as importantly, Burr's indictment prevented him from returning to New York to resume his lucrative law practice. After the fatal dual with Hamilton, Burr described his circumstances as being "under ostracism" and "in New York I am to be disenfran-

---

19 Alexander Hamilton to James Ashton Bayard, August 6, 1800. *The Works of Alexander Hamilton*, Volume X. Henry Cabot Lodge, Editor, pp. 384-388; Catilene was an official in the early Roman Empire. In 63 B.C. he ran against Cicero for consul and was defeated. After his defeat, he plotted an uprising to seize power by force, to plunder and destroy Rome, and to destroy the Senate. Cicero learned about Catilene's plot and delivered an oration against him. Catilene and his followers were forced to leave Rome. Given a death sentence, he was to later die in battle.

20 United States Constitution, Amendment XII, ratified June 15, 1804.

21 John Marshall to James M. Marshall, February 2, 1804. PJM VI, pp. 255-256.

chised, and in New Jersey hanged. Having substantial objections to both, I shall not for the present, hazard either, but shall seek another country."[22]

Although ostracized by the Jefferson administration during his four years as vice president, with the Senate impeachment trial of Associate Justice Samuel Chase pending, President Jefferson and his Administration paid Burr great attention. Senator Plumer of New Hampshire wrote: "I never had any doubts of [Democratic] joy for the death of Hamilton, my only doubts were whether they would manifest that joy, by caressing his murderer. Those doubts are now dispelled—Mr. Jefferson has shown more attention & invited Mr. Burr oftener to his house within this three weeks than ever he did in the course of the same time before."[23] Burr, as president of the Senate, presided over the Chase impeachment trial. In the three month period prior to and during the impeachment trial, Jefferson dined with Burr at least six times: November 9 and December 24 in 1804 and January 11, February 7, March 5, and March 7 in 1805. During this time, two Burr relatives and Burr's friend General James Wilkinson were appointed by President Jefferson to positions in the new Louisiana Territory, appointments that would significantly impact Burr's future intrigues. Following the impeachment trial, Burr's term as vice president concluded: he was now a man without a country.[24]

Aaron Burr was always difficult to understand. John Quincy Adams wrote:

> Burr's life, take it all together, was such as in any country of sound morals his friends would be desirous of burying into sound oblivion. The son and grandson of two able and eminent Calvinistic devines, he had no religious principle, and little, if any, sense of responsibility to a moral Governor of the universe. He lost both his father and mother before he was three years old, and with them appears to have lost all religious education. He lived and died as a man of the world—brave, generous, hospitable, and courteous, but ambitious, rapacious, faithless, and intriguing. The character raised him within a hair's breadth of the Presidency of the United States, sunk him within a hair's breadth of a gibbet and halter for treason, and

---

22   Aaron Burr to Joseph Alston, March 22, 1805. Matthew L. Davis. *Memoirs of Aaron Burr, Volume II*, p. 365. Alston was Burr's son-in-law.

23   William Plumer's *Memorandum of Proceedings*, p. 203.

24   Mary Ellen Scofield. "The Fatigues of His Table: The Politics of Presidential Dining During the Jefferson Administration," *Journal of the Early Republic*, Vol. 26 (Fall 2006), pp. 466-67; *Dictionary of American Biography*, Volume II. Edited by Allan Johnson, and Dumas Malone. pp. 314-321. Although written in a different time and context, Edward Everett Hale's *A Man Without a Country* comes to mind.

left him, for the last thirty years of his life, a blasted monument of Shakespeare's vaulting ambition.[25]

Noted historian Gordon S. Wood recently addressed why both Jefferson and Hamilton opposed Burr:

> In their minds, Burr posed far more than a threat to the American Revolution than either of them ever thought the other did. Burr threatened nothing less than the great revolutionary hope, indeed, the entire republican experiment, that some sort of disinterested politics, if only among the elite, could prevail in America. Because of this threat, Hamilton and Jefferson together eventually brought Burr down. To both men the treason that Burr committed to his class was far more serious than any supposed treason to his country. It was the real treason of Aaron Burr.[26]

BURR'S ADVENTURES

Many Americans, President Jefferson included, had looked toward expansion in the West for years. Some had thoughts about annexing the West and Mexico. Aaron Burr discussed liberation of Spanish colonies with high-ranking officials. For example, he discussed this with John Jay, diplomat and first Chief Justice of the United States. Jay advised Burr that he saw nothing wrong with Burr's ideas about revolutionizing and taking the Spanish Territories.[27] Jefferson had earlier expressed similar sentiments to James Madison in 1786 and 1787.[28] Jefferson opined that the country may be too large and that someday the Appalachian states may desire to go their way.[29] American interest in the west and the Spanish Territories was not unusual.

During negotiations for the Louisiana Territory with France, Jefferson understood that there was a possibility that the western states and territories would choose to separate from the United States. Jefferson was not necessarily opposed to separation, if that was what western settlers desired. President Jefferson wrote: "The future inhabitants of the Atlantic &

---

25 *The Diary of John Quincy Adams, 1794-1845*, p. 487.

26 Gordon S. Wood. *Revolutionary Characters: What Made the Founders Different.* New York: Penquin Press, 2006, p.242. The preceding biographical information was based upon biographies of Burr by Milton Lomask and Nancy Isenberg.

27 Milton Lomask. *Aaron Burr: The Conspiracy and Years in Exile, 1805-1836.* Volume II, p. 7.

28 Thomas Jefferson to James Madison, December 16, 1786; June 20, 1787. *PTJ* 10, pp. 602-606 and *PTJ* 11, pp. 480-484.

29 Lomask, p. 8.

Mississippi States will be our sons. We leave them in distinct but bordering establishments. We think we see their happiness in their union, & we wish it. Events may prove it otherwise; and if they see their interest in separation, why should we take side with our Atlantic rather than our Mississippi descendants? It is the elder and the younger son differing. God bless them both, & keep them in union, if it be for their good, but separate them, if it be better...."[30] President Jefferson expressed similar sentiments to Doctor Joseph Priestly:

> Whether we remain in one confederacy, or form into Atlantic and Mississippi confederacies, I believe not very important to the happiness of either part. Those of the western confederacy will be as much our children & descendants as those of the eastern, and I feel myself as much identified with that country, in future time, as with this; and did I now foresee a separation at a future day, yet I should feel the duty & the desire to promote the western interests as zealously as the eastern, doing all the good for both portions of our future family which should fall within my power.[31]

While still vice president, Burr met with British Ambassador to the United States Anthony Merry in early 1804 and sought British financial assistance for prospective activities in the western territories and Mexico (this meeting was unknown at the time of the Burr trial).[32] In 1804, war with Spain appeared inevitable. While in Europe, James Monroe and John Armstrong advised President Jefferson to abandon hopes for negotiation with Spain and to declare war.[33] As late as a Cabinet meeting on November 12, 1806, war with Spain was discussed.

In 1805, following his vice presidential term, Burr departed on a 3,000 mile trip commencing in Pittsburgh; he planned to travel in a houseboat down the Ohio and Mississippi Rivers. In May 1805, Burr met wealthy Harmon Blennerhassett, who lived on a 179 acre island paradise on the Ohio River near present day Marietta, Ohio and Parkersburg, West Virginia (the island was then part of Virginia). Blennerhassett, born in 1765, was an Irish-born lawyer who immigrated to the United States in 1796. Shortly before his

---

30 Letter from Thomas Jefferson to John C. Breckinridge, August 12, 1803; *Thomas Jefferson: Writings.* Merrill D. Peterson, Editor, pp. 1136-1139.

31 Thomas Jefferson to Doctor Joseph Priestley, January 29, 1804. *Works* X, pp. 69-72.

32 Letter from Anthony Merry to Lord Harrowby, August 6, 1804: Henry Adams. *History of the United States During the Administrations of Thomas Jefferson,* p. 571.

33 Lomask, p. 94; Dumas Malone. *Jefferson the President: Second Term 1805-1809: Jefferson and His Time,* Vol. 5, p. 55.

departure from his native land, he married his niece. Since this was considered an invalid marriage, he fled his native land to avoid gossip and scandal. He chose the western United States and found an island to protect his privacy. Blennerhassett built an estate, an Irish country home with serpentine walkways and landscaped elegantly with flowers and plants.[34] Blennerhassett became an avid supporter of Aaron Burr, both financially and logistically, and wrote a number of newspaper articles supporting him.

After meeting Blennerhassett, Burr continued his westward trip, visiting Cincinnati, Ohio and Lexington and Frankfort, Kentucky. He met with a number of prominent politicians before arriving in Nashville, Tennessee in late May 1805. There he was hosted by General Andrew Jackson and treated as a conquering hero. Burr continued his trip and met with General James Wilkinson, recently appointed Governor of the Louisiana Territory, at Fort Massac, located on the Ohio River near the southern tip of present day Illinois, around June 8, 1805. Wilkinson provided Burr with an elegant barge and letters of introduction for Burr to meet prominent people upon his arrival in New Orleans. Burr was honored at numerous balls and banquets; he stayed for three weeks.

GENERAL JAMES WILKINSON

Perhaps the key player in this drama other than Burr was General James Wilkinson. There is little doubt that Wilkinson was the most duplicitous operative in the affair. Plans later attributed to Burr were most likely crafted by Wilkinson. Wilkinson was the leading military officer of the United States and since the Revolution, lived in the western states and territories of the United States. Wilkinson knew Mexico, the western territories and the western states far better than most Americans; certainly better than Burr. In spite of many signs that would point to Wilkinson's deceit and dishonesty, President Jefferson supported Wilkinson.

James Wilkinson was born in 1757 in Maryland. He became a captain in the Revolutionary Army, where he first gained notoriety. He served under General Benedict Arnold and later General Horatio Gates. Always a self-promoter, he participated in the Conway Cabal, an aborted attempt to remove General Washington from command of the Continental Army. Wilkinson carried a letter to the Continental Congress that called for Washington's removal. During either a drunken conversation at a tavern

---

34   Isenberg, p. 293.

or due to his self-appointed importance, Wilkinson informed the wrong people about the contents of the letter he was delivering. Word of the letter made its way to General Washington and the attempted coup was foiled. Incredibly, Wilkinson landed on his feet and was named Secretary of the Board of War and later Clothier General of the Continental Army. He was later forced to resign after accounting irregularities were uncovered. After the War, Wilkinson moved to Kentucky and opened a mercantile business. While in Kentucky, Wilkinson commenced a treasonous relationship with Spain. He was known to the Spanish government as "Agent-13" and became a Spanish pensioner (on the payroll of the Spanish government). He received payments from Spain for his assistance, payments that continued during the Burr treason prosecution in 1807. Wilkinson submitted a memorial (affidavit) to Spain, declaring his allegiance to the Spanish crown, and provided formal reports.[35]

Wilkinson's loyalty was questioned by four presidents: Washington, Adams, Jefferson, and Madison. Although his illicit relationship with Spain was suspected, it was never proved during his lifetime; his nefarious activity was not confirmed for more than 100 years. In 1805, he was appointed Governor of the Louisiana Territory by President Jefferson in addition to duties as general of the army. It was during this time that Wilkinson commenced discussions with Burr about Mexico and the western territories.[36]

Toward the end of his term as vice president, Burr met General Wilkinson at Burr's home in New York City to discuss western adventures. Wilkinson wrote Burr on May 23, 1804, "to save time of which I need much and have little, I propose to take a Bed with you this night, if it may done without observation or intrusion—Answer me and if in the affirmative I will be with [you] at 30 after the 8th hour."[37] During their meeting, Burr studied maps of the Texas, Mexico, and New Mexico territories provided by Wilkinson, territories controlled by Spain. Invasions by land and sea were discussed. Burr and Wilkinson met a second time in Washington near the conclusion of Burr's term as vice president. Burr and Wilkinson were hardly

---

35   William R. Shepard. "Wilkinson and the Beginnings of the Spanish Conspiracy." *The American Historical Review*, Vol. 9, No. 3 (April 1904), pp. 490-506.

36   *Dictionary of American Biography*, Volume X. Malone, Editor. 1936, pp. 222-226; Andro Linklater. *An Artist in Treason: The Extraordinary Double Life of General James Wilkinson.*

37   James Wilkinson to Aaron Burr, May 23, 1804. *Some Papers of Aaron Burr.* Edited by Worthington C. Ford, pp. 82-83; *Tarnished Warrior-Major General James Wilkinson.* James R. Jacobs, p. 191; Linklater, p. 215.

strangers; they had known each other since service in the Revolutionary War. In an 1805 letter, Burr wrote: "The Governor, General Wilkinson has been long my intimate friend...."[38]

BURR'S ADVENTURES CONTINUE

From July to September 1805, Burr worked his way back up the Mississippi and Ohio Rivers, stopping again in Tennessee, Missouri, and Kentucky. He met again with Wilkinson, this time in St. Louis. Burr returned to Washington in late fall 1805.

Burr's activities and travels began to arouse suspicion. As early as August 2, 1805, *The United States Gazette* (Philadelphia) published an article about Burr's activities:

> How long shall it be before we shall hear of Col. Burr being at the head of a revolution party on the western waters?
>
> Is it a fact that Col. Burr has formed a plan to engage the adventurous and enterprising young men from the Atlantic states to come into Louisiana?
>
> Is it one of the inducements that an immediate convention will be called from the states bordering on the Ohio and Mississippi, to form a separate government?
>
> Is it another that all the public lands are to be seized and partitioned among those states, except what is reserved for the warlike friends and followers of Burr in the revolution?
>
> Is it the plan for the new states to grant these lands in bounties to entice inhabitants from the Atlantic states?
>
> How soon will the forts and magazines, and all the military posts at New Orleans and on the Mississippi be in the hands of Col. Burr's revolution party?
>
> How soon will Col. Burr engage in the reduction of Mexico, by granting liberty to its inhabitants, and seizing its treasures, aided by British ships and forces?[39]

Upon Burr's return to Washington, he met President Jefferson in March 1806. According to Jefferson's notes, Burr requested government employ-

---

38 Aaron Burr to Rufus Easton, March 18, 1805. Aaron Burr. *Correspondence and Public Papers of Aaron Burr, Volume II.* Mary-Jo Kline, Editor, pp. 918-919.
39 *United States Gazette,* August 2, 1805.

ment, possibly as an ambassador. Jefferson was unwilling to make such an offer, advising Burr that he had lost the confidence of the public.[40]

Burr once again moved down the river in fall 1806. Before commencing his trip, he visited Colonel George Morgan, a Revolutionary War veteran. In September, Burr met with Blennerhassett and arranged for food supplies and construction of approximately fifteen boats that could carry up to 500 men. After departing Blennerhassett's Island, Burr met with General Jackson in Nashville. There, he contracted for building six boats. Simultaneously, Burr purchased approximately 400,000 acres on the Washita River located in present day Louisiana and Mississippi, ostensibly for settlement by Burr and his followers.

What was Burr's intent? There are three possibilities. First, his activity may have been perfectly innocent. He purchased 400,000 acres on the Washita River for the purpose of settling this land with friends and supporters. Burr wrote a letter to Treasury Secretary Albert Gallatin in July 1806 inquiring about purchase of the Bastrop lands on the Washita River (present day northwestern Louisiana).[41] Second, until early 1806, war with Spain appeared inevitable.[42] The likely scenario was that Burr contemplated invasion of Mexico and other Spanish territories *after* the United States declared war against Spain. If war was declared, an invasion by Burr and his followers into Mexico would be a "filibuster." (A filibuster is a legal invasion by a private army without government sanction). However, without a formal declaration of war, entry by force and taking of Spanish land by private citizens of the United States was a violation of the Neutrality Act, a high misdemeanor. (Burr was later charged with treason and violation of the Neutrality Act). In October 1806, Burr wrote Governor William Henry Harrison of the Indiana Territory and opined that he considered war with Spain inevitable.[43] Third, Burr and his supporters may have intended to invade Mexico and sever the western portion of the United States, primarily land west of the Alleghany Mountains. This would be treason. Burr directly

---

40 Thomas Jefferson. *The Complete Anas of Thomas Jefferson.* Edited by Franklin B. Swivel, pp. 237-241.

41 Aaron Burr to Albert Gallatin, July 31, 1806. *Correspondence and Public Papers of Aaron Burr, Volume II*, pp. 992-993.

42 Annual Message, December 3, 1805 and Special Message December 6, 1805, *Works X*, pp. 181-205, both issued after Burr left office; Thomas Jefferson to John Breckinridge letter, supra; Albert J. Beveridge III, pp. 283-285.

43 Aaron Burr to William Henry Harrison, October, 1806; *Correspondence and Public Papers of Aaron Burr, Volume II*, pp. 996-998.

addressed this allegation in a letter to Cowles Mead, Secretary of the Mississippi Territory:

> The Reports which charge me with designs unfriendly to the peace and welfare of this and adjacent Territory are utterly false, are in themselves absurd, and are the inventions of wicked men, for evil purposes—I do assure you Sir, that I have no such design, nor any other which can tend to interrupt the peace and welfare of my fellow Citizens, and that I harbor [neither] the wish nor the intention to intermeddle with their Government or concerns—On the Contrary my pursuits are not only justifiable, but laudable, tending to the happiness and benefit of my Country Men and Such every good Citizen and virtuous man ought to promote—These pursuits have very recently been the Subject of investigation before an enlightened Grand Jury in Kentucky whose report is herewith enclosed....[44]

Burr's intent has been the subject of debate among historians. For example, in Walter Flavius McCaleb's *The Aaron Burr Conspiracy* (1903), the author opined that invasion of Mexico, after a declaration of war, was Burr's goal. Further, he believed that the plan to separate the territories outlined to British Ambassador Merry was purely a scheme by Burr to secure funding for his enterprise. In Thomas Perkins Abernathy's *The Burr Conspiracy* (1954), the author opined that Burr intended to foment a separatist movement in the West in 1805. Abernathy concluded that Burr realized that such a plan was not feasible and, therefore, focused more on invasion of Mexico. In the event of war with Spain, he believed that Burr would lead a "filibuster" into the Spanish Territory.[45] In the early 1800s, it was not uncommon for American citizens to engage in personal diplomacy with foreign countries.[46]

When reviewing the treason trial of Aaron Burr and the actions by President Jefferson and Chief Justice Marshall are analyzed, we can only consider evidence that was available and offered by the prosecution at trial. No matter how guilty a defendant, guilt must be proved beyond a reasonable

---

44 Aaron Burr to Cowles Meade. *Correspondence and Public Papers of Aaron Burr*, pp. 1008-1010.

45 Isenberg, 282.

46 Walter Flavius McCaleb. *The Aaron Burr Conspiracy and A New Light on Aaron Burr*; Thomas Perkins Abernathy. *The Burr Conspiracy*: Isenberg, *supra*, 283. In relating events that led to the indictment of Aaron Burr, limited footnotes will be employed. Readers are referred to several excellent treatments of the Burr conspiracy, including the classic works of McCaleb, Abernathy, and Lomask (Milton Lomask. *Aaron Burr: The Conspiracy and Years in Exile, 1805-1836*. Volume II). Lomask's two volume work is the most recent of the three and is, perhaps, the best. (Nancy Isenberg's recently published book, *Fallen Founder: The Life of Aaron Burr*, is of benefit).

doubt with relevant, competent, and admissible evidence. In the Burr trial, the government was unable to prove its case against Burr. A difficult lesson was learned by the government and, in particular, President Jefferson: facts are stubborn things. The Government could not prove its case: witness testimony conflicted and the prosecution was unable to place Burr at the scene of the alleged crime. A brave Judge stood between the government and the accused; civil liberties and the rule of law prevailed.

THE "CIPHER LETTER"

Perhaps the key evidence in the Burr treason case was what became known as the "cipher letter." Wilkinson and Burr communicated in cipher (a written code to avoid detection) until Wilkinson turned "states evidence." At least nine letters were written by Burr to Wilkinson about his activities between March 1805 and the famous "cipher letter" in 1806. Although Burr referred to letters he received from Wilkinson, few are extant. The letters may have been lost at sea in 1813, when the ship carrying Burr's daughter sunk killing her and providing a watery grave for Burr's letters she was transporting. (Copies of letters written by Wilkinson exist but authenticity is suspect).[47]

In September 1806, General Wilkinson received copies of two cipher letter purportedly written by Aaron Burr. One was delivered by sea by Erich Bollman, 35, a Burr associate.[48] The second letter was delivered by land by Samuel Swartwout, 22, another Burr associate. Although Wilkinson was initially a willing participant with Burr, after receiving the letters, Wilkinson turned on Burr and informed President Jefferson in October, 1806, about Burr's activities.

Interestingly, Wilkinson's information about Burr was not the first warning received by President Jefferson. Western newspapers, particularly in Kentucky, published numerous articles about Burr's alleged scheme. Kentucky United States Attorney Joseph Hamilton Daveiss warned Jefferson about Burr's activities in the West in a series of letters (beginning in January 1806) written over a nine month period; the letters received little or no attention from Jefferson. Daveiss later presented evidence to two Grand Juries in Kentucky about Burr's activities. In November 1806, when

47   *Correspondence and Public Papers of Aaron Burr, Volume II*, p.927.
48   Erich Bollman wrote a letter to President George Washington on April 10, 1796, describing his plans to rescue General Lafayette from prison in Europe. *The Writings of George Washington*, Volume XI. Edited by Jared Sparks, pp. 497-500

Burr voluntarily appeared before the Grand Jury, the prosecution collapsed and he was discharged. A month later, another indictment was sought by Daveiss against Burr. Once again, Burr voluntarily appeared, this time with future Kentucky Senator Henry Clay as his attorney. The Grand Jury, once again, declined to indict and returned a special verdict finding that it was unable to "discover that anything improper or injurious to the Government of the United States, or contrary to the laws thereof, is designed or contemplated...."[49]

The cipher letter was considered the "smoking gun" that would convict Burr. By the time Burr faced trial in Richmond, the letter was never offered in evidence. What was this letter? Whatever its source and intent, the cipher letter provided Wilkinson with the means to extricate himself from Burr's plans. What were the contents of the letter? Since Wilkinson admitted that he altered the letter, its exact contents are unknown. The extant "cipher letter" states:

> Your letter post marked thirteenth of May is received. I have at length obtained funds, and have actually commenced. The Eastern detachments, from different points and under different pretences, will rendezvous on the Ohio on 1 November.

> Every thing internal and external favor our views. Naval protection of *England* is secured. Truxton is going to *Jamaica* to arrange with the admiral there and will meet with us at Mississippi. England, a navy of United States, are ready to join, and final orders are given to my friends and followers. It will be a host of choice spirits. Wilkinson shall be second to Burr only and Wilkinson shall dictate the rank and promotion of his officers.

> Burr will proceed westward 1 August, never to return. With him go his daughter and grandson. The husband will follow in October with a corps of worthies.

> Send forthwith an intelligent and confidential friend with whom Burr may confer; he shall return immediately with further interesting details. This is essential to concert and harmony of movement. Send a list of persons known to Wilkinson westward of the mountains who could be useful, with a note delineating their character. By your messenger send me four or five of the commissions of your officers which you can borrow under any pretense you please. They shall be returned faithfully. Already are orders given to the contractor to forward six months provisions to points Wilkinson may

---

49   McCaleb, p. 163; Harold H. Burton. "Justice the Guardian of Liberty': John Marshall at the Trial of Aaron Burr." *American Bar Association Journal*, Vol. 37 (October 1951), pp. 735-738, 785-88; Isenberg, pp. 309-10.

name. This shall not be used till the last moment, and then under proper injunctions.

Our project my dear friend is brought to the point so long desired. Burr guarantees the result with his life and honor, with the lives and honor and the fortunes of hundreds, the best blood of our country.

Burr's plan of operation is to move down rapidly from the Falls on fifteenth November, with the first 500 of 1000 men in light boats now constructing for that purpose; to be at Natchez between the fifth and fifteenth of December, there to meet you; then to determine whether it will be expedient in the first instance to seize or to pass Baton Rouge. On receipt of this send me an answer. Draw on Burr for all expenses.

The people of the country to which we are going are prepared to receive us; their agents, now with Burr, say that if we will protect their religion and will not subject them to a foreign Power, that in three weeks all will be settled.

The Gods invite us to glory and fortune. It remains to be seen whether we deserve the boon.

The bearer of this goes express to you. He is a man of inviolable honor and perfect discretion, formed to execute rather than project, capable of relating facts with fidelity, and incapable of relating them otherwise; he is thoroughly informed of the plans and intentions of Burr, and will disclose to you as far as you may require, and not further. He has imbibed a reverence for your character, and may be embarrassed in your presence; put him at ease, and he will satisfy you.[50]

The exact meaning of this letter has been the subject of debate. A most convincing explanation is provided by Mary-Jo Kline, editor of the *Papers of Aaron Burr*. She submits that the letter was likely never written by Burr. Copies were delivered by Swartwout and Bollman to Wilkinson; the letter delivered by Swartwout was dated July 22, 1806, Bollman's July 29, 1806. Swartwout's and Bollman's versions of conversations with Wilkinson differ greatly from Wilkinson's. It is possible that the letter was not written by Burr at all; most likely it was written by former New Jersey Senator Jonathon Dayton. The bombastic letter is written in the third person and in a style not typical of Burr's. Senator Plumer opined that the letter was not written by Burr. Wilkinson surely knew the handwriting of Burr and Dayton. Kline suggests that it would have better served Wilkinson's purposes

---

50   Beveridge, Vol. III, pp. 614-615; *Correspondence and Public Papers of Aaron Burr, Volume II*, pp. 986-87.

to establish that the letter was written by Burr, in order to establish Burr's wrongful motives. Wilkinson *admittedly altered the letter*. The letter referred to prior correspondence between Wilkinson and Burr; Wilkinson knew the code to decipher the letter. References within the letter reflect Wilkinson's involvement in the plans: his assistance was assumed. The letter expected Wilkinson's cooperation with plans to sever the western states and territories or to invade Mexico, after declaration of war by the United States. Why did Wilkinson wait so long to inform Jefferson and the government about Burr's activities? Why were the cipher letters sent to Wilkinson? How did Wilkinson know the code? The first sentence of the letter referred to prior correspondence between Wilkinson and Burr? Wasn't it obvious that the letter was written in the third person, not Burr's style? Why didn't Jefferson realize that the letter had been altered and that if Burr was guilty, so too was Wilkinson.[51]

Wilkinson was almost indicted by the same grand jury in Richmond that indicted Burr. At Burr's treason trial, the prosecution never called Wilkinson as a witness; the cipher letter was never offered as evidence. After Burr's trials, Wilkinson faced numerous investigations and courts martial; he managed to escape conviction. It was not proved until years later that Wilkinson had been on the payroll of the Spanish government for at least twenty years, all while serving the United States as its chief military officer.[52]

51   Kline, 973-990; Isenberg, 312; Lomask II, 115-22.
52   Andro Linklater. *An Artist in Treason: The Extraordinary Double Life of General James Wilkinson*; Thomas Robson Hay and M. R. Werner, *The Admirable Trumpeter; A Biography of James Wilkinson.*

2. Actions by President Jefferson

President Jefferson received numerous warnings about Burr's activities. *The United States Gazette* (August 1805) earlier propounded numerous questions about Burr's activities. Jefferson received two anonymous letters warning him about intrigues of a new "Catiline," a reference to Burr, in late 1805. The first letter, dated December 1, 1805, warned Jefferson about Burr. The letter charged that Burr was "conspiring against the State," negotiating to overthrow the government and on the payroll of Great Britain. Mention was made of Burr's involvement with England and Spain. A second anonymous letter, apparently from the same source, was sent on December 5, 1805: "Be careful: Although ostensibly directed against a foreign power, the destruction of our government, your ruin and the material injury of the Atlantic states are their true objects." The anonymous writer was aware that Jefferson recently met with Burr at a private dinner.[53]

Beginning in early 1806, President Jefferson received letters from the United States Attorney for Kentucky, Joseph Hamilton Daveiss. Daveiss, a Federalist, was appointed by former President John Adams. Daveiss, married to Chief Justice John Marshall's sister, was a great admirer of his namesake Alexander Hamilton. Although Daveiss advised Jefferson about

---

53 Dumas Malone. *Jefferson the President: Second Term 1805-1809: Jefferson and His Time*, Vol. 5, p. 234. The anonymous letters dated December 1, 1805 and December 5, 1805 may be found at *The Thomas Jefferson Papers* on the Library of Congress digital website, www. memory.loc.gov. The newspaper article was published in the *United States Gazette*, August 2, 1805.

alleged activities of Burr and Wilkinson, Jefferson instead chose to question Daveiss' motives for sending the letters. Daveiss sent his first letter to President Jefferson on January 10, 1806, a month after Jefferson received the two anonymous letters. Daveiss warned Jefferson about traitorous activity in the West involving the Spanish Territories and possible detachment of the western states and territories from the United States. Daveiss identified General Wilkinson as not only a participant in the plan, but as a pensioner of the Spanish government. When Daveiss had not received a reply from President Jefferson, he sent a second letter on February 10, 1806. In that letter, Daveiss advised the President that Burr was deeply involved in a plot with Wilkinson. Jefferson responded to Daveiss first letter (January 10, 1806) on February 15, 1806, indicating that he shared Daveiss first letter with Cabinet members James Madison (Secretary of State), Albert Gallatin (Secretary of the Treasury), and Henry Dearborn (Secretary of War). In Jefferson's February response, he requested that Daveiss keep him informed about activities of those involved. Jefferson assured Daveiss that any information provided would not be shared, "until it shall become necessary to place them in the hands of the law." Daveiss wrote additional letters to Jefferson on March 5, 1806, March 28, 1806, March 29, 1806, April 21, 1806, and July 14, 1806; several letters were forwarded by President Jefferson to Cabinet members. Daveiss sent a letter directly to Secretary of State Madison on August 14, 1806, expressing his displeasure that he had received only one response from President Jefferson. Daveiss provided detailed information about the alleged conspiracy to Secretary of State Madison. Madison acknowledged Daveiss letter on September 18, 1806, and enclosed a letter dated September 12, 1806 from President Jefferson. In Jefferson's letter, he acknowledged receipt of Daveiss' letters and promised that they would remain confidential. Daveiss wrote a final letter to Secretary of State Madison on November 16, 1806. He updated Madison about the activities of Burr and Wilkinson and advised that he had unsuccessfully brought Burr before a Grand Jury in Frankfort, Kentucky. Jefferson placed little credibility in Daveiss' letters; rather, he chose to believe General James Wilkinson, even though Wilkinson had been implicated in the alleged plot by Daveiss and others.[54]

Around the time that President Jefferson received two anonymous letters and the first letters from Daveiss, Aaron Burr, now a private citizen, called upon Jefferson at the President's House (White House). After his duel with Hamilton in 1804, Burr was unable to return to New York to practice law. In his meeting, the President advised Burr that he personally had great confidence in him and thought that he possessed talents that would be beneficial to the public; however he informed Burr that the public had lost confidence in him. Burr hoped that Jefferson would appoint him to an ambassadorship for a European country. Although President Jefferson and Burr met again several days later, nothing came of their conversations.[55] President Jefferson, according to his notes, never questioned Burr about his activities or intentions in the West.

President Jefferson continued to receive reports about Burr. In August 1806, Jefferson received a letter from Thomas Truxton, a former naval commander, offering advice on how to militarily counter Burr's efforts should he attempt to separate the western states and territories. Truxton further suggested that the British may be involved in the alleged scheme. Jefferson ignored Truxton's letter, as he had earlier letters.[56]

A month later, President Jefferson acknowledged receipt of a letter from Colonel George Morgan that warned him about Burr's activities and possible actions against the United States.[57] On the same day, Jefferson re-

---

54 Letters written by Joseph Hamilton Daveiss to Thomas Jefferson (January 10, February 10, March 5, March 28, March 29, April 21, and July 14, 1806); Joseph Hamilton Daveiss to James Madison (August 14 and November 16, 1806); Thomas Jefferson to Joseph Hamilton Daveiss, (February 15 and September 12, 1806); and James Madison to Joseph Hamilton Daveiss (September 18, 1806) may be viewed in a pamphlet written by J. H. Daveiss, *View of the President's Conduct, Concerning the Conspiracy of 1806.* The letters between Jefferson and Daveiss may also be found in the Library of Congress digital website in the Thomas Jefferson Papers.

55 *The Complete Anas of Thomas Jefferson, supra,* pp. 237-241, April 15, 1806.

56 Thomas Truxton to Thomas Jefferson, August 10, 1806. Library of Congress digital website, American Memory (*The Thomas Jefferson Papers*).

57 Thomas Jefferson to George Morgan, September 19, 1806. Library of Congress Digital.

sponded to a letter from John Nicholson of New York, who described the activities of Comfort Tyler, an alleged participant in Burr's plan.[58]

On October 7, 1806, Secretary of State Madison received a letter from Presley Neville and Samuel Roberts of Pennsylvania describing a meeting with Colonel Morgan. Morgan advised them about conversations he and his sons had with Aaron Burr: "To give a correct written statement of these conversations [Burr with the Morgans] ... would perhaps be as unnecessary as it would be difficult.... Indeed, according to our informants, much more was to be calculated from the *manner* in which things were said, and hints given, than from the words used."[59] Around this time, *The Richmond Enquirer* published an article raising numerous questions about Burr's activities.

Jefferson Begins to Act

Several weeks later, after receipt of a letter from Postmaster General Gideon Granger, President Jefferson's attention to Burr was sufficiently aroused. On October 16, 1806, Granger informed Jefferson that he learned about a conversation between Congressman William Ely and General William Eaton. The conversation described Burr's activities and possible actions that Burr might take in Washington, including kidnapping or assassinating the President and overthrowing the government. Jefferson informed Granger, based upon information contained in his letter that he now concluded that action must be taken against Burr. Years later, Jefferson wrote a letter to Mrs. Katherine Duane Morgan informing her that the letter received from Colonel Morgan of September 19, 1806, was his first notification of Burr's "mad project." If true, Jefferson ignored or forgot earlier letters from Daveiss and Truxton, in addition to two anonymous letters and various newspaper articles Jefferson surely must have read.[60] Additionally, Jefferson had been warned about Burr and Wilkinson by General William Eaton. Eaton later

---

58   Thomas Jefferson to John Nicholson, September 19, 1806. *Works* X, p. 292.

59   Presley Neville and Samuel Roberts to James Madison, October 7, 1806. Walter Flavius McCaleb. *The Aaron Burr Conspiracy and A New Light on Aaron Burr*, p. 71; Beveridge III, p. 310.

60   *Memorandum of Proceedings*, December 18, 1806, p. 533: Abernathy, pp. 183-85; Gideon Granger to Thomas Jefferson, October 16, 1806, cited in Malone Vol. V, pp.240-241. (Regrettably, this author was unable to locate this letter on the Library of Congress website. Since *The Papers of Thomas Jefferson* for this date have yet to be published, it is unclear whether this letter is extant): Jefferson to Granger, March 9, 1814. *Works* XI, pp. 383-390 (This letter mentions the October 16, 1806 letter); Jefferson to Mrs. Katherine Duane Morgan, June 26, 1822. *Works* XII, pp. 291-292.

would be the first witness called by the prosecution in the Burr trial. Incredibly, Eaton recommended that Jefferson appoint Burr minister to either Great Britain or another European country as a way to remove Burr from the country. Eaton assured Jefferson that Burr was a patriot and would acquit himself well if given such an assignment.[61]

Upon receipt of Postmaster General Granger's letter, President Jefferson convened his Cabinet on October 22, 1806. Potential problems with Spain, particularly the Louisiana and New Orleans territories were discussed; Burr's activities were on the Cabinet's agenda:

> During the last session of Congress, Col. Burr who was here, finding no hope of being employed in any department of government, opened himself confidentially to some persons on whom he thought he could rely, on a scheme of separating the western from the Atlantic States, & erecting the former into an independent confederacy, he had before made a tour of those states, which had excited suspicions, as every motion does of such a Catalinarian character, of his having made this proposition here we have information from General Eaton, through Mr. Ely & Mr. Granger, he went off this spring to the western country....

Jefferson mentioned information received from Nicholson and Neville and Roberts.[62]

Jefferson's Cabinet agreed that confidential letters should be sent to the Governors of Ohio, Indiana, Mississippi and Orleans and to District Attorneys in Kentucky, Tennessee and Louisiana, directing them to arrest and try any person who committed an overt act of treason. In addition, supporters of the scheme should be arrested and gunboats should stop passage of suspicious persons traveling in force. Finally, the Cabinet discussed what to do with General Wilkinson after he was implicated in the plan with Burr and earlier disobeyed orders to return to New Orleans. Two days later, on October 24th, the Cabinet reconvened. The Navy was to move to New Orleans to assist Governor Claiborne (Territorial Governor of Orleans). John Graham, secretary of the Southern Louisiana Territory, was ordered to follow Burr's trail through Kentucky, consult with Governors, and arrest Burr, if appropriate. Questions about what to do with Wilkinson were deferred.[63]

61　Malone 5, pp. 236, 240-41; Louis B. Wright and Julia H. MacLeod. "William Eaton's Relations with Aaron Burr," pp. 523-536; Beveridge III, pp. 302-307; Isenberg, pp. 330-331.

62　*The Complete Anas of Thomas Jefferson*, pp. 245-246.

63　Ibid., pp. 246-248.

The Cabinet met again the next day, October 25th. Since no additional information had been received about Burr's activities and there was no evidence of an overt act of treason by Burr, orders from the previous day were rescinded. Graham was ordered to confidentially inquire into Burr's movements and place the Governors on notice. The Cabinet's tone from previous Cabinet meetings was more subdued.[64]

As President Jefferson's Cabinet was meeting, General Wilkinson forwarded two confidential messages to the President, not received until November. The first message warned Jefferson that approximately eight to ten thousand men would shortly descend upon New Orleans and proceed with an expedition into Mexico. Wilkinson warned that naval assistance might be provided by the British. In his letter, Wilkinson indicated that he was unable to determine what, if any, authority the enterprise had or what their ultimate intentions were concerning New Orleans. No names were mentioned, but the actors were described as "active influential characters." In his second letter, marked confidential, Wilkinson provided advice to Jefferson about how to combat possible aggression. In light of what we know about Wilkinson's involvement and his knowledge about the plan, Wilkinson had the audacity to write:

> For although my information appears too direct and circumstantial to be fictitious, yet the magnitude of the enterprise, the desperation of the plan, and the stupendous consequences with which it seems pregnant, stagger my belief, and excite doubts of the reality, against the conviction of my senses: and it is for this reason I shall forbear to commit names, because it is my desire to avert a great public calamity, and not to mar a salutary design or to injure any undesignedly. I have never in my whole life found myself under such circumstances of perplexity and embarrassment as at present; for I am not only informed of the prime mover, and ultimate objects of this daring enterprise, but am ignorant of the foundation on which it rests, of the means by which it is to be supported, and whether any immediate or collateral protection, internal or external, is expected.

Wilkinson's letters were received by President Jefferson on November 25.[65]

On November 5, 1806, Andrew Jackson wrote to the President, offering his services in the event of "an insult or aggression" against the government.

---

64 Ibid., p. 248.

65 James Wilkinson to Thomas Jefferson, October 20—21, 1806. General James Wilkinson. *Memoirs of My Own Times.* Volume II (letters found in the appendix with no page numbers).

On December 3, 1806, Jefferson responded: "Whether our difficulties with Spain will issue in peace or war is uncertain, and what provisional measures shall be taken for the latter alternative, is now under consideration by the legislature..." As late as December 3, 1806, Jefferson considered war with Spain possible.[66]

On November 11, 1806, *The Richmond Enquirer* propounded questions about Burr's activities and questioned his intentions. On November 18, *The Enquirer* reported that $40,000 was expended for provisions in support of Burr's alleged plot. Further, the paper alleged that Burr offered General Eaton a commission, which Eaton rejected.[67]

After President Jefferson received Wilkinson's communications on November 25, he quickly convened another Cabinet meeting. The Cabinet determined that a proclamation should be issued to determine whether there was a military enterprise against the Spanish territories. Further, the proclamation directed all persons armed, assembled to travel on the Ohio River, and believed to be engaged in an illegal enterprise to be arrested upon reasonable suspicion. The Governors of the affected states were requested to provide assistance. General Wilkinson was authorized to make arrests.[68]

President Jefferson issued his Proclamation on November 27, 1806 based upon information received from Wilkinson and Granger. Although no suspects were identified, an all points bulletin was issued warning that United States citizens were conspiring to engage in a military expedition against Spain. President Jefferson warned participants in the alleged scheme to immediately withdraw from the enterprise; if not, they would be prosecuted. He directed all public officials (governors, judges, and military officers) to be vigilant and bring violators to justice. Finally, he requested that all citizens assist the government in the discovery and apprehension of those involved, to bring to justice all offenders, and provide information to authorities.[69]

The day after the President's Proclamation, Senator William Plumer recorded:

> Reports have for some time circulated from one end of the United States to the other, that Aaron Burr late Vice President, with others, in the western States are preparing gun boats, provisions, money,

---

66 Thomas Jefferson to Andrew Jackson, December 3, 1806. *Writings*, Volume XIX, pp. 156-157; Andrew Jackson to Thomas Jefferson, November 5, 1806. Andrew Jackson. *The Papers of Andrew Jackson, Volume II, 1804-1813.*.

67 *The Richmond Enquirer*, November 11 and 18, 1806.

68 *The Complete Anas of Thomas Jefferson*, pp. 248-250.

69 Presidential Proclamation, November 27, 1806. *Works* X, pp. 301-302.

men, &c to make war upon the Spaniards in South America—that his intention is to establish a new empire in the western world—& That he contemplates forming this Empire from South America & the western States of North America—

Yesterday the President of the United States issued a proclamation, which is made public today.... There were many things reported against Mr. Burr—some of them too foolish for him to be guilty of.

Wm Eaton has certified, That Mr. Burr last winter desired him (Eaton) to accept a commission under Burr—That Burr told Eaton that General Wilkinson was second in command—& under him, & that Eaton should be third. This is not the language of the cunning, cautious, wily Burr. He would never use such language to a man so imprudent, wild, & raving as Eaton. Burr is capable of much wickedness—but not so much folly.[70]

Simultaneous with events in Washington, Burr wrote letters to assure friends and associates that he had no intention of severing the western states. Burr wrote, for example, to William Henry Harrison, Governor of the Indiana Territory, assuring the Governor that he "had no wish or design to attempt the separation of the Union...."[71]

On December 2, 1806, President Jefferson mentioned the alleged plot in his Sixth Annual Message to Congress, but provided no specifics or names. In the Message, Jefferson provided an update on negotiations with Spain; Jefferson had no progress to report.[72] War was still possible. Jefferson previously identified problems with Spanish territories in earlier reports; specific military measures were taken by the government west of the Mississippi River, particularly in the Louisiana Territory. War with Spain remained a real possibility.

Burr's activity was hardly a state secret. Senator Plumer wrote:

Dr. Park of Boston has a few days since published in this Repertory, a statement purporting to be the conversation of Mr. Burr with William Eaton last winter—& of Eaton's giving information to the President. It appears Mr. Eaton declares this statement published by Park to be correct. From this we are informed. That Burr disclosed to Eaton his intention to attempt a separation of the western states from the Union, & to invade Mexico—& invited him to join the

---

70 *Memorandum of Proceedings*, November 28, 1806, pp. 515-16.

71 Aaron Burr to William Henry Harrison, November 27, 1806. Kline, Ed. *Burr* Papers, pp.1000-1006.

72 Sixth Annual Message to Congress, December 2, 1806. Thomas Jefferson. James D. Richardson, *A Compilation of Messages and Papers of the Presidents* Vol. I. New York: Bureau of National Literature,1897, pp. 393-398.

project.—And yet in this same statement, revised by Eaton himself, we are told that Eaton represented Burr as a dangerous man in this county, & though a traitor—yet he (Eaton) recommended the President to appoint him (Burr) minister either to London or Madrid— for says Eaton "if Burr is put on his honor he would act with fidelity." After this what opinion ought a man to form of Eaton? There are contradictory accounts of Eaton's declarations published. I do not believe his relations either in this or his Mediterranean expedition. He is too light, too fleeting, too unsteady a man to gain my belief—I very much question the soundness of his heart & the correctness of his head—both are distempered.[73]

Senator Plumer later questioned Postmaster General Gideon Granger about information he provided President Jefferson:

In a conversation with Gideon Granger I asked him, if the account published in the newspapers of November last, of his taking down William Eaton's conversation respecting Aaron Burr—& of Eaton's subscribing the same, was true? He replied it was true—& he had delivered the paper, or a copy of it. (I cannot say which) to the President of the United States.... Mr. Granger appears anxious to have people believe he is not friendly to Mr. Burr. He showed me a letter from the western country stating that Burr near Pittsburgh was fitting a number of boats, collecting men & provisions—He, Granger, ordered a Clerk to transcribe a paragraph from this letter....[74]

After the presidential Proclamation, rumors about Burr's activities continued to spread. The *Richmond Enquirer* published an article about Burr's intentions:

The scheme of empire was more comprehensive, than any man not well informed can conceive—but it is demonstrable, that is, the editor of this paper can demonstrate beyond a shadow of a doubt—and in spite of the most confirmed incredulity—that the design conceived and intended by Mr. Burr, extended to:

The establishment of a despotic government on the shores of the Gulf of Mexico.

That Mr. Burr was to be the despot.

That from among his friends in the United States were to be selected, the materials of new nobles—no doubt conservative senates and legions of honor!

That among the designs of empire were fundamentally pre-determined, a formidable military and naval establishment, and that it

---

73 *Memorandum of Proceedings*, December 5, 1806, p. 522.
74 *Memorandum of Proceedings*, December 18, 1806, p. 533.

was to be reared from the materials of the United States, combined with foreign materials.

That, of course, the sea coast, on an extensive line, was to be seized and occupied.

That offers of honor and emolument were to be held forth to adventurers and to every description of persons from all parts of the world.[75]

President Jefferson's Private Correspondence

Although President Jefferson neither publicly identified allegations about the alleged plot nor identified participants, he freely provided details of the plan, particularly Burr's involvement, in his private correspondence. In a letter to Caesar Rodney, soon to become Jefferson's Attorney General, the President wrote, "the designs of our Catiline are as real as they are romantic.... I am confident he will be completely deserted on the appearance of the proclamation, because his strength was to consist of people who had been persuaded that the government connived at the enterprise.... Altho' we shall possibly come to blows with Spain...."[76]

With war with Spain possible, Jefferson wrote son-in-law Thomas Mann Randolph: "In the quarter of Natchitoches I believe every thing will remain quiet. Burr is unquestionably very actively engaged in the westward in preparations to sever that from this part of the Union. We learn that he is actually building 10 or 15 boats able to take a large gun and fit for the navigation of those waters. We give him all the attention our situation admits; *as yet we have no legal proof of any overt act which the law can lay hold of....*"[77] (Emphasis added.)

Several weeks later, Jefferson advised the Governor of Louisiana Territory, William Charles Cole Claiborne: "You already have a general knowledge of the insurrection prepared by Colo. Burr. His object is to take possession of New Orleans, as a station from whence to make an expedition against Vera Cruz and Mexico... We trust that the opposition we have provided at

---

75   *The Richmond Enquirer*, December 11, 1806.

76   Thomas Jefferson to Caesar Rodney, December 5, 1806. *Works* X, pp. 322-23.

77   Thomas Jefferson to Thomas Mann Randolph, November 3, 1806. *Writings* XVIII, pp. 249-250

Marietta, Cincinnati, Louisville & Marsac will be sufficient to stop him; but we are not certain because we do not know his strength...."[78]

President Jefferson wrote Thomas Leiper predicting that the present session of Congress "may become still more important, should the measures we have taken fail to suppress the insurrectionary expedition now going on under Colo. Burr."[79] On the same day, Jefferson wrote John Langdon:

> With England I firmly expect a friendly arrangement. With Spain we shall possibly have blows; but they will hasten, instead of preventing a peaceable settlement. The most instant pressure is now from among ourselves. Our Cataline is at the head of an armed body (we know not its strength) and his object is to seize New Orleans, from thence attack Mexico, place himself on the throne of Montezuma, add Louisiana to his empire, and the Western States from the Alleghany if he can. I do not believe he will attain the crown; but neither am I certain the halter will get its due. A few days will let us see whether the Western States suppress themselves this insurrectionary enterprise, or we shall be objected to make a great armament for it. In the end, I am satisfied it will exhibit to the world another proof that the people of the U.S. are qualified for self government. Our friends, the federalists, chuckle at all this; but in justice I must add we have found some faithful among those in the West....[80]

On December 27, following a dinner with President Jefferson, Senator Plumer recorded the events of that evening: "He told me that Blennerhassett had fled—That he is reputed to be a man of property, worth $100,000.— That he owns & lives on an island in the State of Virginia, adjoining the river Ohio—That governmental agents are in possession of full evidence to convict him of being engaged in conspiracy. *But he thought not enough against the arch traitor Burr.*"[81] (Emphasis added.) Jefferson was aware, at this early date, that prosecution of Burr was problematic, even though he had little difficulty implicating Burr in the scheme.

President Jefferson wrote General Wilkinson and advised him that Blennerhasset had been captured and that the size of Burr's operation was not as large as originally thought. Further, he advised Wilkinson that it appeared that Burr and his followers were either intent on settling the Washita lands (not a crime) or were on their way to fight the Spaniards in Mexico

78   Thomas Jefferson to William C.C. Claiborne, December 20, 1806. *Works* X, pp. 327-329.
79   Thomas Jefferson to Thomas Leiper, December 22, 1806. *Works* X, pp. 329-330.
80   Thomas Jefferson to Gov. John Langdon, December 22, 1806. The Thomas Jefferson Papers, Library of Congress digital.
81   *Memorandum of Proceedings*, December 27, 1806, p. 543.

(a misdemeanor without a declaration of war against Spain). In this letter, Jefferson never suggested that Burr and his followers were engaged in traitorous activity. Jefferson advised Wilkinson that he should not worry about Truxton's involvement, since Truxton was currently in the Caribbean and cooperating.[82] A month later, Jefferson informed Wilkinson that by sending Bollman and Swartwout east, Wilkinson's actions were supported by the public, as would sending Burr and others east upon their capture.[83] Even though Jefferson trusted Wilkinson, the trust was not reciprocated. In a letter to Daniel Coxe, Wilkinson referred to Jefferson as a "fool" and to Governor Claiborne as Jefferson's "contemptible liar."[84]

Perhaps Jefferson's most explicit letter about Burr's activity was sent to Rev. Charles Clay:

> Burr's enterprise is the most extraordinary since the days of Don Quixot [sp]. It is so extravagant that those who know his understanding would not believe it if proofs admitted doubt. He has meant to place himself on the throne of Montezuma, and extend his empire to the Allegany seizing on New Orleans as the instrument of compulsion for our Western States ... our affairs with Spain ... do not promise the result we wish. Not that war will take place immediately; but they may go off without a settlement, and leave us in constant bickering about indemnification for Spoliations, the navigation of the Mobile, and the Limits of Louisiana.[85]

PRESIDENT JEFFERSON PUBLICLY PROCLAIMS BURR'S GUILT

Rumors about Burr's activities were rampant and the public, particularly Congress, wanted to know what the President knew. Jefferson had implicated Aaron Burr in numerous private letters. Public officials sought specific information. Representative John Randolph led the charge: on January 16, 1807, the House passed a resolution calling upon the President to provide Congress with all information about the conspiracy.[86] On January 16th, Senator Plumer recorded that the House of Representatives approved two resolutions proposed by Representative John Randolph that requested

---

82 Thomas Jefferson to James Wilkinson, January 3, 1807. *Works* X, pp. 332-335.

83 Thomas Jefferson to James Wilkinson, February 3, 1807. *Works* X, pp. 335-36.

84 James Wilkinson to Daniel Coxe, January 8, 1807. *The Proof of the Corruption of General James Wilkinson and His Connexion with Aaron Burr*. Daniel Clark. Library of Congress digital, American Memory, First American West: The Ohio River Valley, images 110-111.

85 Thomas Jefferson to Reverend Charles Clay, January 11, 1807. *Works* X, pp. 338-339.

86 Abernathy, pp. 192-93.

the President transmit to Congress information about the western conspiracy and to identify the government's efforts to suppress that conspiracy.[87] Shortly before responding to Congress, Jefferson wrote Governor Charles Pinckney of South Carolina about Burr's alleged plot and warned of the possible involvement of Burr's son-in-law, Joseph Alston, a resident of South Carolina.[88]

On January 22, 1807, Jefferson submitted his Special Message on Burr to the Senate and House of Representatives. The formal title of Jefferson's Message was a: "*Message from the President of the United States, Transmitting Information Touching An Illegal Combination of Private Individuals Against the Peace and Safety of the Union and a Military Expedition Planned by Them Against the Territories of a Power in Amity with the United States; With the Measures Pursued for Suppressing the Same; In pursuance of a Resolution of the House of that Sixteenth Instant.*" (Emphasis added.) In his Message, Jefferson described a conspiracy involving numerous individuals against territories of a foreign nation not at war with the United States. Although the President explained that information in his possession did not constitute formal or legal evidence, he identified Aaron Burr as the prime mover and perpetrator of the scheme. He described Burr's involvement in the conspiracy and alleged that Burr was the "*principal actor, whose guilt is placed beyond question.*" President Jefferson explained that he learned about the conspiracy in September, 1806 and received additional information in October. (Jefferson failed to disclose the two anonymous letters received almost a year earlier, United States Attorney Daveiss' numerous letters, and Truxton's letter; he made only passing reference to letters from Morgan and Nicholson). Jefferson mentioned that the information was voluminous, although the evidence did not rise to the level of formal, legal evidence. Though the evidence consisted of letters filled with rumor, innuendo, conjecture, and suspicions, Jefferson identified Aaron Burr as leader of the conspiracy. Jefferson described General Wilkinson as having the "honor of a soldier and fidelity of a good citizen"; the President failed to mention Wilkinson's involvement in the conspiracy or opine about his truthfulness. Three possible objectives for Burr's enterprise were suggested by President Jefferson: (1) severance of the union west of the Alleghenies, (2) an attack upon Mexico, and (3) settlement of the Washita lands. If the first allegation was proved, treason was the crime; if the second allegation was proved

---

87 *Memorandum of Proceedings*, January 16, 1807, pp. 576-577.
88 Thomas Jefferson to Charles Pinckney, January 20, 1807. *Works* X, pp. 345-346.

without a war against Spain, the crime was violation of the Neutrality Act, a misdemeanor; the third allegation, if true, was no crime at all.[89]

Almost all information describing Burr's involvement in the Special Message was provided to Jefferson by General Wilkinson; it included the "cipher letter," together with letters by Wilkinson to Jefferson in November and December, 1806, and a letter from Erick Bollman to Wilkinson dated September 27, 1806.[90] Jefferson's belief that Burr's "guilt is placed beyond question" was supported only by innuendo, hearsay and inadmissible evidence. Before Burr had even been arrested or charged with a crime, the President of the United States declared Burr guilty, without benefit of trial or the rule of law. Actions taken by President Jefferson, beginning with his January 22 Message to Congress and throughout the subsequent investigation and prosecution of Burr, are inconsistent with Jefferson's reputation as a civil libertarian and proponent of the Bill of Rights. The Fourth, Fifth, and Sixth Amendments of the United States Constitution were stretched, if not outright ignored, by President Jefferson throughout the prosecution of Aaron Burr. Although Jefferson was a serial letter writer and often took contradictory positions within his letters, Jefferson's actions and writings in the Burr case were consistent; they were based upon a prejudiced and misinformed opinion about Aaron Burr's guilt. His blatant animosity toward the judiciary and Chief Justice Marshall permeated subsequent proceedings.

In his Message, President Jefferson credited General Wilkinson not only for his assistance, but for his honor and fidelity. President Jefferson's opinion about Wilkinson was inconsistent with opinions of other governmental officials; many had little confidence in Wilkinson. More than a month before the President's Message, Senator Plumer opined:

> Governor Wilkinson—has long been in habits of intimacy with Burr.... I never had much confidence in the integrity of this same general. I do not know what offers may have been made him to betray his trust. But it is singular that the subtil [sic] cunning Burr should develop his treasonable designs to such men as James Wilkinson, Thomas Truxton & William Eaton. Three vainer men I never saw— Hasty, imprudent, unguarded men—incapable of retaining a secret.

---

89   President Jefferson's Message to Congress, January 22, 1807. *Works* X, pp. 346-356.

90   James Wilkinson to Thomas Jefferson, December 14, 18, 1806; Erick Bollman to James Wilkinson, September 27, 1807 (with attachments). Library of Congress digital website, American Memory Collection, First American West: The Ohio River Valley, 1750-1820, images 1-16.

If Burr has made, or authorized any of his associates to make those overtures to these men, he has acted unlike himself.[91]

Plumer later wrote: "All parties & classes of people who are informed, appear to distrust General Wilkinson the commander of the armies—his friends, distrust him—Their confidence in him is not for his virtues—but they hope his interest will restrain him from committing treason."[92]

91 Abernathy, p. 194; *Memorandum of Proceedings*, December 26, 1806, p. 542.
92 Abernathy, p. 194; *Memorandum of Proceedings*, January 12, 1807, p. 569.

3. Initial Proceedings

Even before President Jefferson publicly implicated Burr in the conspiracy, General Wilkinson began rounding up suspects, with little consideration for civil or Constitutional rights. The first suspects apprehended were Dr. Erich Bollman, an Austrian adventurer who was most famous for his attempt to free the Marquis De Lafayette from imprisonment during the French Revolution, and Samuel Swartwout, a young member of a prominent New York family, both with close ties to Burr. They had traveled to Louisiana to deliver separate copies of the cipher letter to Wilkinson. Wilkinson arrested both and sent them to Washington, without assistance of counsel or Constitutional protections, including failure to specify charges and *habeas corpus* protections. Both men arrived in Washington the day after Congress received President Jefferson's Special Message of January 22, which caused uproar. When Burr's alleged accomplices arrived in Washington under armed guard, Senator William Branch Giles, Jefferson's close ally, presented a resolution to temporarily suspend the Constitutional privilege of *Habeas Corpus*,[93] which provides: "The Privilege of the Writ of *Habeas Corpus* shall not be suspended, unless when in Cases of Rebellion or Invasion the public Safety may require it." This is known as the "suspension clause."

In closed session, the Senate approved Giles' resolution to suspend *Habeas Corpus*; with only one Senator voting against the measure. The Senate

---

93   United States Constitution, Article I, Section 9.

immediately referred the measure to the House and requested prompt action. After several days of debate, the House voted 113–19 against suspension, thus providing some semblance of sanity.[94]

Senator John Quincy Adams of Massachusetts, who voted to suspend *habeas corpus*, wrote his father, former President John Adams, about proceedings in Washington:

> Mr. Burr and his conspiracy have begun to occupy our attention. Last Friday (23rd) the Senate with closed doors passed an act suspending in certain cases the privilege of the writ of *habeas corpus*. The business was finished in one day, with slight opposition from Mr. Bayard, who voted alone against the bill, but did not use his privilege of forbidding the reading of the bill three times on the same day. The House of Representatives adjourned over until Monday before we finished. Yesterday morning the message and the bill were sent to them in confidence. They immediately opened their doors, and almost unanimously rejected the bill at the first reading.... Bollman and Swartwout who were arrested by General Wilkinson are now here, and it seems questionable what can be done with them. The general subject is yet mysterious, but there is a concurrence of testimony establishing facts more important, as they respect *the operation of our Institutions*, and future prospects of this country than most of us appear to be aware of....[95]

Several weeks later, former President Adams wrote Benjamin Rush about the alleged Burr conspiracy and actions taken by President Jefferson:

> What shall I say of the Democratrical Vice-President and the Federal would-be President, Burr? Although I never thought so highly of his natural talents or his acquired attainments as many of both parties have represented them, I never believed him to be a fool. But he must be an idiot or lunatic if he has really planned and attempted to execute such a project as is imputed to him.... At present I suspect that Mr. Jefferson has been too hasty in his message in which he has denounced him by name and pronounced him guilty. But if his guilt is as clear as the noonday sun, the first magistrate ought not to have pronounced it so before a jury had tried him.[96]

On the day the Senate voted to suspend *habeas corpus*, Doctor Erich Bollman met with President Jefferson and Secretary of State James Madison.

---

94 *Memorandum of Proceedings*, January 23, 1807, pp. 585-590; Beveridge III, p. 346-348.

95 John Quincy Adams to John Adams, January 27, 1807. *The Writings of John Quincy Adams*, pp. 158-159

96 John Adams to Doctor Benjamin Rush, February 2, 1807. John A. Schutz and Douglass Adair. *The Spur of Fame: Dialogues of John Adams and Benjamin Rush, 1805-1813*. San Marino, CA: The Huntington Library, 1966, pp. 75-77. A copy of this letter was graciously provided by the Massachusetts Historical Society.

Bollman was hoping to convince Jefferson that Burr had no traitorous intentions and that it was in the best interests of the United States to be at war with Spain and support Burr's proposed expedition into Mexico. Bollman informed Jefferson and Madison that, until recently, General Wilkinson had been part of Burr's enterprise. In notes taken by Secretary of State Madison, Madison recorded that before the interview commenced, President Jefferson assured Bollman that "nothing which he might say or acknowledge should be made use of against himself; and it was further observed to him that it was a settled rule in court, that no communication confidentially made to an officer of the government, in his official capacity, could be extorted from him as a witness." Perhaps, at the time Jefferson made these assurances to Bollman, he intended to honor his pledge. Jefferson would not keep his word. Jefferson further compounded his misrepresentations to Bollman when he wrote Bollman on January 25, 1807, requesting that he commit in writing the information that he earlier provided. In compliance with Jefferson's request, Bollman provided a letter to Jefferson.[97]

PRELIMINARY COURT PROCEEDINGS

In late January, 1807, petitions for Writs of *Habeas Corpus* were filed in the United States Circuit Court in Washington on behalf of Bollman and Swartwout. The Court, in a split decision, denied the petitions and committed both men to jail without bail on the charge of treason.[98] A dissenting opinion was filed by Federalist appointee William Cranch, a United States District Judge for the District of Columbia. Judge Cranch was a respected jurist, enough so that President Jefferson reappointed to the bench in 1806.[99] Judge Cranch's dissent was perceptive and insightful: "In times like these, when the public mind is agitated, when wars and rumors of wars, plots, conspiracies and treasons excite alarm, it is the duty of a court to be particularly watchful lest the public feeling should reach the seat of justice, and thereby precedents be established which may become the ready tools of faction in times more disastrous.... Dangerous precedents occur in dangerous

---

97 James Madison. *Letters and Other Writings of James Madison*. Volume II., pp. 393-401; letters between Thomas Jefferson and Justus Erich Bollman, with attachment from Bollman, January 25-26, 1807. *The Thomas Jefferson Papers*, Library of Congress digital website; Matthew L. Davis. *Memoirs of Aaron Burr, Volume II*, pp. 387-391.

98 Warren, p. 303.

99 Beveridge, III, p. 346.

times. It then becomes the duty of the Judiciary calmly to poise the scales of justice, unmoved by the armed power, undisturbed by the clamor of the multitude."[100]

Judge Cranch later explained his dissent to his father:

> Never in my life have I been more anxious. You will see by the newspapers that I have dared to differ from my brothers on the Bench. I have dared to set the law and the Constitution in opposition to the arm of the Executive power, supported by a popular clamor. I have dared to attempt to maintain principle at the expense of popularity.... In my own mind, I had no doubt whatever that the Constitution did not justify a commitment upon such evidence: and although I felt that the public interest might be benefited by committing these gentlemen for trial, yet I could not consent to sacrifice the most important constitutional provision in favor of individual liberty, to reasons of State. I am not willing that the Executive Department should transfer to us its own responsibility. Never before has this country, since the Revolution, witnessed so gross a violation of personal liberty, as to seize a man without any warrant or lawful authority whatever, and send him two thousand miles by water for his trial out of the district or State in which the crime was committed—and then for the first time to apply for a warrant to arrest him, grounded on written affidavits.... *So anxious was the President to have this prosecution commenced, or, to use his own language, to deliver them up to the civil authority, that he came to the Capitol on the day of their arrival, and with his own hand delivered to the District Attorney, Mr. Jones, the affidavits of General Wilkinson, and instructed the Attorney to demand of the court a warrant for their arrest...*When the circumstance is considered—and the attempt made in the Legislature to suspend the privilege of *Habeas Corpus*... when we reflect on the extraordinary exertions made by all under Presidential influence to exaggerate Burr's conspiracy into a horrid rebellion, so that the Administration may have the merit of quelling it without bloodshed—when they have so far succeeded as to excite the public mind almost to frenzy in many parts of the country—you may form some idea of the anxiety of the Court. But having no doubt as to my duty, I have never once thought of shrinking from my responsibility.[101] (Emphasis added.)

The circuit court decision would now be reviewed by Chief Justice John Marshall and the Supreme Court. The cases were problematic for Chief Justice Marshall for several reasons. First, the principle defendant in the case was former Vice President of the United States Aaron Burr, hardly a person admired by Marshall. Burr killed Alexander Hamilton and although Marshall was a more moderate Federalist than Hamilton, Marshall greatly ad-

---

100 Warren, p. 303.
101 Warren, p. 304.

mired Hamilton's intellect and his loyal and devoted service to General and President George Washington and the nation. Second, Burr was a Republican; Marshall a Federalist. Third, Marshall was a strong supporter of the Constitution and the need for a strong central government; Burr's alleged actions against the United States could not be condoned. Finally, a head-on collision between the President and Chief Justice of the United States would surely result. Marshall and Jefferson were hardly friends; their personalities and political philosophies were polar opposites. Marshall knew no matter how the Burr case played out, the Judiciary would be damaged. If Burr was found not guilty, Jefferson and his supporters might drastically change the judiciary and pursue impeachment against Marshall and other Federalist appointees. If Burr was found guilty, Jefferson would be vindicated even though he disregarded Burr's Constitutional rights.

Supreme Court

Charles Lee and Robert Goodloe Harper, on behalf of their clients, applied to the Supreme Court for a Writ of *Habeas Corpus*. Two issues were presented: whether the Supreme Court had jurisdiction to issue a Writ of *Habeas Corpus* and, if so, should *habeas corpus* relief be granted to Bollman and Swartwout? The Court heard arguments from defense counsel (Luther Martin of Maryland joined the defense) on whether the Court had jurisdiction. The prosecution, led by Attorney General Caesar Rodney, declined to argue this issue and informed the Court that the government would abide by the Court's resolution of this threshold question. On February 13, 1807, Marshall held that the Court had jurisdiction to issue a Writ of *Habeas Corpus*, since review by the Supreme Court of the lower court's decision was appellate. Chief Justice Marshall's opinion was joined by Associate Justices Bushrod Washington and Brockhorst Livingston. Justice William Johnson dissented and advised that Justice Samuel Chase, who was absent, concurred in his dissent. Justice William Cushing did not participate. [102]

After the procedural issue was decided, the Court moved to the substantive legal issue: whether the requests for *habeas corpus* relief should be granted. In addition to *habeas corpus*, the Court considered rights guaranteed by the Sixth Amendment of the United States Constitution, particularly the right of an accused to be informed of accusations against him and the right

---

102 *PJM* VI, pp. 480-85.

to confront witnesses. Resolution of these issues would determine whether these defendants could be tried for treason in Washington, D.C.

Arguments commenced on February 16 and continued for the remainder of the week. Attorney General Caesar Rodney and U.S. Attorney Walter Jones, Jr. argued for the government; Charles Lee, Robert Goodloe Harper, Francis Scott Key, and Luther Martin for the defendants. When arguments concluded, Chief Justice Marshall announced that the Court had yet to reach a decision; the Court was having difficulty with admissibility of General Wilkinson's affidavit, which described the substance of the cipher letter. Bail was granted the Petitioners pending the Court's decision. After the Court admitted the prisoners to bail, Jefferson's Congressional supporters proposed legislation to curb the authority of the Supreme Court to grant Writs of *Habeas Corpus*. This effort to limit the Court's authority failed.[103]

Marshall delivered the Court's opinion several days later. If Petitioner's planned an invasion of Mexico in violation of the Neutrality Act (a high misdemeanor), the Court determined this crime had not been committed within the District of Columbia. Therefore, venue was improper and the Petitioner's could not be tried in the District of Columbia. The Court further found insufficient evidence to establish the crime of treason to justify holding prisoners on that charge. Chief Justice Marshall opined: "As there is no crime which can more excite and agitate the passions of men than treason, no charge demands more from the tribunal before which it is made a deliberate and temperate enquiry. Whether this enquiry be directed to the fact or to the law, none can be more important to the citizen or to the government—none can more affect the safety of both."[104] Marshall reviewed the precise definition of treason found within Article III, Section 3 of the Constitution. To constitute the crime of treason, Marshall opined: "...war must be actually levied against the United States. However flagitious may be the crime of conspiring to subvert by force the government of our country, such conspiracy is not treason. To conspire to levy war, and actually to levy war, are distinct offenses."[105]

One section of the Court's opinion later proved problematic to Marshall during the Burr trial:

---

103 United States Constitution, Amendment VI; Warren, p. 307; *PJM* VI, p. 487; United States Constitution, Article I, Sec. 9 and Article III, Sec. 2.
104 *PJM* VI, p. 488.
105 Ibid.; Constitution of the United States, Article III, Section 3.

> It is not the intention of the court to say that no individual can be guilty of this crime who has not appeared in arms against his country. On the contrary, if war be actually levied, that is, if a body of men be actually assembled for the purpose of effecting by force, a treasonable purpose, all those who perform any part, however minute or however remote from the scene of the action, and who are actually leagued in the general conspiracy, are to be considered traitors. But there must be an actual assembling of men for the treasonable purpose, to constitute a levying of war.[106]

Chief Justice Marshall was describing the British common law doctrine of "constructive treason", a doctrine inconsistent with the Constitutional definition of treason. This portion of Marshall's opinion was unnecessary to the Court's decision (*dicta*). Marshall intended to rule that all parties to a traitorous act can be charged with treason after an overt act of rebellion has first been committed. Unfortunately, when this paragraph is read in isolation, a broader (and incorrect) interpretation of treason may be supported. Burr's prosecutors, including lead prosecutor President Jefferson, chose this incorrect interpretation to support the government's prosecution of Aaron Burr. Chief Justice Marshall later clarified the Supreme Court's *Bollman and Swartwout* decision in the Burr trial, much to the dismay of Jefferson and his prosecution team and to the detriment of the government's case against Burr.[107]

In the *Bollman–Swartwout* opinion, Marshall reviewed evidence provided by President Jefferson, particularly the affidavits of William Eaton and James Wilkinson, together with the cipher letter. Marshall concluded that the crime of treason had not been established. Actions alleged in the proffered documents were directed against Spain; at most, a violation of the Neutrality Act occurred. "Not one syllable" in the cipher letter made reference to any territory of the United States. Marshall found that if the Neutrality Act had been violated, the charges were not brought before the appropriate tribunal.[108] The Writ of *Habeas Corpus* was granted and the prisoners discharged.[109]

Flaws in the government's prosecution were identified by the Court:

> There is a want of precision in the description of the offense which might produce some difficulty in deciding what cases would come within it. But several other questions arise which a court consist-

---

106 *PJM* VI, p. 488.
107 Smith, p. 357.
108 *PJM*, Volume VI, pp. 490-96.
109 *PJM*, Volume VI, pp. 489-496.

ing of four judges finds itself unable to decide, and therefore as the crime which the prisoners stand charged has not been committed, the court can only direct them to be discharged. This is done with the less reluctance because the discharge does not acquit them from the offence which there is probable cause for supposing they have committed, and if those whose duty it is to protect the nation by prosecuting offenders against the laws shall suppose those who have been charged with treason to be proper objects for punishment, they will, when possessed of less exceptional testimony, and when able to say at what place the offence has been committed, institute fresh proceedings against them.[110]

Chief Justice Marshall interpreted the crime of treason consistently with the Constitution. He protected Petitioners from governmental over-reaching and assured the rule of law. A portion of his opinion was unnecessary, later causing Marshall great embarrassment and requiring him to clarify the Court's earlier opinion during the Burr trial. At trial, Marshall would narrow the definition of treason, thus excluding constructive treason from American law. Many historians, including Professor Edwin Corwin, concluded that Marshall's clarification of his earlier decision was politically motivated, particularly against President Jefferson, and represents the low point of his judicial career.[111] More recently, historians and Constitutional scholars have reconciled the two Marshall opinions and concluded that Marshall's actions were appropriate.[112] Professor George Lee Haskins noted:

> Among the points that Marshall was attempting to establish in Bollman were the following: (1) to define treason as an act of levying war against the United States; (2) to make it clear that a military commander, specifically General Wilkinson, could not lawfully imprison men, under the pretense of public safety and martial law, and have them tried in whatever place he selected; and (3) to establish that those who committed acts short of treason could be punished pursuant to criminal sanctions of general applicability enacted by the legislature, "formed upon deliberation," but without particular "resentments" or "passions."[113] The law of treason must be strictly construed in accordance with its Constitutional definition.

---

110 Ibid., pp. 495-96.
111 Edward S. Corwin. *John Marshall and the Constitution: The Chronicle of the Supreme Court.* New Haven: Yale University Press, 1919, pp. 108-109.
112 Robert Kenneth Faulkner. *The Jurisprudence of John Marshall.* Princeton: Princeton University Press, 1968, pp. 269-285; Bradley Chapin. *The American Law of Treason: Revolutionary and Early National Origins;* George Lee Haskins and Herbert A. Johnson. *Foundations of Power: John Marshall, 1801-15.* The Oliver Wendell Holmes Devise: History of the Supreme Court of the United States, Volume II.
113 Haskins, pp. 260-61; Beveridge III, p. 351.

ADDITIONAL HABEAS CORPUS CHALLENGES

Deprivation of Bollman's and Swartwout's Constitutional rights was not an isolated act. When Wilkinson dispatched Bollman and Swartwout by sea from the Louisiana Territory to Washington, Wilkinson sent other alleged conspirators east for prosecution, without benefit of *habeas corpus* rights, counsel or bail. James Alexander was sent east by Wilkinson; upon his arrival in Baltimore, friends applied for a Writ of *Habeas Corpus*, which was immediately granted. In like manner, former United States Senator John Adair and Peter Ogden, alleged conspirators, were sent by Wilkinson to Baltimore and confined at Fort McHenry. Later, local counsel filed petitions for Writs of *Habeas Corpus*. The prisoners were brought before Judge Joseph Hopper Nicholson, a Maryland state judge. After hearing evidence on the writ of *habeas corpus*, Judge Nicholson discharged the prisoners after determining that proof was insufficient. Adair later sued Wilkinson for wrongful arrest and was awarded $2,500, later paid by Congress on Wilkinson's behalf.[114]

Judge Nicholson, after the prisoners were released, wrote President Jefferson to inform him about the legal proceedings in his Court. He explained and apologized for his decision to release the prisoners. Nicholson informed Jefferson that he understood that Adair and Ogden would be in Baltimore for a few more days and that if the President had additional affidavits or evidence that would warrant their arrest, Jefferson should immediately provide it. If additional information or evidence was received, Nicholson would immediately issue a warrant and have Adair and Ogden arrested.[115] President Jefferson responded and informed Judge Nicholson that he had no additional evidence to present against Adair and Ogden that would convict them. He advised Nicholson that Wilkinson was sending a packet that would support the charges against Adair and Ogden. However, Jefferson had yet to receive this information. He advised Nicholson that if the alleged evidence, yet to be received, was conclusive, that the men could be arrested again "if it shall be worth while…. Their crimes are defeated, and whether they shall be punished or not belongs to another department, and is not the subject or even a wish on my part." Jefferson may not have been worried

---

114 Beveridge, III, p. 336.
115 Joseph Hopper Nicholson to Thomas Jefferson, February 18, 1807. *The Thomas Jefferson Papers.* Library of Congress digital.

about Adair or Ogden and, perhaps, even Swartwout or Bollman. Jefferson was, however, intensely interested in the prosecution of Aaron Burr.[116]

After release of five suspects, Senator William Branch Giles, always Jefferson's designated judicial "attack dog," threatened to pursue a Constitutional amendment to remove criminal jurisdiction from the Supreme Court.[117] Reflections of Senator Plumer offer insights into opinions on both sides of the political aisle. The day the Supreme Court granted Swartwout's and Bollman's request for Writ of *Habeas Corpus*, Plumer recorded:

> If Adair, Alexander, Bollman, Ogden & Swartwout, were in fact traitors—they were not convicted—they were but prisoners, & in contemplation of law were presumed innocent—and ought to have been treated with humanity—with respect and with attention due to men of their talents & rank in society. Adair in particular was well known to Wilkinson—he had recently held offices of great importance, & sustained a fair moral character. But this vain intriguing haughty infamous Wilkinson deprived them of the rights which our laws guarantee even to common convicted malefactors.... Wilkinson has done more to destroy our little feeble military establishment, than its bitterest enemies have been able for years to effect. The President ought instantly to remove him from his two offices of Governor of Upper Louisiana & commander of the army. If he does not do it, Wilkinson will damn him & his administration. Thomas M. Randolph told me he thought Wilkinson must be removed or his father-in-law's (Jefferson) administration would fall.
>
> The public indignation seems now to be transferred from Burr to Wilkinson. And I expect in a few days to hear that the former has been tried & legally acquitted.
>
> It is now very apparent Wilkinson himself has created much of the alarm, & has greatly exaggerated the force & importance of Burr. I think Burr's object was the Mexican provinces—not a separation of the Union. And I rejoice the bill to suspend the writ of *habeas corpus* did not pass into a law. I hope that I shall never again consent to the passing an important law in haste.[118]

---

116 Thomas Jefferson to Joseph Hopper Nicholson, February 20, 1807. *Works* X, pp. 369-370.

117 Adams, p. 837; Beveridge III, p. 357.

118 *Memorandum of Proceedings*, February 21, 1807, pp. 617-619.

4. THE LAW OF TREASON

Treason is the only crime specifically defined in the Constitution. Treason is "the offense of attempting to overthrow the government of the state to which one owes allegiance, either by making war against the state or materially supporting its enemies."[119] According to medieval English law, "treason" is a word for an ancient crime—the betrayal of one's tribe, nation, or God. Treason was considered so reprehensible that the bitter punishment visited on Satan in *Paradise Lost* for his revolt against God, being cast into Hell, was scarcely worse than the gruesome price paid by real traitors during Milton's time."[120] Although the law of treason finds its roots in English law, the Roman Republic, long before the birth of Christ, developed the notion of *maiestas*, an insult to public authority.[121]

It has been said that "we are a rebellious nation: our whole history is treason."[122] Montesquieu wrote "that if the crime of treason be indeterminate, this alone is sufficient to make any government degenerate into arbitrary power."[123] If we had lost the Revolutionary War, the most famous violators of treason in the 18th century would have been those who partici-

---

119 Bryan A. Garner. *West's Law Dictionary, 7th Edition.* St.Paul: West Group, 1999, p. 1506.

120 Joseph Wheelan. *Jefferson's Vendetta: The Pursuit of Aaron Burr and the Judiciary*, p. 175.

121 Buckner Melton, *Aaron Burr: Conspiracy to Treason*, pp. 161-162.

122 1848 quote by Reverend Theodore Parker. Milton Metzger. *Henry David Thoreau: A Biography.* Minneapolis: Twenty-First Century Books, 2007, p. 78.

123 Joseph Story. *Commentaries on the Constitution of the United States*, p. 669.

pated in the American Revolution. Our ultimate act of rebellion was the Declaration of Independence:

> The history of the present King of Great Britain is a history of repeated injuries and usurpations, all having in direct object the establishment of absolute tyranny over these States...In every stage of these Oppressions, We have petitioned for Redress in the most humble terms; Our repeated petitions have been answered only by repeated injury. A Prince whose character is thus marked by every act which may define a Tyrant, is unfit to be the ruler of free people... We, therefore, the Representatives of the United States of America, in General Congress Assembled, appealing to the Supreme Judge of the world for the rectitude of our intentions, do in the name, and by Authority of the good people of these Colonies, solemnly publish and declare, that these United Colonies are, and of Right ought to be free and independent states; and that they are absolved from all allegiance to the British Crown.

Colonists knew what they were doing was a hanging offense; the Declaration concluded by pledging to one another "*...our Lives, our Fortunes, and our sacred Honor.*" Benjamin Franklin astutely observed: "Yes, we must, indeed, all hang together, or most assuredly we shall all hang separately."[124] (Emphasis added.)

BRITISH LAW OF TREASON

The restrictive and narrow definition of treason in the Constitution protects the rights of our citizens more precisely than did British law. The law of treason in Great Britain was derived from the Statute of 1351, 25 Edward III, st.5, c.3. This law established that treason was, among other things, that "if a man do levy war against our lord the King in his realm, or be adherent to the King's enemies in his realm, giving to them aid and comfort in the realm, or elsewhere, and thereof be probably attainted of open deed by the people of their condition."[125]

The definition of treason in Great Britain was expanded over time, often at the Crown's whim. For instance, it was considered treason (1) to commit murder of the monarch, (2) to take up arms against the monarch, his consort, or his eldest son, (3) to violate the monarch's consort, his eldest son's consort, or his eldest unwed daughter, (4) to murder the monarch's eldest

---

124 *The Works of Benjamin Franklin and the Life of Benjamin Franklin*, Jared Sparks, Volume I, p. 407.

125 Richard L. Perry and John C. Cooper, Editors. *Sources of Our Liberties: Documentary Origins of Individual Liberties in the United States Constitution and Bill of Rights*, pp. 240-241.

son, or (5) to murder a principal officer of the state. Further, it was treasonable (6) to compass or imagine the death of the monarch, his consort, or his eldest son as well as (7) to give aid to his enemies at home or abroad.[126] In later British statutes, the law of treason required that there must be two witnesses against the defendant and that they must testify before the defendants' testimony was given.[127] The two witness requirement was confirmed during the Restoration by the Treason Act of 1661.[128] In 1696, an act of treason required that there must be "two lawful witnesses, either both of them to the same overt act, or one of them to one, and the other of them to another overt act of the same treason."[129] In an effort to provide fair trials, British law after the Restoration provided certain procedural safeguards. An accused was permitted to have a copy of the indictment, right to counsel, and right to compulsory process.[130] When British authorities realized that the definition of venue for treason was too narrowly drawn, rules for venue were clarified and broadened, not only for treason, but for other crimes.[131] For several centuries after the 1351 Act, the law of treason was expanded and contracted by Parliament, often temporarily. During the reign of Henry VIII, for example, the scope of treason was extended to words, writings or conspiracy, even though an overt act may not have been committed.[132]

During Elizabethan times, Crown lawyers stretched the meaning of treason. In times of stress, the parameters of the law of treason were expanded, in an effort to stamp out resistance. For example, Algernon Sidney was condemned for sentiments that he expressed in a book that he never published and, in effect, was prosecuted for treason for merely thinking dangerous thoughts. Many American revolutionaries and statesmen in the 18th Century considered Sidney a patriotic martyr.[133]

Thomas Jefferson was well aware of British treason law. A case of particular interest involved Colonel Richard Rumbold. Rumbold was charged

---

126 L.M. Hill. "The Two-Witness Rule in English Treason Trials: Some Comments on the Emergence of Procedural Law," pp. 95-111.
127 *Sources of Our Liberties*, p. 241; I Edward 6, c. 12; 5 and 6 Edward 6, c. 11.
128 Ibid., 13 Caroline 2, c. 1.
129 Ibid., Trial of Treasons Act, 7 & 8 William 3, c. 3.
130 Bradley Chapin. *The American Law of Treason: Revolutionary and Early National Origins*, p. 4; The Trial of Treasons Act, 1696.
131 Chapin, p. 13. Act of 1543, during the reign of Henry VIII.
132 Hill, p. 101.
133 Edward Dumbauld. *The Constitution of the United States*. Norman: University of Oklahoma Press, 1964,p. 374; Chapin, p. 4.

in the "Rye-House plot" together with other extremist Whigs who plotted to ambush King Charles II and his brother James. Rumbold fled England, returning two years later. Upon his return, he was tried, convicted, and hanged for treason. Before his execution, Rumbold famously said: "There was no man born marked of God above another; for none comes into the world with a saddle on his back, neither any booted and spurred to ride him." In one of Thomas Jefferson's final letters, he paraphrased Rumbold's dying statement: " All eyes are opened, or opening, to the rights of man. The general spread of the light of science has already laid open to every view the palpable truth that the mass of mankind has not been *born with saddles on their backs, nor a favored few booted and spurred ready* to ride them legitimately by the grace of God...."[134] (Emphasis added.) Thomas Jefferson was well aware of abuses of British abuses of the law of treason.

Over the years, British court rulings expanded the parameters of the law of treason. One led to "constructive treason," defined by Sir Edward Coke: "In treason all the *participles criminis* are principals; and every act, which in the case of a felony, would render a man an accessory, will, in the case of treason, make him a principal."[135] St. George Tucker, a leading attorney in Virginia and a friend of both Thomas Jefferson and John Marshall, concluded that the doctrine of "constructive treason" was not part of our Constitutional definition of treason. He opined that British cases and common law could be reviewed by American courts. However, they must not be relied upon as binding precedent. Tucker continued: "It is probable that no part of the Constitution of the United States, was supposed to be less susceptible of various interpretations than that which defines and limits the offense of treason against the United States; the text is short, and until comments upon it appeared, might have been deemed explicit."[136] Tucker cited *The Federalist Papers* and early Federal cases that interpreted the treason clause, including the first *Fries case* heard by Supreme Court Associate Justice James Iredell and District Judge Peters in 1799 and the second *Fries* case heard by Supreme Court Associate Justice Samuel Chase and District Judge Peters

---

134 Douglass Adair. Rumbold's Dying Speech, 1685, and Jefferson's Last Words on Democracy, 1826. The William and Mary Quarterly. 3rd Series, Volume 9, Number 4 (October, 1952), pp. 521-31.

135 St. George Tucker's Blackstone's Commentaries, Volume 5, (1803), Note B, pages 272-297. Electronic Edition provided by the Lonang Institute, www.lonang.com.

136 Tucker, p. 272.

in 1800, both in Federal Circuit Court in Pennsylvania. In another case, Supreme Court Associate Justice James Wilson charged the jury on the law of treason: "It well deserves to be remarked, that with regard to treason a new and great improvement has been introduced to the government of the United States; under that government, the citizens have not only a legal, but a constitutional security against the extension of that crime, or the imputation of treason. Treasons, capricious, arbitrary, and constructive, have often been the most tremendous engines of despotic or legislative tyranny."[137]

TREASON BEFORE THE CONSTITUTION

As early as 1774, in a draft of Instructions to Deputies appointed to meet in General Congress, Jefferson considered the definition of treason.[138] Jefferson castigated General Gage for not understanding the Treason statute of Edward III and the importance of removing the doctrine of constructive treason from hands of despots. During the Revolution, the issue of disloyalty in the military was frequently addressed. The first American law to punish treasonable acts was in the Articles of War of the Continental Army, passed by the Continental Congress in 1775. This law established that mutiny, sedition, and providing assistance to the enemy were treasonable acts punishable by death.[139] On June 24, 1776, shortly before the Declaration of Independence was adopted, the Committee of Spies (a committee formed within the Continental Congress) addressed civilian treason:

> Resolved, That all persons abiding within any of the United Colonies, and deriving protection from the laws of the same, owe allegiance to the said laws, and are members of such colony; and that all persons passing through, visiting or making a temporary stay in any of the said colonies, being entitled to the protection of the laws during the time of such passage, visitation, or temporary stay, owe during the same time allegiance thereto:

> That all persons, members of, or owing allegiance to any of the United Colonies, as before described, who shall levy war against any of the said colonies within the same, or be adherent to the King of Great Britain, or others the enemies of the said colonies, or any of them, within the same, giving to him and them aid and comfort, are guilty of treason against such colony:

---

137 Tucker, pp. 272-73.
138 Thomas Jefferson. *PTJ* I, pp. 141-144. Instructions by the Virginia Convention to Their Delegates in Congress (August, 1774).
139 Chapin, pp. 29-30.

> That it be recommended to the legislatures of the several United Colonies to pass laws for punishing such persons before described, as shall be proveably [sic] attainted of open deed, by people of their own condition, of any of the treasons before described.[140]

Contemporaneously, Joseph Hawley wrote Elbridge Gerry urging prosecution of loyalists and Tories for treason: "I have often said that I supposed a declaration of independence would be accompanied with a declaration of treason.... I never desire to see high treason extended here further than it is now extended in Britain. But an act of high treason we must have instantly...."[141] Shortly thereafter, upon urging of the Continental Congress, individual state treason statutes were adopted. States defined treason in one of three ways: 1) treason was incorporated into laws of the state or common law; 2) specific acts were defined within treason laws that constituted levying war and adherence to enemies; or 3) statutes were enacted for crimes less than treason.[142] In contrast to the gruesome punishment for treason in Great Britain, the punishment adopted by the States was hanging.[143]

While drafting a general criminal statute for Virginia in 1778, Thomas Jefferson wrote that he understood the relation of the statute of Edward III to the judicially constructed treasons that later developed. Jefferson's draft statute provided for levying war and adherence as treason "and no others" in order to "prevent an intimidation of common law treasons."[144] Jefferson thus defined treason: "If a man do levy war against the Commonwealth, or be adherent to the enemies of the Commonwealth, giving to them aid or comfort in the Commonwealth, or elsewhere, and thereof be convicted of open deed, by the evidence of two sufficient witnesses, or his own voluntary confession, the said cases, and no others, shall be adjudged treasons which extend to the Commonwealth, and the person so convicted shall suffer death, by hanging, and shall forfeit his lands and goods to the Commonwealth."[145] Not a traitor suffered death in Virginia during the Revolution: the State General Assembly pardoned all those sentenced to hang.[146]

---

140 Chapin, pp. 36-37; John Adams. *The Works of John Adams.* Charles Francis Adams, Editor. Volume I, pp. 224-225.

141 Joseph Hawley to Elbridge Gerry, July 17, 1776; James T. Austin. *The Life of Elbridge Gerry, with Contemporary Letters.* Boston: 1829-1830. Volume I, pp. 206-208.

142 Chapin, pp. 38-39.

143 Chapin, p. 45.

144 Chapin, p. 40; *PTJ* 2, pp. 492-507.

145 *PTJ* 2, pp. 493-494.

146 Chapin, p. 62.

Jefferson attached several footnotes to his draft statute on treason that are of interest. Jefferson wrote: "Though the crime of an accomplice in treason is not here described, yet, Lord Coke says, the partaking and maintaining a treason herein described, makes him a principal in that treason: it being a rule that in treason all are principals." Next, Jefferson wrote:

> The stat. 25 E. 3 directs all other cases of treasons to await the opinion of Parliament. This has the effect of negative words, excluding all other treasons. As we drop that part of the statute, we must, by negative words, prevent an inundation of common law treasons. I strike out the word "it", therefore, and insert "the said cases, and no others." Quaere, how far those negative words may affect the case of accomplices above mentioned? Though if their case was within the statute, so as that it needed not to await the opinion of Parliament, it should seem to be also within our act, so as not to be ousted by the negative words.[147]

As of 1778, Thomas Jefferson favored limiting the scope of treason:

> In its style, I have aimed at accuracy, brevity, and simplicity, preserving, however, the very words of the established law, whenever their meaning had been sanctioned by judicial decisions, or rendered technical by usage.... And I must pray you to be as watchful over what I have not said, as what is said; for the omissions of this bill have all their positive meaning. I have thought it better to drop, in silence, the laws we mean to discontinue, and let them be swept away in the general negative words of this, than to detail them in clauses of express repeal...[148]

TREASON AFTER THE CONSTITUTION

At the Constitutional Convention, the Framers understood the importance of defining treason narrowly, so that it could not be used as a political weapon. The Constitution provides:

> Treason against the United States, shall consist *only* in levying War against them, or in adhering to their Enemies, giving them Aid and Comfort. No person shall be convicted of Treason unless on the Testimony of two Witnesses to the same overt Act, or on Confession in open Court.

> The Congress shall have power to declare the Punishment of Treason, but no Attainder of Treason shall work Corruption of Blood, or

---

147 James Willard Hurst. *The Law of Treason in the United States*, p. 88; PTJ 2, pp. 493-494..

148 Thomas Jefferson to George Wythe, November 1, 1778. *PTJ*, Volume 2, pp. 229-30.

Forfeiture except during the Life of the Person attainted.[149] (Emphasis added.)

The word "only" in the treason clause is the sole time that word appears within the Constitution.[150]

Since treason is specifically defined by the Constitution, it cannot be modified without a Constitutional Amendment. Its precise definition insures that treason will not be used against political adversaries or expanded during times of stress. Although the Legislative branch has authority to prescribe punishment for treason, it cannot alter its terms. The Supreme Court, in *Cramer v. United States*, 325 U.S. 1, 28 (1945), noted: "The concern uppermost in the framers' minds, that mere mental attitudes or expression should not be treason, influenced both the definition of the crime and procedure for its trial." Since Bills of Attainder were prohibited by the Constitution (Article I, Sections 9 and 10), judicial process was the only method permitted by the Constitution to resolve allegations of treason. During the Constitutional Convention, Benjamin Franklin spoke about treason, particularly the requirement for testimony of two persons: "... prosecutions for treason were generally virulent; and perjury too easily made use of against innocence." During the Pennsylvania Ratification Convention, James Wilson opined: "Congress can neither define nor try the crime" of treason.[151]

In *Cramer*, Justice Jackson wrote, "the basic law of treason in this country was framed by men who ... were taught by experience and by history to fear abuse of the treason charge almost as much as they feared treason itself."[152] It was important to protect against the abuses of treason that occurred under British rule; in particular, the use of treason against those who participated in political activities.

Treason was discussed in *The Federalist Papers*. In *Federalist No. 43*, James Madison wrote:

---

149 United States Constitution, Article III, Section 3.

150 Akhil Reed Amar. *America's Constitution: A Biography*. New York: Random House Trade Paperbacks, 2005, p.243.

151 Max Farrand, *The Records if the Federal Convention of 1787*. New Haven: Yale University Press, 1911, Volume III, p. 163; Edward Dumbauld, *The Constitution of the United States*, p. 375; James Madison. *Notes of the Debates in the Federal Convention of 1787*. Reported by James Madison; Edited by Adrienne Koch. New York: W.W. Norton & Company, 1966, p. 492.

152 *Cramer v. United States*, 325 U.S. 1, 76: Hamilton further discussed the law of treason in *Federalist* Nos. 74 and 84, pp. 447-449, 510-520.

As treason may be committed against the United States, the authority of the United States ought to be enabled to punish it. But as new-fangled and artificial treasons have been the great engines by which violent factions, the natural offspring of free government, have usually wreaked their alternate malignity on each other, the convention have, with great judgment, opposed a barrier to this particular danger, by inserting a constitutional definition of the crime, fixing the proof necessary for conviction of it, and restraining the Congress, even in punishing it, from extending the consequences of guilt beyond the person of its author.[153]

Not only was the charge of treason feared; punishment was downright frightening. This is how Britain punished treason: "...the culprit should be drawn prostrate at the tails of horses through the jagged and filthy streets from the court-room to the place of execution; that he be hanged by the neck and then cut down alive, the legs, arms, nose and ears then cut-off; the intestines ripped out and burned 'before the eyes' of the victim; and finally the head cut off, that his body be divided in four parts, and that his head and quarters be at the King's disposal...."[154] In 1790 Congress established hanging as the penalty for treason. Further, procedural guarantees were afforded all criminal defendants, including those charged with treason—the accused was entitled to a copy of the indictment, a list of witnesses and jurors was to be provided at least three days before trial, the right to counsel, the right to compulsory process, and the right to 35 peremptory challenges to the petit jury. Finally, a plea of standing mute to a charge was considered a plea of not guilty.[155] A year later, many of these same rights were incorporated into the Bill of Rights.

Among the first treason charges brought under the Constitution were against participants in the Whiskey Rebellion in the 1790s. The Whiskey Rebellion involved resistance of farmers in Western Pennsylvania against the new federal excise tax on whiskey.[156] After Phillip Vigol and John Mitchell were convicted of treason, President Washington pardoned them. In the Vogel and Mitchell cases, the term "to levy war" was interpreted as an assembly of men who used violence for the purpose of resisting execu-

---

153 *The Federalist Papers*. Clinton Rossiter, Editor. New York: The New American Library of World Literature, Inc., 1961, pp. 271-280, at 273.

154 Beveridge III, p. 402.

155 Chapin, pp. 84-85; 1 Stat. 112 (1790) 18 U.S.C. 1.

156 Chapin, pp. 85-90; Stanley Elkins and Eric McKitrick,. *The Age of Federalism: The Early American Republic, 1788-1800*, pp. 461-474.

tion of a law. During the Whiskey Rebellion, Thomas Jefferson wrote James Madison:

> And with respect to the transactions against the excise-law, it appears to me that you are all swept away in the torrent of governmental opinions, or that we do not know what these transactions have been. We know of none which according to the definitions of the law have been any thing more than riotous. There was indeed a meeting to consult about a separation. But to consult on a question does not amount to a determination of that question in the affirmative, still less to the acting on such a determination; but we shall see I suppose what the court lawyers, and courtly judges and would-be Ambassadors will make of it....

Thomas Jefferson argued that prosecution of those involved in the rebellion was an overreaction by the government. Interestingly, Jefferson's opinion on whether participants in the Whiskey Rebellion were guilty of treason mirrored John Marshall's later interpretation of the law of treason in the Burr case, a position that Jefferson roundly criticized. Although Burr may have been involved in a meeting of the participants, no direct action was taken against the state.[157]

John Fries was charged with treason in 1799. Fries was the leader of forcible resistance in Northeastern Pennsylvania against a 1798 federal law that levied a direct tax on houses. Supreme Court Associate Justice James Iredell and District Judge Richard Peters charged the jury that intent to prevent execution of a federal law with forcible opposition amounted to levying war within the definition of treason. Fries was convicted, but later granted a new trial after a problem was discovered with a juror. In his second trial, Supreme Court Associate Justice Samuel Chase, who had replaced Justice Iredell, sat with Judge Peters. Chase opined that conspiracy to oppose the execution of a federal law was a misdemeanor; forcible action in opposition to law amounted to levying war as required by the Constitutional definition of treason. Fries was convicted of treason, but later pardoned by President John Adams. Chief Justice Marshall cited this case during the Burr treason trial, holding that force was a necessary element of levying war.[158]

Supreme Court Associate Justice Story later wrote:

> Treason is generally deemed the highest crime, which can be committed in civil society, since its aim is an overthrow of the government and public resistance of its powers by force. Its tendency is to

---

157 Thomas Jefferson to James Madison, December 28, 1794. *PTJ* 28, pp. 228-230.
158 Dumbauld, pp. 376-377; Tucker, pp. 273-274. Justice Chase's actions in the *Fries* case became the basis for Article I of his impeachment.

create universal danger and alarm; and on this account is peculiarly odious, and often visited with the deepest resentment. Even a charge of this nature, made against an individual, is deemed so opprobrious, that, whether just or unjust, it subjects him to suspicion and hatred; and in times of high political excitement, acts of a very subordinate nature are often, by popular prejudices, as well as by royal excitement, magnified into this ruinous importance.

Story observed that since the law of treason had been misused and abused in England, the Framers of our Constitution wanted to insure that arbitrary constructions of treason by Courts or Congress could not occur, particularly in times of stress.[159]

The evolution of Thomas Jefferson's interpretation of the law of treason is interesting. There is no indication that Jefferson supported the doctrine of "constructive treason" prior to the Burr trial. Chief Justice Marshall's opinions in the Burr case were consistent with Thomas Jefferson's earlier writings on treason. Why, then, did Jefferson change his opinion? Was he so intent on convicting Burr that he was willing to change his earlier views and adopt the doctrine of constructive treason?[160]

---

159 Joseph Story. *Commentaries on the Constitution of the United States*. Durham: Carolina Academic Press, 1987, pp. 669-70.
160 Thomas Jefferson to George Wythe, November 1, 1778. *PTJ* 2, pp. 229-231; Thomas Jefferson to James Madison, December 28, 1794, *PTJ* 28, pp. 228-230.

5. COMMENCEMENT OF LEGAL PROCEEDINGS AGAINST AARON BURR

President Thomas Jefferson's orders to General Wilkinson and civilian authorities in the Louisiana and Mississippi Territories to thwart the alleged conspiracy, as interpreted and executed by General Wilkinson, turned into a dragnet operation. The result was that associates of Burr (Bollman, Swartwout, Adair, Armstrong, and Ogden) and, later, Burr himself, were taken into custody and deprived of basic Constitutional rights. After Bollman, Swartwout, Adair, Armstrong, and Ogden were discharged by the Courts, the stage was set for Burr's prosecution. Burr appeared before two separate Grand Juries in Kentucky to answer charges of treason and violation of the Neutrality law; true bills of indictment were not returned. Burr was later arrested in the Mississippi territory and once again, brought before a Grand Jury. In that case, the Grand Jury was incensed with numerous abuses of civil rights within their territory committed by governmental officials, including Wilkinson, against private individuals. As a result, the Grand Jury, after it denied issuance of an Indictment, took the unusual step of issuing a report. An account in the *Mississippi Messenger* reported that Burr appeared before the Grand Jury on February 2, 1807, and the Grand Jury reached its decision on February 4, 1807:

> The Grand Jury of the Mississippi Territory, on a due investigation [of the evidence] brought before them, are of the opinion that Aaron Burr has not been guilty of any crime or misdemeanor against the laws of the United States or of this Territory, or given any just occasion for alarm or inquietude to the good people of this Territory.

The Grand Jury present as a grievance, the late military expedition, unnecessarily as they conceive, fitted out against the person and property of said Aaron Burr, where no resistance has been made to the ordinary civil authority.

The Grand Jury also present as a grievance, destructive of personal liberty, the late military arrests made without warrant, and as they conceive without other lawful authority: and they do seriously regret that so much cause should be given to the enemies of our glorious Constitution, to rejoice in such measures being adopted in a neighboring Territory, [which] if sanctioned by the Executive of our country, must sap the vitals of our political existence, and crumble this glorious fabric into dust.[161]

It was now Aaron Burr's turn to be deprived of Constitutional rights by General Wilkinson and, later, President Jefferson. After the Grand Jury refused to indict Burr, he requested the Judge discharge him from custody. The Judge was the father of Caesar Rodney, soon to be appointed Attorney General by President Jefferson. The Judge required Burr to post bond. After posting bond, Burr immediately went into hiding, fearing for his life. Several weeks later, Burr was arrested by military authorities, housed in a federal stockade, and subsequently sent north for trial. When Burr and his military guards arrived in Fredericksburg, Virginia, they were redirected to proceed to Richmond for trial. President Jefferson and his advisers determined that the Federal Circuit Court in Richmond, Virginia was the appropriate location for Burr's trial. Blennerhassett's Island, the scene of Burr's alleged crimes, was located in Wood County, Virginia. (Blennerhassett's Island is today located in West Virginia).

Even before Burr's arrival in Richmond, President Jefferson anticipated what would happen. According to Senator Plumer, President Jefferson informed him:

... that he expected Aaron Burr had a trial in the Mississippi territory and was acquitted. But that Wilkinson had orders to arrest him & send him to this city—& he presumed he was now on his way as a prisoner for Wilkinson had many spies around Burr. But that he feared he would be discharged, the Courts being inclined to construe the law too favorably for the accused & too rigidly against the Government. That it was difficult to say where he ought to be tried—but on the whole thought in the State of Virginia—And there the judges were Marshall [Chief Justice John Marshall] who had already, in the case of Bollman & Swartwout, given an unfavorable

---

161 *The Mississippi Messenger*, February 26, 1807; Kline, p. 1020.

opinion—And that Griffin [Cyrus Griffin, United States District Judge for Virginia] the district judge was a poor creature.[162]

In March, Jefferson received a letter with an enclosed a pamphlet written by Judge Workman of New Orleans, a supporter of war against Spain and the taking of Mexico. On March 18, Jefferson wrote that Judge Workman released Peter Ogden on a writ of *habeas corpus*. Ogden was considered a Burr co-conspirator. Jefferson wrote that Workman was a member of the Mexican League, an organization that shared the alleged co-conspirator's desire for war with Spain: "This insurrection will probably show that the fault in our Constitution is not that the executive has too little power, but that the judiciary either has too much, or holds it under too little responsibility."[163]

An interested party, Representative John Randolph of Virginia, observed Burr's travels while under house arrest:

> Colonel Burr ... passed by my door the day before yesterday, under a strong guard. So I am told, for I did not see him, and nobody hereabouts is acquainted with his person. The soldiers escorting him, it seems, indulged his aversion to be publicly known, and to guard against inquiry as much as possible he was accoutred in a shabby suit of homespun, with an old white hat flapped over his face, the dress in which he was apprehended. From the description, and indeed the confession of the commanding officer to one of my neighbors, I have no doubt it was Burr himself. His very manner of traveling, although under arrest, was characteristic of the man, enveloped in a mystery.[164]

President Jefferson, in a letter to Robert Livingston, wrote: "Burr indeed made a most inglorious exhibition of his much over-rated talents. He is now on his way to Richmond for trial."[165] In a letter to Colonel Morgan, President Jefferson said:

> Burr is on his way to Richmond for trial; and if the judges do not discharge him before it is possible to collect the testimony from Maine to New Orleans, there can be no doubt where his history will end. To what degree punishments adherents shall be extended, will be decided when we shall have collected all the evidence, and seen who were cordially guilty. The Federalist's appear to make Burr's cause their own, and to spare no efforts to screen his adherents. Their great mortification is at the failure of his plans. Had a little success

162 *Memorandum of Proceedings*, March 4, 1807, p. 641.
163 Thomas Jefferson to Joseph Cabell, March 18, 1807. *The Thomas Jefferson Papers*, Library of Congress digital, image 62.
164 John Randolph to Joseph H. Nicholson, March 25, 1807. Henry Adams. *John Randolph*. Boston: Houghton, Mifflin & Company, 1882, pp. 217-218
165 Thomas Jefferson to Robert Livingston, March 24, 1807. *Works* X, pp. 170-172.

dawned on him, their openly joining him might have produced some danger. As it is, I believe the undertaking will not be without some good effects, as a wholesome lesson to those who have more ardor, than principle. I believe there is reason to expect that Blennerhasset will also be sent by the judges of Mississippi to Virginia. Yours was the first intimation I had of this plot, for which it is but justice to say you have deserved well of your country.[166]

In his letter to Morgan, Jefferson acknowledged that there was a problem with the evidence against Burr (this problem was previously addressed during a Cabinet meeting on March 17).[167] Jefferson should have been well aware of the correct interpretation of the Supreme Court's decision in *United States v. Bollman and Swartwout*. Dicta in that opinion, which later become the basis for the prosecution's case against Burr (constructive treason), had not yet been contemplated by either Jefferson or the prosecution. Albert Beveridge, in *The Life of John Marshall*, opined: "A personal antagonism, once formed, became with Thomas Jefferson a public policy."[168] Beveridge's comment was applicable not only to Aaron Burr and John Marshall but to anyone who politically disagreed with him. When one disagreed with Thomas Jefferson, he became Jefferson's enemy and would remain an enemy.

President Jefferson stirred up hysteria after he publicly declared Burr's guilt in January, 1807, media coverage spread rumors and gossip about Burr and speculated about what the government would do. Public perceptions were inflamed and opinions formed about Burr; an impartial trial would be difficult, if not impossible. Although the State Capitol of Richmond was not Jefferson's base of power, Virginia was, after all, Jefferson's home state. Richmond was approximately ninety miles from the seat of the federal government in Washington and Jefferson was President.

A number of newspapers speculated about what would happen to Burr. *The Richmond Enquirer*, a newspaper published in the city where Burr was to be tried, published a lengthy article on March 31, 1807, about Burr's apprehension and arrest. It described Burr's detention at Fort Stoddard in Mobile, Alabama, his armed military escort to Washington, and, subsequently, Richmond:

> He is conducted to this city, to undergo an examination before Chief Justice Marshall—several circumstances concur to recom-

---

166 Thomas Jefferson to Colonel Morgan, March 26, 1807. *Writings* XI, pp. 173-74.
167 *The Complete Anas of Thomas Jefferson*, pp. 254. "Persons were named for conducting enquiries into Burr's treasons."
168 Beveridge, III, p. 384.

mend the choice of this tribunal. The most material of them is that, the overt act of treason, on which he may be charged, was most probably committed at Blennerhassett's Island, in the river Ohio and within the limits of Virginia. His crime therefore will fall within the jurisdiction of the Federal District Court of this state. He will be brought before the highest judicial minister in this country—the chief justice of the United States.

He will be examined in a judicial district, among the nearest to the seat of government of the United States; and should he be sent on for further trial, he will have the advantage of being brought before one of the district courts, whose sessions come on the soonest. In these respects, Aaron Burr will possess all the privileges secured to him by the Constitution of the United States. He will "enjoy the right to a speedy and public trial, by an impartial jury of the state and district wherein the crime shall have been committed, which district shall have been previously ascertained by law."

Whether we consider the nature of the crime or the character of the criminal; the witnesses who will be brought up, the counsel by whom it will be argued, or the eager curiosity of the nation; this will be one if the most impressive spectacles which this or any other city in the United States was ever witnessed in.

The criminal was once the Vice President of the United States; and a man who ranks at all times among men of the ascendant talents in this country.

The crime likely to be alleged against him is the foulest and most atrocious that can possibly disgrace the inhabitant of a free country. It is the crime of a traitor. It is the crime of a parricide in arms against his country; who has labored to excite a gallant people against the very best government that ever existed; who has plotted to destroy that great ark of our political safety, our union; in fact, one who has whetted the poisoned daggers of civil insurrection, to "levy war" against his country. In comparison of such a crime, what is murder; what is robbery that clandestinely empties my purse; or the felon that boldly prowls upon the highway, and at the same blow deals robbery and murder?... If upon this ground, even, he be acquitted, perhaps he may still be indicted and tried by laws of the United States for preparing an expedition against Mexico; the colony of a foreign state with whom we are now at peace.[169]

Burr was held to answer in Richmond, for the fourth time, for the same alleged crimes. Burr was arrested in the Mississippi Territory on February 19, 1807 and held in a military stockade for almost two weeks. He was transported under armed guard to Washington. Upon arrival in Fredericksburg,

---

169 *The Richmond Enquirer*, March 31, 1807.

Burr's guards were intercepted and re-directed by the Jefferson Administration to transport Burr to Richmond for legal proceedings. Burr arrived in Richmond on March 26, 1807. There he remained under armed guard until his arraignment at the Eagle Tavern. The tavern was located at the foot of a hill in Richmond above the James River. He appeared before the Chief Justice of the United States, John Marshall.

6. Judiciary Acts

> *The judge of course stands till the law shall be repealed, which we trust will be at the next Congress.*
> —Thomas Jefferson to Archibald Stuart, April 8, 1801

Why did the Chief Justice of the United States sit as a trial judge in the Burr trial? In recent memory, the only time a chief justice acted apart from his brethren was during the impeachment trial of President William Clinton. The first great battle between President Jefferson and his supporters and the judiciary and Chief Justice Marshall directly led to Chief Justice Marshall presiding as circuit judge in the Burr trial. How did this happen?

The Constitution established the Judiciary as a third co-equal branch of government in Article III. Although the Judicial Branch was intended to be a co-equal branch, it was thought to be the "least dangerous" branch.[170] Alexander Hamilton wrote in *Federalist* No. 78:

> ... the judiciary, from the nature of its functions, will always be the least dangerous to the political rights of the Constitution; because it will be least in a capacity to annoy or injure them...The judiciary, on the contrary, has no influence over either the sword or the purse; no direction either in the strength or of the wealth of the society, and can take no active resolution whatever. It may truly be said to have neither FORCE nor WILL but merely judgment; and must ultimately depend upon the aid of the executive arm for the efficacy of its judgments....[171]
> (Emphasis added.)

---

170 *The Federalist Papers*, No. 78. Rossiter, pp. 464-472.
171 Ibid., p. 465.

JUDICIARY ACT OF 1789

Since Article III of the Constitution outlined a bare framework for the Judicial Branch, Congress was left with the task of giving life to the judiciary. The Senate's first order of business was to draft the Judiciary Act of 1789, signed into law by President Washington on September 24, 1789.

The Judiciary Act of 1789 created a three-tiered structure for Federal courts, a structure that survives today. Six justices were to sit on the Supreme Court, one of whom was to be designated Chief Justice. The Supreme Court met twice a year. Two inferior Federal courts were created: district and circuit courts. Each state was assigned a district court; the district court held sessions four times a year. An intermediate court was established, consisting of three circuit courts—eastern, middle, and southern circuits. Each circuit was comprised of one district judge and two Supreme Court Justices. Circuit court duties were known as "circuit riding." The circuit courts served as the chief trial courts for the Federal judicial system.[172]

CIRCUIT RIDING

As the Supreme Court commenced operation, it had little to do. The Court first met in February 1790 in New York City; no cases were yet filed with the Court and only two filed in 1791. In the early years of the Court, approximately five cases were filed per year. As a result, Justices primary responsibility was to ride circuit.[173]

> Circuit riding for the Justices was required for several reasons. First, it saved money for litigants and the Federal government. Second, since interpretation of the Constitution and federal law was in its infancy, interpretation of the law by Justices at the trial level would result in consistent and accurate legal opinions. Third, circuit riding would bring the Federal Judiciary to local courts and provide better communication with its citizens. Finally, circuit riding would enhance communication between the Supreme Court and other Federal judges.[174]

Circuit riding became the bane of existence for the Justices. To a man, they hated it. The primary complaint was travel, particularly for older Jus-

---

172 The Judiciary Act of 1789, 1 U.S. Stats. 73, adopted September 24, 1789: Maeva Marcus, Editor. *The Documentary History of the Supreme Court of the United States, 1789-1800*. Volume 4. New York: Columbia University Press, 1992, pp. 22-35.

173 William R. Casto. *The Supreme Court in the Early Republic: The Chief Justiceships of John Jay and Oliver Ellsworth*, pp. 54-55.

174 Joshua Glick. "Comment: On the Road: The Supreme Court and the History of Circuit Riding." *Cardozo Law Review*, Vol. 24 (April 2003), pp. 1753.

tices. Travel in the 1790s was hazardous and tedious. Another complaint was that, when sitting on the Supreme Court, Justices frequently heard cases on appeal after that they had decided the case in the circuit court. Although several changes were made to accommodate the Justices in the first ten years of the Court, circuit riding responsibilities would continue for almost one hundred years.

Riding circuit required Justices to travel great distances, with assignments anywhere from Maine to Georgia. All were inconvenienced; many suffered injuries. For example, Justice William Paterson was once so badly injured while riding circuit that he was unable to move after an accident, resulting in his absence from the Supreme Court and circuit court. Most of the Justices hated riding circuit. Future Supreme Court Justice Joseph Story's biographer referred to circuit riding as a "wretched system." Story, who was appointed to the Court in 1811 and later became Chief Justice Marshall's great friend and collaborator, often traveled more than 2,000 miles a year while riding circuit and attending sessions of the Supreme Court. Justice James Iredell of North Carolina was referred to as a "traveling post boy."[175]

ATTEMPTS TO REFORM THE JUDICIARY ACT OF 1789

As early as 1790, Chief Justice John Jay, on behalf of the Court, wrote President Washington expressing the Justices' displeasure with circuit court responsibilities. Jay requested that the Judiciary Act be amended, since it was inconsistent and incompatible for a Justice to sit on both the Circuit and Supreme Court.[176] President Washington brought reform of the judiciary to the attention of Congress in 1790: "...The laws you already passed for the establishment of the judiciary system have opened the doors of justice to all descriptions of persons. You will consider in your wisdom whether improvements in that system must yet be made..." Congress requested the Attorney General to prepare a report on the administration of justice. Attorney General Edmond Randolph recommended that Supreme Court Justices be relieved of circuit riding responsibilities. When Congress

---

175 Charles Warren. *The Supreme Court in United States History*, Volume I, p. 86; Washington to Thomas Johnson, August 7, 1791, *The Papers of George Washington*, Volume 31, pp. 332-333.

176 Justices of the Supreme Court to President Washington. Maeva Marcus, Volume 2, pp. 89-92.

failed to act, President Washington wrote another letter to Congress requesting relief from burdensome circuit court travel of the Justices.[177]

Much to the dismay of the Supreme Court and the Washington Administration, judicial reform was not a priority for Congress. It was still not a Congressional priority when John Adams became President. Although a Senate Committee in 1798 drafted a bill to create five additional districts and eliminate Justices from circuit court responsibility, no action was taken. President Adams, in a 1799 Message, recommended that Congress:

> ... give due effect to the civil administration of government, and to ensure a just execution of the laws, a revision and amendment of the judiciary system is indispensably necessary. In this extensive country it cannot but happen that numerous questions respecting the interpretation of the laws and the rights and duties of officers and citizens must arise. On the one hand, the laws should be executed; on the other, individuals should be guarded from oppression. Neither of these objects is sufficiently assured under the present organization of the judicial department. I therefore earnestly recommend the subject to your serious consideration.

In response, Congressional committees were appointed to consider revisions to the Judiciary Act; once again, the law was unchanged.[178]

President Adams, in his final Address to Congress in late 1800, once again urged amendment of the judicial system:

> In every point of view of such primary importance to carry the laws into prompt and faithful execution, and to render that part of the administration of justice which the Constitution and laws devolve on the Federal Courts, as convenient to the People as may consist with their present circumstances, that I cannot omit, once more, to recommend to your serious consideration the Judiciary System of the United States. No subject is more interesting than this to the public happiness, and to none can those improvements which may have been suggested by experience, be more beneficially applied....[179]

JUDICIARY ACT OF 1801

The Judiciary Act of 1801 became law on February 13, 1801, just three weeks before President-elect Jefferson was to take office. Long desired

---

177 Maeva Marcus, Volume 4, pp. 122-127; President Washington's Second Annual Address, December 8, 1790. James D. Richardson, Editor. *A Compilation of the Messages and Papers of the Presidents.* Volume I, pp. 73-76.

178 Kathryn Turner. "Federalist Policy and the Judiciary Act of 1801", pp. 3-32; Maeva Marcus, Volume 4, pp. 223-226; Richardson, Volume I, pp. 279-282.

179 Maeva Marcus, Volume 4, pp. 288-289; President John Adams Fourth Annual Address to Congress, November 22, 1800. Richardson. Volume I, pp. 295-298.

reforms were realized with passage of this Act. When portrayed as a last minute Federalist law, enacted in the closing days of a lame-duck administration, the Judiciary Act of 1801 appears political; when viewed in light of reforms requested for more than ten years by the Washington and Adams Administrations and the Supreme Court, the Act was prescient and necessary. Unfortunately, politics got in the way. The uproar caused by "midnight appointments" by President John Adams of judges and court officials created by the new law on his way out of office diverted attention from its merits. The timing of the Act could not have been worse.

Shortly before enactment of the Judiciary Act of 1801, Chief Justice Ellsworth submitted his resignation to President Adams. After former Chief Justice John Jay declined reappointment, President Adams surprised everyone when he nominated his Secretary of State, John Marshall. President Adams would never regret his appointment of John Marshall. Adams is reported to have said: "My gift of John Marshall to the people of the United States was the proudest act of my life." Adams, late in life, wrote Chief Justice Marshall: "There is no act of my life that I look back upon with more pleasure, than the short time I spent with you. And it is the pride of my life that I have given to this nation a Chief Justice, equal to Coke or Hale, Holt or Mansfield."[180] John Quincy Adams, upon Marshall's death in 1835, wrote: "...He was one of the most eminent men that this country has ever produced. He has held this appointment thirty-five years. It was the last act of my father's Administration, and one of the most important services rendered by him to his country...."[181]

The Judiciary Act of 1801 revised circuit courts, relieving Supreme Court Justices from dreaded circuit riding. Since Justices no longer had circuit court responsibilities, the Act reduced the number of Justices by one; the reduction was to occur upon the next vacancy on the Court. Thomas Jefferson considered this a political trick intended to deprive him, as the next President, with the opportunity to appoint a Republican to the Court. The Act revised the terms of the Court: the Court would now convene on the first Mondays in June and December, rather than the first Mondays in February and August. Its major focus was reconfiguration of the circuit court system. Six circuit courts were established. Five circuits would have three

---

180 John Adams to John Marshall, August 17, 1825. *PJM* X, p. 197.

181 John Quincy Adams. *The Diary of John Quincy Adams, 1794-1845.* Allan Nevins, Editor, pp. 460-461.

Judges; the fifteen new positions were to be appointed by the President. The Sixth Circuit (Kentucky, Tennessee and the territories of Indiana and Ohio) had one new circuit Judge and two new district judges. In total, the Judiciary Act of 1801 created five district judges and sixteen circuit judges.[182] All newly created positions were filled by President Adams in the closing days of his Administration, angering Thomas Jefferson and his supporters.

THOMAS JEFFERSON'S FIRST ATTACK ON THE JUDICIARY

Ironically, President Jefferson's opposition to the Judiciary Act of 1801 and its subsequent repeal led directly to Chief Justice Marshall presiding in the Burr trial. The Judiciary Act of 1801 united Republicans in opposition to the judiciary. When President Adams appointed judges, government attorneys, and court personnel to newly established positions, Republicans were appalled.

From the early stages of his Administration, President Jefferson expressed disgust with the judiciary; Republican's would take action against the Judiciary Act of 1801. At first, there was little President Jefferson could do. The newly elected Republican Congress would not convene until December 1801, nine months after President Jefferson took office. Jefferson complained bitterly: "[the Federalists] stand at present almost without followers. The principal of them have retreated into the judiciary as a strong hold. The tenure of which renders it difficult to dislodge them."[183] Treasury Secretary Albert Gallatin prepared a budget for Jefferson early in his Administration, in part based upon the assumption that the recent judiciary bill would be repealed.[184]

Several weeks after President Jefferson's Inauguration, William Branch Giles, the Virginia firebrand who served as President Jefferson's point man in the House of Representatives and later in the Senate, wrote Jefferson to offer advice on "purgation" from office as a benefit of a new administration:

> It appears to me, that the only check upon the Judiciary system as it is now organized and filled, is the removal of all its executive officers indiscriminately—The Judges have been the most unblushing violators of constitutional restrictions, and their officers have been the humble echoes of all their vicious schemes, to retain them in office would be to sanction the pollution of the very fountain of

---

182 Max Farrand. "The Judiciary Act of 1801." *The American Historical Review*, Vol. 5, No. 4 (July 1900), pp. 682-686.
183 Thomas Jefferson to Joel Barlow, March 14, 1801. *PTJ* 33, pp. 274-275.
184 Albert Gallatin to Thomas Jefferson, March 14, 1801, *PTJ* 33, pp. 275-277.

justice, taking it for granted therefore, that this salutary check will be applied....[185]

A week later, President Jefferson responded:

All appointments to civil offices during pleasure, made after the event of the election was certainly known to Mr. Adams are considered as nullities. I do not view the persons appointed as even candidates for the office, but make others without noticing or notifying them. Mr. Adams' best friends have agreed this is right...Good men, to whom there is no objection but a difference of political principle, practiced only as far as the right of a private citizen will justify, are not proper subjects of removal, except in the case of Attorneys & Marshals. The courts being so decidedly federal, & irremovable, it is believed that republican Attorneys & Marshals, being the doors of entrance into the courts, are indispensably necessary as a shield to the republican part of our fellow citizens, which I believe is the main body of the people....[186]

Several months later, Giles offered additional advice to President Jefferson:

But the circumstance, which most attracts the attentions and employs the reflections of the thinking republicans here, is the situation of the judiciary as now organized.—It is constantly asserted, that the revolution is incomplete, so long as that strong fortress is in possession of the enemy; and it is surely a most singular circumstance, that the public sentiment should have forced itself into the Legislative and Executive departments, and that the Judiciary should not only not acknowledge its influence, but should pride itself in resisting its will under the under the misapplied idea "Independence". I have bestowed some reflections upon this subject, and under my present impressions it appears to me that no remedy is competent to redress the evil, but an absolute repeal of the whole judiciary system, terminating the present *offices* and creating an entire new system defining the common law doctrine, and restraining to the proper constitutional extent the jurisdiction of the Courts.[187]

President Jefferson's intent to seek repeal of the Judiciary Act of 1801 was most clearly expressed in a letter to Archibald Stuart:

Mr. Adams, who continued filling all the offices till 9 oclock of the night, at 12 of which he was to go out of office himself, took care to appoint for this district also. *The judge of course stands till the law shall be repealed, which we trust will be at the next Congress.* But as to all others, I made it immediately known, that I should consider them as nullities, and appoint others: as I think I have a preferable right to

---

185 William Branch Giles to Thomas Jefferson, March 16, 1801, *PTJ* 33, pp. 310-312.
186 Thomas Jefferson to William Branch Giles, March 23, 1801, *PTJ* 33, pp. 413-414.
187 William Branch Giles to Thomas Jefferson, June 1, 1801, *PTJ* 34, pp. 227-228.

name agents for my administration, at least to the vacancies falling after it was known that Mr. Adams was not naming himself.... The only shield for our Republican citizens against the federalism of the courts is to have the Attorneys & marshals republicans....[188] (Emphasis added.)

REPEAL OF THE JUDICIARY ACT OF 1801

Until the new Congress convened in December 1801, little action could be taken. President Jefferson, in his First Annual Message to Congress, recommended:

> *The Judiciary system of the United States, and especially that portion of it recently erected, will of course present itself to the contemplation of Congress;* and that they may be able to judge of the proportion which the institution bears to the business it has to perform, I have caused to be procured from the several States, and now lay before Congress, an exact statement of all the causes decided since the first establishment of the courts, and those which were depending when additional courts and judges were brought in to their aid. (Emphasis added.)

This Message provided marching orders to the newly convened, Republican controlled Congress.[189] Repeal of the Judiciary Act of 1801 had been in the cross-hairs of Republicans since enactment.

In December, 1801, an original action was filed in the Supreme Court requesting that an order be issued to Secretary of State James Madison to show cause why a *writ of mandamus* should not be issued requiring him to deliver four undelivered commissions to Justice of the Peace appointees. (*Mandamus* is a writ issued by a superior court to compel a lower court or a government officer to perform mandatory or purely ministerial duties).[190] The four men were appointed by President Adams in the waning hours of his Administration and come to be the most famous of the "midnight appointees." Although their Commissions were signed by President Adams and sealed by the Secretary of State (John Marshall), the commissions were never delivered. Upon assuming office, President Jefferson found the undelivered commissions and ordered that they not be delivered. A brief hearing on the show cause motion was held. After the Government presented

---

188 Thomas Jefferson to Archibald Stuart, April 8, 1801. *PTJ* 33, p. 555; *Dictionary of American Biography*, Volume XVIII. Edited by Dumas Malone, pp. 161-162.

189 President Jefferson's First Message to Congress, December 8, 1801, *PTJ* 36, pp. 57-65.

190 Bryan A. Garner. *West's Law Dictionary*, 7th *Edition*. St. Paul, MN: West Group, 1999, p. 973.

no argument, the Court granted the preliminary motion for a rule to show cause. The Supreme Court scheduled argument on the *writ of mandamus* for the fourth day of the next regularly scheduled term of the Supreme Court in June 1802; however, due to subsequent repeal of the Judiciary Act of 1801, the next term of the Supreme Court would not convene until February 1803.[191]

President Jefferson never understood the judiciary; he believed it should be as representative and responsive to the people as the legislative and executive branches.[192] Judges, however, have never been expected to be representative or responsive to popular opinion. In fact, just the opposite is true. The judiciary's responsibility is to be representative and responsive to the law, not political pressures or public opinion.[193]

President Jefferson wrote John Dickinson:

> On their part, they have retired into the judiciary as a stronghold. There the remains of federalism are to be preserved and fed from the treasury and from that battery all the works of republicanism are to be beaten down and erased. By a fraudulent use of the Constitution, which has made judges irremovable, they have multiplied useless judges merely to strengthen their phalanx.[194]

Congressional argument on repeal of the Judiciary Act of 1801 was heated. Republicans, led by Senators Breckinridge (Kentucky) and Mason (Virginia), argued against expansion of the judiciary as authorized by the Judiciary Act of 1801. Federalists, led by Senator Gouverneur Morris of Pennsylvania, argued that the newly appointed judges were protected by the Constitution, which ensured an independent judiciary; judges could only be removed from office by impeachment. During Senate debate, upon third reading of the Bill, Vice President Aaron Burr, serving as President of the Senate, broke a tie (two Republican Senators were absent) on a motion to refer the Bill for repeal of the Judiciary Act of 1801 to a select committee in an effort to improve the bill and make it more palatable to Federalists. Although Burr's actions were appropriate, another nail was driven into the coffin of his relations with Jefferson. The bill passed the Senate on February 3, 1802 by a vote of 16–15. The bill later passed the House 59–32. When

---

191 Warren, pp. 200-203.
192 Dumas Malone, *Jefferson the President: First Term, 1801-1805*. Volume IV, pp. xix-xx.
193 Baker, p. 372.
194 Thomas Jefferson to John Dickinson, December 19, 1801, *PTJ* 36, pp. 165-166.

President Jefferson signed the bill, repeal of the Judiciary Act of 1801 was now law.[195]

A revised Judiciary Act, passed in April 1802, and provided that the Supreme Court would now have one annual session, commencing on the first Monday in February. In most respects, other than composition of the circuits and one annual Supreme Court term, the Judiciary Act of 1789 had been re-implemented. Supreme Court Justices would again be required to ride circuit, although accommodation for excessive travel was made. Six regional circuits (consisting of the local District Judge and one Supreme Court Justice) were established, thus reducing the size of circuits and easing travel requirements. Each Justice was assigned a specific circuit court, usually in proximity to his home. For example, Chief Justice Marshall was assigned to the Fifth Circuit, consisting of Virginia and North Carolina. The Virginia circuit court met in Richmond, Marshall's home. He traveled twice a year to Raleigh, North Carolina.

REACTION TO REPEAL

After repeal of the Judiciary Act of 1801, letters between the Justices provide an interesting glimpse into the workings of the early Marshall Court. Contrary to the opinions of those who opposed him, Chief Justice Marshall did not always prevail in every argument with his brethren. Letters reveal that Marshall reconciled his opinions with those of his fellow Justices; at a minimum, he knew how to count votes. For example, Chief Justice Marshall wrote Justice William Paterson:

> You have I doubt not seen the arrangement of our future duties as marked out in a bill lately reported to the Senate. They are less burthensome than heretofore, or than I expected. *I confess I have some strong constitutional scruples. I cannot well perceive how the performance of circuit duty by the Judges of the Supreme Court can be supported.* If the question was new I should be unwilling to act in this character without a consultation of the Judges; but I consider it as decided & that whatever my own scruples may be I am bound by the decision. I cannot however but regret the loss of the next June term. I could have wished the Judges had convened before they proceeded to execute the new system....[196] (Emphasis added.)

Several weeks later, Chief Justice Marshall rethought his earlier position on acquiescence with Congressional action:

---

195 Warren, pp. 208-209; Beveridge III, 65-66.
196 John Marshall to William Paterson, April 6, 1802, *PJM* VI, pp. 105-106.

It having now become apparent that there will be no session of the Supreme Court of the United States holden in June next & that we shall be directed to ride the circuits, before we can consult on the course proper to be taken by us, it appears to me proper that we Judges should communicate their sentiments on this subject to each that they may act understandingly & in the same manner.

I hope I need not say that no man in existence respects more than I do, those who passed the original law concerning the courts of the United States, & those who first acted under it. So highly do I respect their opinions that I had not examined them & should have p(roceed)ed without a doubt on the subject, to perform the duties assigned to me if the late discussions had not unavoidably produced an investigation of the subject which from me it would not otherwise have received. *The result of this investigation has been an opinion which I cannot conquer that the Constitution requires distinct appointments & commissions for the Judges of the inferior courts from those of the Supreme Court. It is however my duty & inclination in this as in all other cases to be bound by the opinion of the majority of the Judges & I should therefore have proceeded to execute the law so far as that task may be assigned to me; had I not supposed it possible that the Judges might be inclined to distinguish between the original case of being appointed to duties marked out before their appointments & of having the duties of administering justice in new courts imposed after their appointments.* I do not myself state this because I am myself satisfied that the distinction ought to have weight, for I am not—but as there may be something in it I am induced to write to the Judges requesting the favor of them to give me their opinions which opinions I will afterwards communicate to each Judge. My own conduct shall certainly be regulated by them.

This is a subject not lightly resolved on. The consequences of refusing to carry the law into effect may be very serious. For myself personally I disregard them, & so am I persuaded does every other Gentleman on the bench when put in competition with what he thinks his duty, but the conviction of duty ought to be very strong before the measure is resolved on. The law having been once executed will detract very much in the public determination, not now to act under it....[197] (Emphasis added.)

John Marshall was not pleased with the actions by the Republican Congress and the President. Writing to Rufus King, Marshall voiced displeasure with repeal of the Judiciary Act of 1801 and renewal of circuit riding responsibilities:

---

197 John Marshall to William Paterson, April 19, 1802, *PJM* VI, pp. 108-109. Marshall enclosed in his letter to Justice Paterson a similar letter to Justice Cushing that he requested Justice Paterson pass along to Cushing. John Marshall to William Cushing, April 19, 1802, *PJM* VI, p. 108.

"...Public opinion in this quarter of the union has sustained no es-sential change. That disposition to coalesce with what is, now, the majority in America as well in this state, which was strongly dis-played by the minority twelve months past, exists no longer. It has expired. But the minority is only recovering its strength & firmness. It acquires nothing. Our political tempests will long, very long, exist, after those who are now tossed about by them shall be at rest..."[198]

Chief Justice Marshall's handling of this crisis speaks volumes about his leadership and moderation. Although he believed that circuit riding duties of Supreme Court Justices should be abolished and repeal of the Judiciary Act of 1801 raised constitutional issues, he sought the opinions and advice of his colleagues and subordinated his personal opinions to the collective opinion of his brethren. Wisely, Marshall chose to lose this battle so that the Court would later prevail.

STUART V. LAIRD

The Supreme Court affirmed repeal of the Judiciary Act of 1801 and enactment of the Judiciary Act of 1802 in *Stuart v. Laird,* 1 Cranch 299, 309 (1803). This case arose out of Virginia Federal Circuit Court, where Chief Justice Marshall presided with District Judge Cyrus Griffin. In the *Stuart* case, a direct challenge was made to the constitutionality of repeal of the Ju-diciary Act of 1801. John Laird won a judgment against Hugh Stuart prior to repeal of the Judiciary Act of 1801. The judgment was challenged on several grounds, including Supreme Court justices sitting as circuit judges. After Chief Justice Marshall rejected this argument, the case was appealed to the Supreme Court. Since Chief Justice Marshall heard this case in the Rich-mond Circuit Court, he did not participate in the Supreme Court decision. Associate Justice William Paterson, writing for the Court, held that objec-tion to justices sitting as circuit judges was untimely. He noted that there was a notion being discussed,

... that the judges of the Supreme Court have no right to sit as cir-cuit judges, not being appointed as such, or in other words, that they ought to have distinct commissions for that purpose. To this objec-tion, which is of recent date, it is sufficient to observe, that practice and acquiescence under it [the Judiciary Act of 1789] for a period of several years, commencing with the organization of the judicial system, afford an irresistible answer, and have indeed fixed the con-struction. It is a contemporary interpretation of the most forcible nature. This practical exposition is too strong and obstinate to be

---

198 John Marshall to Rufus King, May 5, 1802. *PJM* VI, pp. 119-120.

shaken or controlled. Of course, the question is at rest, and ought not now to be disturbed.

In a later decision, *United States v. Daniel,* 19 U.S. 542 (1821), Chief Justice Marshall referred to the Judiciary Act of 1802 as a "great improvement of the preexisting system" at least in respect to the requirement that Supreme Court Justices be assigned to circuits in proximity to their residence.

After passage of the Judiciary Act of 1802, Chief Justice Marshall was assigned to the Federal Circuit Court in Richmond, Virginia and sat with Federal District Judge Cyrus Griffin. After Republicans had returned Supreme Court Justices to circuit court duties, it was more than ironic that John Marshall, perhaps Thomas Jefferson's greatest nemesis, would sit as circuit judge in the Burr trial.

7. Marshall's First Ruling in the Burr Trial

Chief Justice Marshall drafted, signed, and issued the warrant that charged Burr with treason and violation of the Neutrality Act. Burr first appeared before the United States Circuit Court in Richmond on March 30, 1807 for arraignment. United States Attorney for the Commonwealth of Virginia George Hay and United States Attorney General Caesar Rodney appeared on behalf of the government; Burr's initial defense team consisted of Richmond attorneys John Wickham, the leading attorney in Richmond, and Edmund Randolph, former governor of Virginia and attorney general under President Washington. Aaron Burr, an accomplished attorney in his own right, played a prominent role in his defense throughout the proceedings.

Chief Justice Marshall issued the first of his many opinions in the Burr case on April 1, 1807. The Burr trial was, probably, Marshall's most difficult case. The case ultimately turned on the admissibility of evidence and insufficiency of proof. When the transcript of the trial is reviewed and the depth and quality of Marshall's opinions are considered, Marshall's management of the case and his application of law to the facts was unquestionably one of his greatest achievements. Marshall was called upon, time after time, to decide ground-breaking legal issues; at the same time, throughout trial, he responded to high octane counsel and witnesses with the greatest deference and respect. Perhaps Chief Justice Marshall's greatest achievement throughout the trial was to insure that the rule of law prevailed.

CHIEF JUSTICE MARSHALL'S RULING ON PROBABLE CAUSE

The initial hearing was conducted in a back room of the Eagle Tavern in Richmond. United States Attorney Hay offered the same evidence that had been presented two months earlier in the Supreme Court *Bollman–Swartwout* cases to support the charges against Aaron Burr. The Supreme Court had earlier found the evidence insufficient to hold Bollman and Swartwout for trial. The only additional evidence now offered was provided by the arresting officer, Major Nicholas Perkins, who described how he apprehended Burr and transported him to Richmond. After Prosecutor Hay requested that the Court commit Burr to jail on charges of treason and violation of the Neutrality Act, the Court requested legal argument. Interest in the case resulted in an overflow crowd in the tiny makeshift courtroom; thus, to permit more spectators to observe the hearing, legal proceedings were moved from the Eagle Tavern to the State Capitol building in Richmond. Burr was released on $5,000 bond pending the Court's ruling.

After legal arguments concluded, Chief Justice Marshall delivered the first of many judicial opinions in the Burr case. His rulings would expose Chief Justice Marshall and the judiciary to attacks by President Jefferson and his supporters. Wounds between Jefferson and Marshall were deep, particularly after repeal of the Judiciary Act of 1801, the landmark decision of *Marbury v. Madison* in 1803, and the unsuccessful attempt to impeach Associate Justice Samuel Chase in 1805. During the Burr trial, Marshall wrote to a fellow Justice: "It has been my fate to be engaged in the trial of a person whose case presents many real intrinsic difficulties which are infinitely multiplied by extrinsic circumstances."[199] The battle, however, was now joined and Chief Justice Marshall had no choice but to proceed. The competence of the attorneys, the theatrics of participants, the active involvement by President Jefferson, and Chief Justice Marshall's management of the Burr case were unrivaled in American legal history.

Chief Justice Marshall's first opinion was delivered on April 1, 1807. He found that the standard of proof required for this hearing was establishment of probable cause by sufficient evidence to believe that a crime was committed by the person charged; proof sufficient to convict was not required. Marshall cited Blackstone, the noted British legal commentator, for the proposition that if probable cause is established, the suspect should be

---

199 John Marshall to Justice William Cushing, June 29, 1807. *PJM* VII, pp. 60-62.

committed to jail or must provide bail. Quoting Blackstone, Marshall said: "I do not understand him as meaning to say that the hand of malignity may grasp any individual against whom its hate may be directed, or whom it may capriciously seize, charge him with some secret crime, and put on the proof of his innocence."

Chief Justice Marshall examined the evidence; the evidence consisted of the same affidavits by Wilkinson and Eaton that were considered by the Supreme Court in *Ex Parte Bollman and Swartwout*. The Chief Justice found probable cause to support the misdemeanor charge (violation of the Neutrality Act). However, Chief Justice Marshall was not satisfied that there was probable cause to support the treason charge. The only evidence implicating Burr of the crime of treason was the cipher letter. The Chief Justice questioned its admissibility, at least at this stage of the proceedings.

Marshall addressed the treason charge:

> As this is the most atrocious offense which can be committed against the political body, so it is the charge which is most capable of being employed as the instrument of those malignant and vindictive passions which may rage in the bosoms of contending parties struggling for power. It is that, of which the people of America have been most jealous, and therefore, while other crimes are unnoticed, they have refused to trust the national legislature with the definition of this, but have themselves declared in their Constitution that "it shall consist only in levying war against the United States, or in adhering to their enemies giving them aid and comfort." The high crime consists of overt acts which must be proved by two witnesses or by confession in open court.

Marshall cited the Constitutional definition of treason (Article III, Section 3) and clarified his understanding of the proof necessary to establish treason:

> It has been already observed, that to constitute this crime, troops must be embodied, men must be actually assembled; and there are facts which cannot remain invisible. Treason may be machinated in secret, but it can be perpetrated only in open day and in the eye of the world. Testimony of a fact which in its own nature is so notorious ought to be unequivocal. The testimony now offered has been laid before the Supreme Court of the United States, and has been determined in the cases of *Bollman* and *Swartwout*, not to furnish probable cause for the opinion that war had been actually levied. Whatever might have been the inclination of my own mind in that case — I should feel much difficulty in departing from the decision then made, unless the case could be clearly distinguished from it....

Chief Justice Marshall next challenged the Jefferson Administration for its failure to present additional evidence from that offered in the earlier *Bollman and Swartwout* cases:

> Several months have elapsed, since this fact did occur, if it ever occurred. More than five weeks have elapsed, since the opinion of the Supreme Court has declared the necessity of proving the fact, if it exists. Why is it not proved?

> To the Executive government is entrusted the important power of prosecuting those, whose crimes disturb the public repose or endanger its safety. It would be easy in much less time than has intervened since Colonel Burr has been alleged to have assembled his troops, to procure the affidavits establishing the fact. If in November or December last a body of troops had been assembled on the Ohio, it is impossible to suppose that affidavits establishing the fact could not have been obtained by the last of March. I ought not to believe, and I do not believe that there has been any remissness on the part of those who prosecute, on this important and interesting subject; & consequently, when at this late period no evidence, that the troops have been actually embodied, is given, I must say that the suspicion, which in the first instance might have been created, ought not to be continued, unless this want of proof can be in some manner be accounted for.

The Court ruled that Burr should be held on the misdemeanor charge; bail was set at $10,000. Burr was ordered to next appear in court on May 22, 1807. Bond was posted and Burr set free. Chief Justice Marshall made it clear that the prosecution was not prohibited from seeking an indictment for the crime of treason if it presented sufficient testimony to the Grand Jury at the next session of Court.[200]

Chief Justice Marshall's opinion dismayed the prosecution and President Jefferson. The term "the hand of malignity" was interpreted as a direct reference to President Jefferson and his Administration. After Chief Justice Marshall became aware of this interpretation, he clarified his ruling. He informed several reporters that when he made these observations, he made no allusions about the conduct of the government; he only intended to elucidate the general doctrine of Blackstone.[201]

One additional portion of his opinion raised questions: Chief Justice Marshall's comment about the failure of the Jefferson Administration to produce additional and sufficient admissible evidence to support the

---

200 *PJM* VII, pp. 13-21 (This cite applies to the proceeding five paragraphs that quote from the April 1, 1807 decision in *United States v. Burr*).
201 *PJM* VII, pp. 20-21.

charges against Burr. President Jefferson was aware, after the *Bollman* and *Swartwout decision*, that it was incumbent upon the prosecution to gather additional evidence and locate witnesses to support the charges against Burr. Even though President Jefferson's privately acknowledged that the government did not have sufficient evidence to support the charges against Burr, Jefferson took umbrage with that portion of Chief Justice Marshall's opinion that suggested additional evidence was needed.[202]

THE ILL-FATED DINNER

Several days after Chief Justice Marshall delivered his initial opinion in the Burr case, an incident arose that would cause him great embarrassment and provide ammunition to his opponents. It may have been his biggest mistake in the Burr proceedings. Marshall attended a dinner at the home of his good friend, Richmond attorney and neighbor John Wickham (co-counsel for Burr); Burr also attended. Today, similar fraternization between a judge and a defendant and his counsel during trial would require a trial judge to recuse himself from hearing the case; at a minimum, the trial judge would be subjected to an embarrassing motion for removal and mistrial. However, at the time of the Burr case, there were no Canons of Judicial Ethics or Rules of Professional Conduct for Attorneys. Recently, a judicial ethics panel in Florida went so far as to rule that lawyers and judges should no longer "friend" each other on Facebook if an attorney appears before a judge.[203] However, at the time of the Burr trial, it was not unusual for local members of the bar to socialize with members of the bench. In Richmond, John Marshall was well-liked and a respected member of the Bar. Marshall enjoyed social engagements, was an active member of a local men's social group, the Barbecue Club, and was renowned for his active and aggressive participation in the game of "quoits," a game similar to horseshoes. Marshall and Wickham were close friends, frequently socialized, and lived close to one another. Wickham looked after Marshall's law practice on several occasions (during Marshall's mission to Paris, when he was a member of the House of Representatives, and during his term as Secretary of State). Dinner parties at the Marshall and Wickham houses with members of the local bar were common and invitations were prized. Unfortunately, this din-

---

202 Thomas Jefferson to Colonel Morgan, *Writings* XI, pp. 173-174 March 26, 1807; *Anas*, p. 254.

203 Florida Judges, Lawyers Must 'Unfriend' on Facebook." *The Miami Herald*, December 11, 2009.

ner became a major *faux pas* for Chief Justice Marshall due to Aaron Burr's attendance.

Wickham, a brilliant attorney, used poor judgment when he invited Chief Justice Marshall to dinner. It is unclear whether Marshall knew that Burr would be present prior to accepting the invitation; most evidence indicates that Marshall was unaware. Most likely, Marshall learned that Burr would be in attendance after he accepted the invitation but before attending the dinner. Since Marshall and Wickham were good friends, Marshall may not have wanted to appear rude and embarrass Wickham by withdrawing his acceptance of the invitation. St. George Tucker, a prominent attorney and friend of Chief Justice Marshall's (although a better friend of President Jefferson's), attended the dinner and reported that Marshall "had no communication whatever with Burr; he sat at the opposite end of the table; and withdrew at an early hour after dinner." Tucker suggested that although it was improper for Marshall to attend the dinner, no one felt worse about the incident than did Marshall. Unfortunately Marshall's presence further inflamed President Jefferson and his supporter's distrust of Federalist judges, particularly John Marshall.[204]

The press had a field day with Chief Justice Marshall's attendance. The *Virginia Argus* reprinted an article believed written by President Jefferson's friend, Samuel Pleasants:

> It is reported, and we are sorry to say, that the fact appears indisputable, that Colonel Aaron Burr and the Chief Justice of the United States, dined together at Mr. Wickham's, since his examination, and since his honor had himself solemnly decided that there were probable ground to believe him guilty of a high misdemeanor against the United States. We acknowledge that the rites of hospitality ought not to be refused to this unfortunate gentleman by those who believe him innocent; but confess our astonishment that men, whose intellects are so penetrating as those of Mr. Wickham and Mr. Marshall, did not perceive the extreme indelicacy and impropriety of such respect being paid him by the Judge, who is to sit hereafter on his trial, and, who, by his own opinion officially pronounced, had affixed a stigma on his character, which can only be wiped off by his future acquittal.[205]

---

204 Baker, pp. 467-69: Beveridge III, pp. 394-97; Francis F. Bierne. *Shout Treason: The Trial of Aaron Burr*. New York: Hastings House,1959, pp. 57-61.
205 *Virginia Argus*, April 7, 1807.

Several days later, *The Richmond Enquirer* published an article by "A Stranger to the Country," believed written by Jefferson friend Thomas Ritchie:

> In the Argus of the 7th, it is stated, and the fact is now too generally notorious to be doubted, that Chief Justice Marshall has dined with Aaron Burr at Mr. Wickham's, since he himself solemnly decided, that there was probable cause to believe Burr guilty of a high misdemeanor against his country. The story has indeed excited some surprise in Richmond, but none of these sentiments of lively indignation, which a stranger from the country would naturally have expected.
>
> Let me inform the conscience of the Chief Justice, that the public do not view his dining with Burr, as a circumstance so trivial as he himself may incline to consider it. It is impossible to separate the judge from the man. We regard such conduct as a willful prostration of the dignity of his own character, and a wanton insult he might have spared his country. How has Burr entitled himself to be the social companion of the Chief Justice? Is he not still suspected of the blackest crimes? How has lie manifested his innocence? Has he ever thrown off that cloak of mystery, which truth, innocence, and virtue were never known to wear, and in which all his words and actions have been enveloped?
>
> Has the Chief Justice forgotten or neglected the maxim, which is in the mouth of every tyro of the law—that the administration of justice should not only be pure but unsuspected? I warn him to have it constantly in his remembrance, and to beware how lie inconsiderately betrays motives which may expose him to further scrutiny....?[206]

Other newspapers, particularly those less supportive of the Administration, did not think the Chief Justice committed an ethical lapse of judgment. *The Virginia Gazette* reprinted an article from *The United States Gazette*, published in Philadelphia:

> The democratic papers of Richmond have commenced a most furious attack upon the character of Chief Justice Marshall. They say that his conduct has been "excited sentiments of lively indignation," &c. &c. It will immediately be asked what has the Chief Justice done to merit their accusations? Why, forsooth, he dined with a gentleman in Richmond, and Colonel Burr was at the table!!! And the Chief Justice neither kicked Colonel Burr out of doors, nor ran away himself; but sat and ate his dinner as deliberately and to all appearance with as little concern as though perfectly unconscious that the

---

206 *The Richmond Inquirer*, April 10, 1807.

presence of Colonel Burr could either contaminate his principles, or blast his reputation! This is the head and front of the offending.[207]

In retrospect, Chief Justice Marshall should not have attended the dinner. If he learned about Burr's presence before the dinner, he should have politely informed John Wickham that he could not attend. There is no evidence that Marshall interacted with Burr at the dinner; in fact, local attorney St. George Tucker reported that Marshall never conversed with Burr and removed himself from the dinner as soon as practicable. Unfortunately for Marshall, the dinner provided raw meat for President Jefferson and his supporters, who already detested the Chief Justice.

---

207 *The Virginia Gazette*, April 29, 1807.

8. Interval Between the Preliminary Hearing and the Grand Jury

Between the preliminary hearing in early April and the next scheduled court date of May 22, President Jefferson and his Administration were actively involved with the Burr case. The day after Chief Justice Marshall's first opinion, Jefferson wrote a letter to Spanish Ambassador James Bowdoin. Jefferson updated him on the status of the Burr case:

> No better proof of the good faith of the U.S. could have been given, than the vigor with which we have acted, & the expense incurred in suppressing the enterprise meditated lately by Burr against Mexico.... *Yet he very early saw that the fidelity of the Western country was not to be shaken, and turned himself wholly towards Mexico* and so popular is an enterprise on that country in this, that we had only to be still, & he could have had followers enough to have been in the city of Mexico in 6 weeks. You have doubtless seen my several messages to Congress, which give a faithful narrative of that conspiracy. Burr himself, after being disarmed by our endeavors of all his followers, escaped from the custody of the court of Mississippi, but was taken near Fort Stoddard, making his way to Mobile, by some country people, who brought him on as a prisoner to Richmond, where he is now under a course for trial. Hitherto we have believed our law to be that suspicion on probable grounds was sufficient to commit a person for trial, allowing time to collect witnesses till the trial, but the judges here have decided that conclusive evidence of guilt must be ready in the moment of arrest, or they will discharge the malefactor. If this is still insisted on, Burr will be discharged, because his crimes having been sown from Maine thro' the whole line of the Western waters to New Orleans, we cannot bring the witnesses here under 4 months.

The fact is that the Federalists make Burr's cause their own, and exert their whole influence to shield him from punishment....And it is unfortunate that federalism is still predominant in our judiciary department, which is consequently in opposition to the legislative & Executive branches, & is able to baffle their measures often.[208] (Emphasis added.)

Interestingly, President Jefferson stated that he no longer believed Aaron Burr to be guilty of treason, no matter what Burr may have originally intended; most certainly, Jefferson knew that Burr could not be convicted of treason. Whether for revenge, hatred, inability to admit a mistake—President Jefferson continued to press forward with prosecution of Burr for treason. The most important reason may have been Jefferson's public declaration that Burr's "guilt is placed beyond question."

On April 6, 1807, Senator Giles wrote Jefferson about prosecution of Burr. Senator Giles, it will be remembered, instigated suspension of *habeas corpus* in the Senate. Giles offered this advice:

> The late enquiry into the charges vs. Colonel Burr, has excited a very great degree of sensibility in this part of the country and will probably have the same effect in all parts of the United States. The real friends of the administration are universally anxious for a full and fair judicial investigation into his conduct, and rely with great confidence upon the executive for taking all measures for affecting that object. The new, as well as the old opposers of the administration, are anxious to smother the investigation, and have already suggested doubts respecting the measures heretofore pursued in relation to Burr; and intimate that the executive are not possessed of evidence to justify those measures, or if they are, that they have been extremely delinquent in not producing it at the examination. It is even said that General Wilkinson will not be ordered to attend the trial.... These considerations, I am confident cannot receive too much of your attention.[209]

Jefferson, in response to Giles' letter, attacked Chief Justice Marshall and the Judiciary:

> That there should be anxiety & doubt in the public mind, in the present defective state of the proof, is not wonderful; and this has been sedulously encouraged by the tricks of the judges to force trials before it is possible to collect the evidence, dispersed through a line of 2000 miles from Maine to Orleans. The federalists, too, give all their aid, making Burr's cause their own....

208 Thomas Jefferson to James Bowdoin, April 2, 1807. *Works* X, pp. 379-383.
209 William Branch Giles to Thomas Jefferson, April 6, 1807. Dice Robbins Anderson. *William Branch Giles: A Study in the Politics of Virginia and the Nation from 1790 to 1830*, Menasha, WI: George Banta Publishing Co., 1915, pp. 110-111.

... We have set on foot an inquiry through the whole of the country which has been the scene of these transactions, to be able to prove to the courts, if they will give time, or to the public by way of communication to Congress, what the real facts have been.... Aided by no process or facilities from the federal courts [this was not true], but frowned on by their new born zeal for liberty of those whom we would not permit to overthrow the liberties of our country, we can expect no revealments from the accomplices of the chief offender. Of treasonable intentions, the judges have been obliged to confess there is probable appearance. What loophole will they find in it, when it comes to trial, we cannot foresee. Eaton, Stoddard, Wilkinson, and two others whom I must not name, will satisfy the world, if not the judges, on that head. And I do suppose the following overt acts will be proved....

But a moment's calculation will show that this evidence cannot be collected under 4 months, probably 5, from the moment of deciding when & where the trial shall be.... Marshall says, "more than 5 weeks have elapsed since the opinion of the Supreme Court has declared the necessity of proving the overt acts, if they exist." Why are they not proved? ... I understand, said the judge, "probable cause of guilt to be a case made out by proof furnishing good reason to believe." Speaking as a lawyer, he must mean legal proof, i.e., proof on oath, at least. But this is confounding probability and proof. We had always before understood that where there was reasonable ground to believe guilt, the offender must be put on his trial. That guilty intentions were probable, the judge believed. And as to the overt acts, were not the bundle of letters and facts published in the local newspapers, Burr's flight, & the universal belief or rumor of his guilt, probable ground for presuming the facts of enlistment, military guard, rendezvous, threats of civil war, or capitulation, so as to put him on trial? Is there a candid man in the United States who does not believe some one, if not all, of these overt acts to have taken place?

If there ever had been an instance in this or the preceding administrations, of federal judges so applying principles of law as to condemn a federal or acquit a republican offender, I should have judged them in the present case with more charity. *All this, however, will work well. The nation will judge both the offender & judges for themselves. If a member of the Executive or Legislature does wrong, the day is never far distant when the people will remove him. They will see then & amend the error in our Constitution, which makes any branch independent of the nation. They will see that one of the great co-ordinate branches of the government, setting itself in opposition to the other two, and to the common sense of the nation, proclaims impunity to that class of offenders which endeavors to overturn the Constitution itself; for impeachment is a farce which will not be tried again. If their protection of Burr produces this amendment, it will do more good than his condemnation would have done.* Against Burr, personally, I never had one hostile sentiment.

> I never indeed thought him an honest, frank-dealing man, but considered him as a crooked gun, or other perverted machine, whose aim or stroke you could never be sure of. Still, while he possessed the confidence of the nation, I thought it my duty to respect in him their confidence, & to treat him as if he deserved it; and if this punishment can be commuted now for any useful amendment of the Constitution, I shall rejoice in it....[210] (Emphasis added.)

President Jefferson once again acknowledged that the government could not establish overt acts necessary to prove the crime of treason. After arresting and transporting five Burr associates to Washington and Baltimore, all of whom were subsequently released by the Courts, Burr was sent east for trial. The government still did not have sufficient evidence to charge Burr with treason and it was now more than three months since Jefferson had first declared Burr's guilt to the world. The government's investigation continued. Apparently, President Jefferson had not anticipated that Chief Justice Marshall would require competent and admissible evidence, would strictly construe criminal statutes, and protect the rights of the accused, as guaranteed by the Constitution. Rather than enhance his image as a champion of individual rights, Jefferson blatantly disregarded those rights, blinded by the opportunity to continue his fight against the Judiciary and seek revenge against Burr. Even if the Burr case was lost, Jefferson advised Giles that "this will work well" in the effort to dismantle and weaken the Judicial Branch.

President Jefferson became the Chief Prosecutor in the Burr case. He was hell-bent on bringing the full weight, power, and resources of the government to bear against Burr. Jefferson ignored Constitutional guarantees and reprised the litany of governmental abuses that he so compellingly described in the Declaration of Independence. Jefferson's letter to Giles evidenced his disregard for the rule of law and guarantee of constitutionally protected rights, at least in Burr's case. Jefferson was more interested in trying Burr in the court of public opinion than convincing a judge and jury of Burr's guilt with legally admissible evidence. The prosecution of Aaron Burr was not Thomas Jefferson's shining hour.

In preparation for Burr's trial, President Jefferson was without the assistance of his Attorney General Caesar Rodney. Rodney was elected to Congress in 1802 and was a House manager in the impeachment trials of Federal District Judge John Pickering and Supreme Court Justice Samuel

---

210 Thomas Jefferson to William Branch Giles, April 20, 1807. *Works* X, pp. 383-389.

Chase. On January 20, 1807, Rodney became Jefferson's Attorney General, a position he occupied until December 5, 1811, well into the Madison Administration.[211] Attorney General Rodney had family issues to address, thus requiring lengthy absences from Washington. As importantly, due to his long-standing friendship with Burr, Rodney had little desire to take an active role in the prosecution. As subsequent events unfolded, Rodney was one of the few government officials who expressed concern that Burr should receive a fair trial. At Burr's preliminary hearing in Richmond in April, Rodney's only court appearance in the Burr case, Rodney advised the Court:

> For my part, I wish for nothing but that justice may be done, and not to avail myself of any testimony but such as is perfectly correct.... I rejoice that, on this occasion men of talents and liberality have been found of sufficient independence of mind to come forward to defend the prisoner, notwithstanding the general appearance of his guilt. And I wish it were possible that the walls of this room could expand, and that, not only those who hear me, but all the people of America were present, and could hear this discussion.—They would then be convinced that there is no predisposition in the government or in myself, to persecute Col. Burr.[212]

To insure that justice be done is the responsibility of a public prosecutor.

At an April 2, 1807 Cabinet meeting, preparation of interrogatories for prospective witnesses and discussion of efforts to secure witnesses for the Burr trial took place.[213] In Attorney General Rodney's absence, President Jefferson relied upon Secretary of State James Madison. Jefferson requested that Madison assist in bringing witnesses to trial and secure payment for them.[214] He further sought Madison's advice about where General Wilkinson should send certain suspects and defendants, including Blennerhassett. Jefferson provided Madison with a Treasury warrant for $5,000 to cover allowances for witnesses authorized by the Attorney General.[215]

Attorney General Rodney transmitted a circular letter to federal agents. The letter included a list of questions to be propounded to potential witnesses to ascertain whether they had knowledge of Burr's conspiracy. For

211 *Dictionary of American Biography*, Volume VII, Part 2. Edited by Dumas Malone, 1935, pp. 82-83.

212 Smith, p. 359; Malone V, p. 299.

213 *Anas*, p. 254.

214 Thomas Jefferson to James Madison, April 14, 1807, *Republic of Letters*, Volume 3, pp. 1466-67.

215 Thomas Jefferson to James Madison, April 25, 1807, *Republic of Letters*, Volume 3, pp. 1471-72.

instance, one circular letter was sent to Jonathon Clark of Louisville: "It is unnecessary to add any incentive to the discharge of a patriotic task. You must be sensible that our country calls for a complete investigation of those projects which have threatened its peace and safety. At such a time it becomes not only the duty, but the interest of every good citizen to step forward, and communicate to the government any information he may possess which may contribute to the general welfare." Twelve interrogatories were attached to the circular letter with multiple sub-questions; there were more than fifty questions in all. In addition, an all-points bulletin sought witnesses, evidence, and testimony that might assist in proving Burr's guilt—months after the President of the United States publicly declared to Congress and the nation that former Vice President Aaron Burr was guilty of the most detestable crime that one can commit against his nation—treason.[216]

Burr and his defense team vigorously prepared for the scheduled court hearing in May. Burr completed his defense team and trial strategy was discussed. Burr carefully reviewed composition of the Grand Jury, composed primarily of men supportive of the Jefferson Administration. In a letter to daughter Theodosia, Burr advised:

> The grand jury is composed of twenty democrats and four federalists. Among the former is W.C. Nicholas, my vindictive and avowed personal enemy—the most so that could be found in this state [Virginia]. The most indefatigable industry is used by the agents of government, and they have money at command without stint. If I were possessed of the same means, I could not only foil the prosecutors, but render them ridiculous and infamous. The democratic papers teem with abuse against me and my counsel, and even against the chief justice. Nothing is left undone or unsaid which can tend to prejudice the public mind, and produce a conviction without evidence.[217]

THE ATTORNEYS

The prosecution and defense teams were composed of the leading attorneys of the day, several of whom would be considered the greatest attorneys in the history of the United States. Most of the attorneys and judges lived within several blocks of one another in Richmond: Chief Justice John Mar-

---

216 Circular letter, May 2, 1807; The Thomas Jefferson Papers, Library of Congress American Memory digital.
217 Nathan Schachner. *Aaron Burr: A Biography*, p. 407; Matthew L. Davis. *Memoirs of Aaron Burr*, Volume II, pp. 405-406.

shall, defense attorneys John Wickham and Edmund Randolph; and prosecutors George Hay, Alexander MacRae, and William Wirt.[218]

District Judge Cyrus Griffin

As Chief Justice of the Supreme Court, John Marshall was assigned to preside over Federal circuit courts in Virginia and North Carolina. Sitting on the Circuit bench in Richmond with Marshall was District Judge Cyrus Griffin. Judge Griffin was appointed Federal District Judge for Virginia by President Washington.[219] During the Burr trial, in the transcript prepared by David Robertson, Judge Griffin did not make a single ruling (he concurred with Marshall) and uttered few words.[220] An example of President Jefferson's contempt for the Judiciary is found in a comment he made in anticipation of Judge Griffin's impending death in 1810; Jefferson expressed his desire that President Madison appoint a more favorably inclined judge: "From what I can learn Griffin cannot stand it long, and really the state has suffered long enough by having such a cipher in so important an office, and infinitely more from the want of any counterpoint to the rancorous hatred which Marshall bears to the government of his country, & from the cunning & sophistry within which he is able to enshroud himself. It will be difficult to find a character of firmness enough to preserve his independence on the same bench with Marshall ... a milk & water character ... would be seen as a calamity ... for so wretched a fool as Griffin...."[221]

THE PROSECUTION TEAM

United States Attorney George Hay

No trial was ever blessed with so many talented attorneys, great orators and interesting personalities. The prosecution was led by the United States Attorney for Virginia George Hay, who was assisted by William Wirt and Virginia Lieutenant Governor Alexander MacRae. The senior and chief

---

218 Samuel Mordecai. *Richmond in By-Gone Days: Being Reminiscences of an Old Citizen.* Philadelphia: King & Baird,1856, pp. 64-69, 76-79.

219 *Dictionary of American Biography*, Volume VIII. Edited by Allan Johnson and Dumas Malone, pp. 618-619.

220 Baker, p. 470: Beveridge IV, pp. 104-105.

221 Thomas Jefferson to James Madison, May 25, 1810. *PTJ-Retirement* 2, pp. 416-417. This letter relates to the *Batture* case and is an example of Jefferson's contempt for the Judiciary. Further, it was an attempt by Jefferson to have a favorable judge appointed who would hear a case that involved him as the defendant. This was not the first time that Jefferson would wish for someone's death. He earlier expressed similar sentiments about Patrick Henry.

prosecutor was President Jefferson. In the early 1800s, there was no Depart-ment of Justice as we know it today. At that time, the Department of Justice consisted of the Attorney General and United States Attorneys appointed for each state by the President. There was no "Main Justice" in Washington, comprised of scores of top-notch attorneys available to address the myriad criminal and civil legal issues that confront the government. Caesar Rodney, recently appointed Attorney General, played virtually no role in the pros-ecution of Burr. At that time, the Attorney General was, in effect, a one-man Department of Justice. In the Burr case, the defense had the glamour attor-neys; the government had the resources and the bully pulpit.

Born in 1765, George Hay was 42 years old at the time of trial. He was the son of the proprietor of the famous Raleigh Tavern in Williamsburg. Hay studied law and became a member of the Virginia House of Delegates. Hay was a Jefferson acolyte who first drew Jefferson's attention in 1799 when he wrote a pamphlet defending freedom of the press and opposing the Sedition Acts. Hay represented James Callender in his Sedition trial in Virginia before Justice Samuel Chase. To reward Hay's support of Repub-lican causes, President Jefferson appointed him United States Attorney for Virginia in 1801, a position he held for a number of years. Since he was the Chief Federal Prosecutor in Virginia, it was his duty to prosecute Aaron Burr. Hay tried the Burr case with a heavy heart: his wife passed away a few days before Burr was first brought before Chief Justice Marshall. Hay later married the daughter of James Monroe, further solidifying his ties to Jeffer-son and Republicans. Hay was a competent, although not brilliant attorney and proved a poor match for Burr's high-powered defense team. After with-drawal of Attorney General Rodney from the case, Hay was the principal prosecutor, subject to President Jefferson's dictates. Hay was the only attor-ney in this case who did not have great respect for Chief Justice Marshall. After spending ten additional years as United States Attorney for Virginia and several years as a state legislator, Hay practiced law in the Washington, D.C. and provided advice to his father-in-law, President James Monroe. Hay was later appointed United States District Judge for the Eastern District of Virginia by President John Quincy Adams; ironically, he sat with Chief Justice John Marshall on the United States Circuit Court in Richmond.[222]

---

222 *Dictionary of American Biography*, Volume VIII. Dumas Malone, Editor, 1932. pp. 429-430; Charles Hobson, Federal Judicial Center article—digital; Whelan, p.103; Beveridge III, 407; Isenberg, p. 335, n.49 (p. 501).

William Wirt

The two attorneys who assisted United States Attorney Hay were appointed special prosecutors, with President Jefferson's approval. The first was William Wirt, who would later become the most famous member of the prosecution team. At the time of trial, he was 35 years old and the least experienced attorney for the prosecution. He was a brilliant orator with an outgoing personality. Wirt, who was known for his eloquence, overcame a pronounced stutter at an early age that almost prevented him from pursuing a life in the law.[223]

Wirt was a gifted writer and published *The Letters of a British Spy* in 1803. This work consisted of a series of sketches depicting prominent Virginians, including three key participants in the Burr trial: Chief Justice Marshall and defense attorneys John Wickham and Edmund Randolph. He later published *Sketches of the Life and Character of Patrick Henry*. Wirt's closing argument in the Burr trial depicted Burr as a villain, who duped the unwitting Blennerhassett into his unlawful scheme. His flowery oratory was typical of his eloquence and the closing argument was, for many years, read by school children in rhetoric classes. He was later appointed Attorney General by President Monroe, a post he held during Monroe's eight years in office and for four additional years during the administration of President John Quincy Adams. As Attorney General, Wirt argued the famous cases of *McCullough v. Maryland* (1819) and *Gibbons v. Ogden* (1824) on behalf of the government. He was respected by Chief Justice Marshall and the feeling was mutual, with one exception; Wirt was not pleased with Marshall's decisions in the Burr case. Marshall was impressed with Wirt's judgment and genius. Wirt had an insightful legal mind.[224]

William Wirt depicted Chief Justice Marshall four years prior to the Burr trial in his *The Letters of a British Spy*, written around the time of the *Marbury v. Madison*:

> The Chief Justice of the United States is, in his person, tall, meager, emaciated; his muscles relaxed, and his joints so loosely connected as not to disqualify him, apparently, for any vigorous exertion of the body, but to destroy everything like elegance and harmony in his air and movements. Indeed, in his whole appearance and demeanor,

223 Bruce Chadwick. *I am Murdered: George Wythe, Thomas Jefferson and the Killing that Shocked a Nation*. Hoboken, NJ: John Wiley & Sons, Inc.,2009, pp. 143-145

224 *Dictionary of American Biography*, Volume X. Dumas Malone, Editor, !936, pp. 418-421; Hobson-Federal Judicial Center digital; Baker, p. 470; Beveridge, p 407.; Whelan, p. 103.

dress, attitudes, gestures—sitting, standing or walking—he is as far removed from the idolized graces of Lord Chesterfield, as any other gentleman on earth. To continue this portrait: his head and face are small in proportion to his height; his complexion swarthy; the muscles of his face, being relaxed, give him the appearance of a man fifty years of age, nor can he be much younger; his countenance has a faithful expression of great good humor and hilarity; while his black eyes—that unerring index—possess an irradiating spirit, which proclaims the imperial powers of the mind that sits enthroned within.

This extraordinary man, without the aid of fancy, without the advantages of person, voice, attitude, gesture, or any of the ornaments of an orator, deserves to be considered as one of the most eloquent men in the world; if eloquence may be said to consist in the power of seizing the attention with irresistible force, and never permitting it to elude the grasp, until the hearer has received the conviction which the speaker intends.

... He possesses one original, and almost, supernatural faculty: the faculty of developing a subject by a single glance of his mind, and detecting at once, the very point on which every controversy depends. No matter what the question, though ten times more knotty than the gnarled oak, the lightning of heaven is not more rapid nor more resistless than his astonishing penetration. Nor does the exercise of it seem to cost him an effort. On the contrary, it is as easy as vision. I am persuaded that his eyes do not fly over a landscape and take in its various objects with more promptitude and facility than his mind embraces and analyzes the most complex subjects.

... From this impression I have never seen any cause to wonder at what is called universal genius; it proves only that the man has applied a powerful mind to the consideration of a great variety of subjects, and pays a compliment rather to his superior industry, than his superior intellect. I am very confident that the gentleman of whom we are speaking, possesses the acumen which might constitute him a universal genius....[225]

Alexander MacRae

The third member of the prosecution team was Alexander MacRae, then Lieutenant Governor of Virginia. Little is known about MacRae, although he had a temper, was sarcastic, and did not care whom he offended. During the trial, MacRae acquitted himself well and proved a competent attorney.[226]

---

225 William Wirt. *The Letters of a British Spy*, pp. 177-185.
226 Beveridge, pp. 407-8; Whelan, p. 103.

THE DEFENSE ATTORNEYS

The defense team consisted of John Wickham, Luther Martin, Edmund Randolph, Benjamin Botts, John Baker, and Charles Lee. Aaron Burr was active in his own defense; he was a skilled litigator and made many strategic decisions. The primary defense attorneys were Wickham and Martin; others provided strong support.

John Wickham

John Wickham, age 44, was the leading attorney in the Richmond and Virginia Bars at the time of the Burr trial, particularly after John Marshall became Secretary of State and Chief Justice. Wickham was a friend and colleague of Marshall's and assumed Marshall's law practice while he was away from Richmond during his assignments for the government. Wickham was from a family of loyalists and was one of the few from loyalist families who obtained prominence in post-war United States. He studied law under George Wythe and was admitted to practice in 1786. He never ran for public office and devoted his entire career to the practice of law. He was sophisticated and became the richest man in Richmond. Much of his lucrative law practice involved assisting British merchants collect debts from American businessmen. He lived close to Marshall and built a house that later became a National Historic Landmark. Wickham and Marshall gave numerous dinners and socialized frequently, typical of the legal community at the time. Wickham was the ablest and best prepared of all the attorneys in the Burr case, with the exception of the presiding judge and, perhaps, the defendant.[227] Wirt described Wickham in his *The Letters of a British Spy*:

> ...The qualities by which Mr. Wickham strikes the multitude, are his ingenuity and his wit. But those who look more closely into the anatomy of his mind, discover many properties of much higher dignity and importance. This gentleman, in my opinion, unites in himself a greater diversity of talents and acquirements than any other at the bar of Virginia. He has the reputation and I doubt not a just one, of possessing much legal science. He has an exquisite and highly cultivated taste for polite literature; a genius quick and fertile; a style pure and classic; a stream of perspicuous and beautiful elocution; an ingenuity which no difficulties can entangle or embarrass; and a wit whose vivid and brilliant coruscation can gild and decorate the darkest subject. He chooses his ground, in the first instance, with great judgment; and when, in the progress of a cause, an unexpected

---

227 *Dictionary of American Biography*, Volume X. Dumas Malone, Editor, 1936, pp. 181-182.

evolution of testimony, or intermediate decisions from the bench, have beaten that ground from under him, he possesses a happy, an astonishing versatility, by which he is enabled at once to take a new position, without appearing to have lost an atom, either in the measure or the stability of his basis. This is a faculty which I have observed before in an inferior degree; but Mr. Wickham is so adroit, so superior in the execution of it, that in him it appears a new and peculiar talent; his statements, his narrations, his arguments, are all as transparent as the light of day. He reasons logically, and declaims very handsomely....[228]

At trial, Wickham argued that overt acts of treason must first be established before admission of testimony of the defendant's intent. His successful argument limited trial testimony and excluded evidence that failed to establish overt acts. He convinced the Court that no one may be convicted of levying war without being personally present. Since Burr was not present at the scene of the alleged crime at the time charged in the indictment, he could not be convicted of treason. Wickham's argument led to exclusion of the doctrine of constructive treason from the American law of treason.[229]

Luther Martin

The most colorful and bombastic attorney in the Burr trial was Luther Martin, age 59. He was admitted to the practice of law in 1771 in Virginia; he moved to Maryland three years later to continue his legal career. At the time of the Burr trial, Martin was considered the foremost trial lawyer in the United States. He was appointed Maryland's first Attorney General, a post he held off and on for forty years. Although he was a delegate to the Constitutional Convention, he opposed ratification; he later became a Federalist and strong supporter of Presidents Washington and Adams. He disliked Thomas Jefferson for a number of reasons, including the inaccurate portrayal of his father-in-law in Jefferson's *Notes on the State of Virginia*. In *Notes*, Jefferson described the murder of an Indian Chief by a group of European's who included Colonel Michael Cresap, the father of Martin's wife. Martin spent many years seeking a retraction from Jefferson, a retraction never received. Martin's favorite phrase, when denouncing someone, was "Sir! He is as great a scoundrel as Thomas Jefferson." Martin was a life-long friend of Supreme Court Associate Justice Samuel Chase, whom he represented in his impeachment trial. Martin's representation of Chase drew the admira-

228 William Wirt. *The Letters of a British Spy*. New York: Harper & Brothers, Publishers, 1875, pp. 214-17.
229 Beveridge III, 407; Baker, 470; Whelan, 13.

tion of Aaron Burr, who presided at the Chase trial. Martin was well-known for his love of drink and was often publicly drunk, sometimes during trials. His personal appearance was disheveled, which earned him the nickname "Lawyer Brandy Bottle." Samuel Chase would later remember his life-long friendship and Martin's representation of him in trial. Martin appeared years later before Justice Chase in Federal Circuit Court in Baltimore. Martin was overcome with alcohol and treated the Court with less than respect. The District Judge who sat with Chase drew up a commitment for contempt against Martin and submitted it to Chase for signature. Chase refused to sign the commitment, stating: "Whatever may be my duties as judge, Samuel Chase can never sign a commitment against Luther Martin."

Martin and Burr vigorously pursued a trial strategy of unremitting attacks on President Jefferson. Following the Burr trial, Martin continued to practice law, most prominently appearing on behalf of the State of Maryland in *McCullough v. Maryland*. After suffering a severe stroke, Burr took Martin in and cared for him for the remainder of his life.[230]

Perhaps the best description of Martin was provided by friend Henry Brackenridge:

> Luther Martin was a *sui generis*. In his appearance there could be nothing more common.... His voice was thick and disagreeable, his language and pronunciation rude and uncouth. With all these defects he possessed extraordinary powers. He had the finest capacity for discrimination and analysis, the faculty which, perhaps more than any other, distinguishes the lawyer. He also had wit, philosophy, a prodigious memory, and stores of learning, which were unsuspected until the occasion called for their display. On the different occasions on which I heard him speak, he seemed to blunder along for an hour or two; as if he were merely meditating his subject.... It was in his recapitulation that he appeared to be great. He became warm, his language more happy, his leaden eyes seemed to kindle, and for fifteen minutes or half an hour he spoke with admirable force and power. This would probably have been his speech if he had prepared himself in his closet. But his usual preparation was drinking enormous quantities of brandy. For twenty or thirty years he was a

---

230 *Dictionary of American Biography*, Volume XII. Edited by Dumas Malone, 1933, pp. 343-345; Paul S. Clarkson, and R. Samuel Jett. *Luther Martin of Maryland*. Baltimore: The Johns Hopkins Press, 1970. William L. Reynolds, "Luther Martin, Maryland and the Constitution." *Maryland Law Review*, Vol. 47, (1987-1988), pp. 291-321; Baker, pp. 470-1: Beveridge III, pp. 186-7. In the story about Justice Chase almost holding Martin in contempt, Chase supposedly said to Martin: "I am surprised that you can so prostitute your talents." Martin allegedly replied: "Sir, I never prostituted my talents except when I defended you and Colonel Burr." Smith. *John Marshall: Definer of a Nation*, p. 343.

perfect sot, and it is wonderful how both his constitution and his intellect could withstand the destructive habit.[231]

Edmund Randolph

Edmund Randolph, age 54, was the former Governor and Attorney General of Virginia and Attorney General and Secretary of State in the Washington Administration. He served as senior counsel for the defense team. Randolph, while sitting as Governor of Virginia, was a member of the Constitutional Convention, although he did not initially support the Constitution. However, by the time the Constitution was submitted for ratification to the Commonwealth of Virginia, Randolph became an advocate. President Washington appointed him the first Attorney General of the United States and, upon the resignation of Thomas Jefferson, Randolph was appointed Secretary of State. After leaving the Washington Administration under questionable circumstances in 1795 (it was alleged that he assisted the French government without authority of the Administration), he resumed the practice of law in Richmond and became a leader in the legal community. He died six years after the Burr trial.[232] This is how Wirt described Randolph in his *The Letters of a British Spy*:

> Mr. Randolph has great personal advantages. A figure large and portly; his features uncommonly fine; his dark eyes and his whole countenance lighted up with an expression of the most conciliating sensibility; his attitudes dignified and commanding; his gesture easy and graceful; his voice perfect harmony; and his whole manner that of an accomplished and engaging gentleman. I have reason to believe that the expression of his countenance does no more than justice to his heart. If I be correctly informed, his feelings are exquisite; and the proofs of his benevolence are various and clear beyond the possibility of doubt. He has filled the highest offices in this Commonwealth, and has very long maintained a most respectable rank in his profession. His character, with the people, is that of a great lawyer and eloquent speaker....[233]

Other defense attorneys included Benjamin Botts, John Baker, and Charles Lee, all excellent attorneys. Botts, a young man who practiced law in Richmond, was known for his fearlessness and played a prominent role in the trial. He died tragically in a Richmond theater fire in 1811. Baker, a handicapped attorney from Richmond, together with Botts, assisted the defense

---

231 *Luther Martin of Maryland*, pp. 246-7.
232 *Dictionary of American Biography*, VIII, Part 1. Dumas Malone, Editor, 1935, pp. 353-355); Baker, p. 470; Whelan, p. 103; Beveridge III, p. 407.
233 *The Letters of a British Spy*, p.207

with jury selection since they were both from the Richmond area. Charles Lee, a former Attorney General in the Washington and Adams Administrations, was the final attorney and played a minor role. He was actively involved in the earlier *Swartwout–Bollman* case and was a friend of Chief Justice Marshall.[234]

Hearings Begin

On May 22, 1807, at high noon, legal proceedings against Aaron Burr resumed. Chief Justice Marshall and Judge Griffin presided over the Fifth United States Circuit Court in Richmond, Virginia. Perhaps no judge ever made as many important legal rulings in so short a time as did Marshall. There were at least fifteen written opinions in addition to rulings made from the bench. With high profile attorneys, the importance of the case, and the intersection of politics and law, Marshall's control of the courtroom, particularly his fairness in permitting counsel to make voluminous motions with extended legal arguments, must surely rank as one of the most impressive performances ever by a trial judge. Many issues decided by Marshall were of first impression—rights provided criminal defendants by the Constitution and guaranteed by the Bill of Rights. Marshall understood, as Supreme Court Justice Felix Frankfurter later wrote, that "The history of liberty has largely been the observance of procedural safeguards."[235]

Selection and Composition of the Grand Jury

When proceedings commenced, Burr first challenged the selection and composition of the Grand Jury. The Grand Jury consisted primarily of Jefferson's Republican supporters. Burr challenged irregularities that occurred during selection of prospective Grand Jurors by the United States Marshal. Burr, Botts, Randolph, and Wickham argued for the defense; Hay for the prosecution. The Judiciary Act of 1789 provided that for selection of Federal Grand Jurors, procedures used for selection of juries in state courts should be followed.[236] Under Virginia law, the Marshal of the court was to summon 24 freeholders for the Grand Jury. The Marshal, however, was without authority to strike names off the original panel of grand jurors selected and, further, had no authority to substitute new jurors for those excused or re-

---

234 Beveridge III, p. 407; Baker, p. 470.
235 Baker, p. 474.
236 The Judiciary Act of 1789, 1 Stat. 73, section 29 (adopted September 24, 1789).

moved. The Marshal's responsibility was purely ministerial; he could not act outside the scope of his authority. During selection of the Grand Jury in the Burr case, the Marshal improperly permitted changes to the original composition of the Grand Jury without Court approval.[237]

After hearing arguments, Chief Justice Marshall issued an opinion. He ruled that the Marshal had no authority to go beyond the original twenty-four grand jurors without express authority of the Court.[238] The Chief Justice observed that the law provided procedures for protection of the accused and the Court would not permit abuse.

Burr next questioned the specific composition of the grand jury, challenging the inclusion of Senator William Branch Giles and William Cary Nicholas (an avowed opponent of Burr's), staunch Republicans both. Burr's challenge resulted in the voluntary withdrawal by Giles and Nicholas as grand jurors. The Court replaced them with U.S. Representative John Randolph (appointed foreman) and William Foushee (later replaced by James Barbour).[239]

After the Grand Jury was sworn, Burr requested that the Court instruct the Grand Jury on legal issues, particularly admission of evidence. Prosecutor Hay opposed Burr's request and urged the Court to proceed as usual, that no particular "indulgences be granted to Colonel Burr" and that Burr "should stand on the same footing with every other man charged with a crime." In the first of many dramatic moments during trial, Burr exploded: *"Would to God that I stand on the same ground with every other man. This is the first time that I have ever been permitted to enjoy the rights of a citizen.* How have I been brought hither?" (Emphasis added.) He said he wanted to be treated like any other citizen and expected the same rights and privileges.[240]

JEFFERSON/HAY LETTERS

After Aaron Burr's term as Vice President concluded in March 1805, President Jefferson monitored Burr's travels and activities. Jefferson's pronouncement of Burr's guilt without benefit of legal process or trial was unprecedented. Perhaps as egregious was the extraordinary communication

---

237 *PJM* VII, pp. 21-22; Beveridge, III, p. 408-9; Malone, V, p. 311; Robertson I, 1-8 (The Burr trial).
238 *PJM*, VII, 21-22; Robertson I, 8-9.
239 Beveridge III, pp. 409-413; *PJM*, VII, 22; Malone, 311; Robertson I, 9-13.
240 David Robertson. *Transcription of Trial of Aaron Burr* I, pp. 13-15; Beveridge III, 413-15.

that took place between President Jefferson and United States Attorney Hay. Correspondence commenced in May 1807 and continued throughout the Burr trial. Jefferson provided legal advice, guidance, and opinions on law to Hay. Additionally, he provided opinions about Chief Justice Marshall, the judiciary, and politics. Approximately thirty-five letters were exchanged between Jefferson and Hay.[241]

Throughout his life, Thomas Jefferson wrote extensive and exhaustive letters intended not only for communication, but for posterity. To paraphrase James Madison, Jefferson, like many brilliant men, was far more expressive in his letters than he was in public and sometimes wrote outrageous things that he probably didn't mean: "[A]llowances ... ought to be made for the habit of Mr. Jefferson, as in others of great genius, of expressing in strong and round terms, impressions of the moment." As an example of Jefferson's thoughts about his letters, consider this attempt by Jefferson to discourage the writing of his biography while still living: "It is impossible that the writer's delicacy should permit him to speak as freely of the faults or errors of a living, as of a dead character. There is still a better reason. The letters of a person, especially one whose business has been chiefly transacted by letters, form the only full and genuine journal of his life; and few can let them go out of their own hands while they live. A life written after these hoards become opened to investigation must supersede any previous one." Jefferson intended that his letters be read and reviewed after his death.[242] The letters between Jefferson and Hay did not become public until after Jefferson's death in 1826, almost twenty years after the Burr trial.

In President Jefferson's first letter to United States Attorney Hay, dated May 20, 1807, he advised that:

---

241 This list of letters was obtained by reviewing letters in the Library of Congress digital and was supplemented by various histories of the Burr trial and compilations of Jefferson's writings — *Works, Writings*, etc.. Unfortunately, the definitive *Papers of Thomas Jefferson*, published by Princeton University, is only complete through early 1802 at the time of this writing. Perhaps when this definitive work is completed, we will discover additional letters between Jefferson and Hay. In addition, correspondence between Jefferson and others about Burr's activities may be uncovered that will further explain the actions taken by Jefferson and his Administration during the Burr case.

242 James Madison to Nicholas Trist, May 15, 1832, The Papers of James Madison. Charlottesville: University of Virginia Press, 1990, pp. 644-645; Thomas Jefferson to Robert Walsh, April 5, 1823, Library of Congress digital, The Thomas Jefferson Papers.

Dr. Bollman, on his arrival here in custody in Jan., voluntarily offered to make communications to me, which he accordingly did, Mr. Madison, also being present. *I previously & subsequently assured him, (without, however, his having requested it) that they should never be used against himself.* Mr. Madison on the same evening committed to writing, by memory, what he had said; & I moreover asked of Bollman to do it himself, which he did, & I now enclose it to you. The object is as he is to be a witness, that you may know how to examine him, & draw everything from him. I wish the paper to be seen & known only to yourself and the gentlemen who aid you, & returned to me. *If he should prevaricate, I should be willing for you should go so far as to ask him whether he did not say so & so to Mr. Madison and myself.* In order to let him see that his prevarications will be marked, Mr. Madison will forward to you a pardon for him, which we mean should be delivered previously. It is suspected by some he does not intend to appear. If he does not, I hope you will take effectual measures to have him immediately taken into custody. *Some other blank pardons are sent on to be filled up at your discretion,* if you should find a defect of evidence & believe that this would supply it, by avoiding to give them to the gross offenders, unless it be visible that the principal will otherwise escape. I send you an affidavit of importance received last night. If General Wilkinson gets on in time, I expect he will bring Dunbaugh on with him. At any rate it may be a ground for an arrest & commitment for treason....[243] (Emphasis added.)

This is an incredible letter; it certainly does nothing to enhance Jefferson's standing as a civil libertarian. In his desire to convict Burr, Jefferson was willing to trample on the rights of others (in this case Bollman) to achieve his objective. The information he provided Hay was less than truthful. In the January meeting with Jefferson, Madison, and Erick Bollman, President Jefferson promised Bollman about use of any information that he provided. Jefferson not only reneged on his promise to Bollman, but instructed the trial prosecutor on how Bollman should be cross-examined and how to impeach Bollman's testimony, if necessary. Even more incredible, Jefferson provided Hay with a presidential pardon for Bollman and additional blank pardons to be used at Hay's discretion. The Constitution provides that the President is solely authorized to grant pardons.[244] Pardon authority is non-delegable; lower-level governmental officials are not authorized to issue pardons. A pardon must be personally authorized by the President, not the United States Attorney. Alexander Hamilton wrote about the pardon authority in the *Federalist Papers*:

---

243 Thomas Jefferson to George Hay, May 20, 1807. *Works X*, pp. 394-401.
244 United States Constitution, Article II, Section 2.

Humanity and good policy conspire to dictate the benign preroga-
tive of pardoning should be as little unfettered or embarrassed.... As
the sense of responsibility is always strongest in proportion as it is
divided, it may be inferred that a single man would be most ready to
attend to the force of those motives which might plead for a mitigation of the rigor of the law, and least apt to yield to considerations
which were calculated to shelter a fit object of its vengeance. The
reflection that the fate of a fellow-creature depended on the *sole fiat*
would naturally inspire scrupulousness and caution; the dread of
being accused of weakness or connivance would beget equal cir-
cumspection, though of a different kind. On the other hand, as men
generally derive confidence from their numbers, they might often
encourage each other in an act of obduracy, and might be less sensible to the apprehension of suspicion or censure for an injudicious
of affected clemency. On these accounts, one man appears to be a
more eligible dispenser of the mercy of the government than a body
of men.[245]

President Jefferson's delivery of blank pardons becomes more surpris-
ing when contrasted with his earlier correspondence. On August 16, 1806,
less than a year earlier, Jefferson wrote Treasury Secretary Albert Gallatin:
"I have made it a rule to grant no pardons in any criminal case but on the
recommendation of the judges who sat on the trial, or the district attorney,
or two of them. I believe it a sound rule, and not to be departed from but in
extraordinary cases."[246] Here, neither the judge nor the district attorney recommended a pardon. Jefferson issued a pardon for Bollman and additional
blank pardons, to be used at Prosecutor Hay's discretion.

Prosecutor Hay, on May 25, 1807, wrote his first letter to President Jefferson. Hay acknowledged receipt of Bollman's pardon. He was unsure how
the pardon was to be used and reported that his prosecution team decided
that the Bollman pardon should be held until clarifying instructions were
received. Hay advised the President that General Wilkinson had yet to arrive and the prosecution would not present evidence to the Grand Jury until
his arrival. Hay was confident that there was sufficient evidence to convict Burr of treason and violation of the Neutrality Act. He believed, however, that Wilkinson's presence was necessary to negate Burr's belief that
Wilkinson would never appear. Hay advised Jefferson about Marshall's ruling on the composition of the Grand Jury. Hay next expressed surprise at
the degree of local support for Burr:

---

245 *Federalist Papers*, No. 74.
246 Thomas Jefferson to Albert Gallatin, August 16, 1806. *The Thomas Jefferson Papers*.
 Library of Congress digital, American Memory.

I am not surprised that Burr should be a traitor. Employment however vicious must have afforded him some relief, from the torment of reflection. When he looked abroad, he saw nothing but hatred and scorn: when he retired within himself, he would find nothing but reproach and despair. I am not therefore surprised at the magnitude of his crime, or at the low, petty, and dirty deceits to which he has occasionally resorted, for their accomplishment. But I am surprised, and afflicted, when I see how much, and by how many, this man has been patronized and supported. There is among mankind, sympathy for villainy, which sometimes, shows itself in defiance of every principle of patriotism and truth. In the present instance, this observation humiliating as it may be, is, most deplorably, exemplified.

Finally, Hay advised the President that he would move to commit Burr for treason with the additional evidence now available.[247]

MOTION TO COMMIT

As promised, when Court convened on May 25th, Hay moved to commit Burr for treason. The prosecution was not prepared to present evidence to the Grand Jury; they awaited the arrival of General Wilkinson. The motion to commit was a request by the prosecution for additional bail in anticipation of the treason charge. The prosecution team was concerned that Burr might abscond. The defense argued the motion was inappropriate since the Grand Jury had assembled and was in session. The defense was concerned that a ruling by the Court might unduly influence the action of the Grand Jury.[248] Burr presented the defense's final argument:

> *Our president is a lawyer and a great one too. He certainly ought to know what it is that constitutes a war. Six months ago, he proclaimed that there was a civil war. And yet, for six months have they been hunting for it, and it still can not find one spot where it existed.* There was, to be sure, a most terrible war in the newspapers; but nowhere else. When I appeared before the grand jury in Kentucky, they had no charge to bring against me, and I was consequently dismissed. When I appeared for a second time, before a grand jury, in the Mississippi Territory, there was nothing to appear against me; and the judge even told the United States Attorney that if he did not send up his bill before the grand jury, he himself would proceed to name as many witnesses as he could, and bring it before the court. Still there was no proof of war. At length, however, the Spaniards invaded our territory, and yet there was no war. *But, sir, if there was a war, certainly no man can pretend to say that the government is*

---

247 George Hay to Thomas Jefferson, May 25, 1807, The Thomas Jefferson Papers, Library of Congress digital. (All letters from George Hay to Thomas Jefferson are the Author's transcription.)
248 Robertson I, pp. 15-52; Beveridge, pp. 415-420.

---

*able to find it out. The scene to which they have now hunted it, is only three hun-
dred miles distant, and still there is no evidence of war.*[249] (Emphasis added.)

The next morning, Chief Justice Marshall delivered the Court's opinion. Marshall permitted the prosecution to proceed and present evidence in
support of its motion for bail. The Court opined:

> The court perceives and regrets that the result of this motion may
> be publications unfavorable to the justice, and to the right decision
> of the case; but if this consequence is to be prevented, it must be by
> other means, than by refusing to hear the motion. No man feeling a
> correct sense of the importance which ought to be attached by all
> to a fair and impartial administration of justice; especially in crimi-
> nal prosecutions, can view without extreme solicitude, any attempt
> which may be made, to prejudice the public judgment, and to try any
> person, not by the laws of his country and the testimony exhibited
> against him—but by public feelings, which may be and often are ar-
> tificially excited against the innocent, as well as the guilty. But the
> remedy, for a practice not less dangerous than it is criminal, is not to
> be obtained by suppressing motions, which either party may have a
> legal right to make.[250]

After the Court ruled, the merits of the motion to commit were argued.
Before any testimony or evidence was presented, the defense questioned the
order of proof. Defense attorney John Wickham insisted that there must
be a strict order of proof for a treason charge: the prosecution must first
prove that an overt act occurred before evidence may be presented linking
Burr to the crime. The order of proof would become the pivotal issue in the
Burr trial. The parties next argued about evidence provided by President
Jefferson: Wilkinson's affidavit (earlier ruled inadmissible since it failed to
establish an overt act of treason) and the affidavit of Jacob Dunbaugh (the
Army sergeant who accompanied Burr on his trip to Fort Massac in December, 1806). On May 28, the Court ruled that the Dunbaugh affidavit was
defective and, therefore, inadmissible since it was not given under oath or
duly authenticated.[251]

Defense attorney Luther Martin appeared for the first time on Burr's behalf on May 28, appearing without fee. A few hours later, Chief Justice Marshall delivered his second opinion on bail. Marshall ruled that additional
bail would be ordered solely to assure Burr's appearance at future proceedings. After Burr voiced opposition to additional bail, he voluntarily agreed

---

249 Robertson I, pp. 51-52.
250 *PJM* VII, pp. 23-25; Robertson I, pp. 52-56.
251 *PJM* VII, pp.25-30; Robertson I, pp. 75-81.

to bail in the amount of $10,000, as long as it was understood that the Court had not ruled on the issue of probable cause to commit treason. Bail was posted immediately by four men, one of whom was Martin.[252]

While Chief Justice Marshall was delivering his opinions, the President was writing to Hay. Jefferson was unhappy with Burr's challenge to the composition of the Grand Jury and the Court's resolution of this issue. Jefferson was particularly incensed with rejection of Giles and Nicholas from the Grand Jury. He wrote that these men were "far above all exception as any two members of the Grand Jury.... I suppose our informant is inaccurate in his terms, and has mistaken an objection by the criminal & voluntary retirement of the gentlemen with the permission of the court, for a challenge & rejection, which, in the case of the Grand Jury is impossible." Although President Jefferson had retired from the practice of law in 1774 (33 years before the Burr trial) and tried very few criminal cases when he did practice,[253] he did not hesitate to extensively advise Hay on the law. Jefferson then wrote:

> Be this as it may, and the result before the formal tribunal, fair or false, it becomes our duty to provide that full testimony be laid before the Legislature & through them to the public. For this purpose, it is necessary that we be furnished with the testimony of every person who shall be with you as a witness. If the Grand Jury find a bill [Bill of Indictment] the evidence given in court, taken as verbatim as possible, will be what we desire. If there be no bill, & consequently no examination before court, then I beseech you to have every man privately examined by way of affidavit, and to furnish me with the whole testimony. In the former case, the person taking down the testimony as wholly delivered in court, should make oath that he believes it to be substantially correct. In the latter case, the certificate of the magistrate administering the oath, and signature of the party will be proper; and this should be done before they receive their compensation, that they may not evade examination. Go into any expense necessary for this purpose & and meet it from the funds provided by the Attorney General for the other expenses....[254]

Why would President Jefferson request court testimony or sworn affidavits for submission to Congress? Perhaps Jefferson wanted Congress to review the law of treason and determine whether a Constitutional Amendment or legislative action was needed. More likely, Jefferson intended to submit statements to Congress for its consideration as to whether changes

---

252 *PJM* VII, pp. 30-31; Robertson I, pp. 85-86; Baker, pp. 474-75.
253 R.B. Bernstein. *Thomas Jefferson*. New York: Oxford University Press, 2003, p. 8.
254 Thomas Jefferson to George Hay, May 26, 1807. *Works* X, pp. 394-395.

to the Judicial Article were necessary, including term limitations for Federal judges, establishing an easier method to remove Federal judges, or, perhaps, filing articles of impeachment and conducting a Senate trial against recalcitrant Federal judges, including Chief Justice John Marshall. One thing is certain: President Jefferson was concerned that the government could not convict Burr, the man he publicly declared guilty four months earlier.

During the wait for General Wilkinson, Jefferson wrote the Marquis de Lafayette:

> Burr is now under trial for a misdemeanor, that is for his projected Mexican enterprise, and will be put on his trial for treason as soon as the witnesses can be collected, for his attempt to sever the Union, and unless his federal patrons give him an opportunity of running away, he will unquestionably be convicted on both prosecutions. The enterprise has done good by proving that the attachment of the people in the west is as firm as that in the East of the union of our country, and by establishing a mutual & universal confidence....[255]

Contrary to earlier letters, Jefferson here voiced great confidence in Burr's conviction.

Jefferson wrote two additional letters. The first was to son-in-law, Representative John W. Eppes, a Congressional defender:

> The news is now with you. We have heard as yet only the proceedings of the 1st day of Burr's trial, which from the favor of the marshal & judge promises him all which can depend on them. A grand jury of 2 feds, 4 Quids & 10 republicans does not seem to be a fair representation of the state of Virginia. *But all this will show the original error of establishing a judiciary independent of the nation,* and which, from the citadel of the law can turn its guns on those they meant to defend, & control & fashion their proceedings to it's own will. I have always entertained a high opinion of the marshal's integrity & political correctness. But in a state where there are no more than 8 Quids, how 5 of them should have been summoned on one jury is difficult to explain from accident.[256] (Emphasis added.)

("Quids" is a term of Latin derivation; initially it referred to a third party movement in Pennsylvania within the Republican Party. "Quid" was later used to describe John Randolph and his supporters in Congress who broke with Jefferson. The term was sometimes used to refer to Burr and his supporters.[257])

---

255 Thomas Jefferson to Marquis de Lafayette, May 26, 1807. *Works* X, pp. 406-412.
256 Thomas Jefferson to John W. Eppes, May 28, 1807. *Works* X, pp. 412-413.
257 Isenberg, p. 299.

Jefferson, acting as a senior partner, advised Hay on how to question Bollman if he did not cooperate:

> If the grand jury do not find a bill against Burr, as there will be no examination before a petty jury, Bollman's pardon need not in that case to be delivered; but if a bill be found, and a trial had, his testimony is deemed entirely essential & in that case his pardon is to be produced before he goes to the book. In my letter of the day before yesterday, I enclosed you Bollman's written communication to me, & observed you might go so far, if he prevaricated, as to ask him whether he did not say so & so to Mr. Madison and myself. On further reflection, I think you may go farther, if he prevaricates grossly, & show the paper to him, and ask if it is not his handwriting, & confront the contents. I enclose you some other letters of Bollman to me on former occasions, to prove by similitude of hand that the paper I enclosed on the 26th was of his handwriting....[258]

Jefferson's letter was a legal primer on evidence, including impeachment of a witness and verification and admissibility of a document. He advised Hay on how to cross-examine and impeach Bollman through the legal methods of refreshing recollection, past recollection recorded, and prior recorded statement. These legal principles are today codified in the Federal Rules of Evidence.[259]

Hay provided a chronology of trial events to President Jefferson on May 31, 1807:

> The trial of Burr has indeed commenced under inauspicious circumstances, and I have no doubt that its progress will be as unfavorable as its commencement. What the issue may be it is impossible to foretell. The delay on the part of Wilkinson is a matter of great triumph to the numerous partisans of Burr, who are strenuous persevering in their efforts to produce a belief that he will never dare attend.

> ...Burr's conduct shows that he believes his situation to be desperate. He takes every advantage, denies every position advanced in the prosecution, acquiesces in no decision, however solemnly made, as frequently repeated, and while he boldly asserts his innocence, adopts every measure within his power to bar the door to an inquiry. My associates in the prosecution and myself have determined not to present the bills until Wilkinson's arrival. If he does not come by tomorrow (two o'clock) the grand jury will probably be discharged, a special court will be called, and a day fixed which the General may be confidently expected.

---

258 Thomas Jefferson to George Hay, May 28, 1807. *Works X*, pp. 395-396.
259 See, Federal Rules of Evidence (FRE) 607, 612-13, 701, 901, 1002, 1005. http://www.uscourts.gov/rules/Evidence.

If the whole truth comes out Burr must be convicted of treason. But how is this to be expected? Bollman has refused to accept the pardon, or rather has said that he neither takes it nor rejects it. His object is to refuse answers to important questions, on the ground of his not being obliged to implicate himself. His evidence, if he will give it, I deem conclusive as to the treasonable design and perfectly coincident with Eaton's: but I am inclined to believe that he is as unprincipled as his leader.

There is one decision of the judges (or rather *the Judge*) in this case which will evidence to Congress the propriety of making some general and effectual provision for the arrest and examination of offenders, in cases similar to that of Aaron Burr.

The affidavit of Dunbaugh has been rejected. Its materiality was ascertained in spite of every effort to prevent it. The Counsel wished to see the form of the authentication and under the pretext run through the statement. Their knowledge of the contents excited the most ardent opposition and they finally prevailed. The exceptions were, first, that "B. Cenas" who is certified by the Governor ... a justice of the peace, does not appear to be the same "B. Cenas" by whom the affidavit is certified. Secondly, that "B. Cenas" does not certify that he performed this official act within the territory of Orleans. The arguments, in support of this affidavit founded on common sense, public good, the admission in the Supreme Court of Wilkinson"s affidavit authenticated in the same way, a principle laid down by that Court in the case of *Bollman* and *Swartwout*, and the decision of our Court of Appeals ... who urged with great force and specificity were totally unavailing. This decision is a specimen of the doctrine against which we must fight every inch of the way. *I do not say, because I do not believe that the Chief Justice does wrong with his eyes open, but that his eyes are almost closed, in a position of which no man can doubt who has observed his conduct before and since the examination.* I do not despair, however, of bringing Aaron Burr to justice. Every possible difficulty will be thrown in our way, but I trust that neither energy nor patience to encounter and to surmount them will be wanted.

Your direction as to taking down the evidence will be directly attended to.[260] (Emphasis added.)

Awaiting Wilkinson

The Grand Jury was unable to proceed since Wilkinson had yet to arrive. President Jefferson was still concerned about the Grand Jury. On June 5, Jefferson responded to a Hay letter:

---

260 George Hay to Thomas Jefferson, May 31, 1807. *The Thomas Jefferson Papers*, Library of Congress digital, American Memory.

I think it will be fortunate if any circumstance should produce a discharge of the present scanty grand jury and a future summons of a fuller; though the same views of protecting the offender may again reduce the number to 16 in order to lessen the chance of getting 12 to concur. It is understood, that wherever Burr met his subjects who did not choose to embark on his projects, unless approved by their government, he asserted that he had that approbation. Most of them took his word for it, but it is said that with those who would not, the following stratagem was practiced. A forged letter, purporting to be from General Dearborn, was made to express his approbation, and to say that I was absent at Monticello, but that there was no doubt that, on my return, my approbation of his enterprises would be given. This letter was spread open on his table, so as to invite the eye of whoever entered his room those who he wished to become witnesses of his acting under sanction. By this means he avoided committing himself to any liability to prosecution for forgery, & gave another proof of being a great man in little things, while he is really small in great ones. I must add General Dearborn's declaration that he never wrote a letter to Burr in his life, except that when here, once in a winter, he usually wrote a billet of invitation to dine. The only object of sending you the enclosed letters is to possess you of the fact, that you may know how to pursue it, if any of your wit-nesses should know anything of it. My intention in writing to you several times, has been to convey facts or observations occurring in the absence of the Attorney General, and not to make the dreadful drudgery you are going through the unnecessary addition of writing me letters in answer, which I beg you to relieve yourself from, except when some necessity calls for it...[261]

While awaiting Wilkinson, a young New York writer, Washington Ir-ving, covered the Burr trial for a New York newspaper. In a letter to a friend, Irving wrote:

[W]e are now enjoying a kind of suspension of hostilities; the grand jury having been dismissed the day before yesterday for five or six days.... As yet we are not even on the threshold of a trial; and, if the great hero of the south does not arrive, it is a chance if we have any trial this term. I am told the Attorney General talks of moving the Court next Tuesday for a continuance and a special Court, by which the present grand jury (the most enlightened, perhaps, that has ever assembled in this country) will be discharged; the witness-es will be dismissed; many of whom live such a distance off that it is a chance if half of them will ever again be collected. The Govern-ment will again be subjected to immense expense, and Colonel Burr, besides being harassed and detained for an additional space of time, will have to repeat the enormous expenditures which this trial has already caused him. I am very much mistaken, if the most under-handed and ungenerous measures have not been observed towards

---

261 Thomas Jefferson to George Hay, June 5, 1807, *Works* X, pp. 397-398.

him. He, however, retains his serenity and self-possession unshaken, and wears the same aspect in all times and situations. I am impatient for the arrival of this Wilkinson, that the whole matter may be put to rest; and I never was more mistaken in my calculations, if the whole will not have a most farcical termination as it respects the charges against Colonel Burr.[262]

During this interval, Jefferson wrote Hay on June 2, 1807: "While Burr's case is depending before the court, I will trouble you, from time to time, with what occurs to me." What troubled Jefferson this date was Chief Justice Marshall's opinion in *Marbury v. Madison*, issued four years earlier. Jefferson noted that this decision may have been cited in the Burr proceedings, although he may have been mistaken:

> I think it material to stop at the threshold the citing of that case as authority, and to have it denied to be law. 1. Because the judges, in the outset, disclaimed all cognizance of the case, although they then went on to say what would have been their opinion, had they had cognizance of it. This, then, was confessedly an extrajudicial opinion, and as such, of no authority. 2. Because it had been judicially pronounced, it would have been against law; for to a commission, a deed, a bond, delivery is essential to give validity. Until, therefore, the commission is delivered out of the hands of the Executive & his agents, it is not his deed. He may withhold or cancel it at pleasure, as he might his private deed in the same situation. The Constitution intended that the three great branches of the government be co-ordinate, & independent of each other. As to acts, therefore, which are to be done by either, it has no control to another branch. A judge, I presume, cannot sit on a bench without a commission, or a record of a commission; & the Constitution having given to the judiciary branch no means of compelling the executive branch either to deliver a commission, or to make a record of it, shows it did not intend to give the judiciary that control over the executive, but that it should remain in the power of the latter to do it or not....

Jefferson next argued that the three branches of government should independently determine the constitutionality of their respective actions, employing his tri-partite theory of government. He then concluded:

> I have long wished for a proper occasion to have the gratuitous opinion in *Marbury v. Madison* brought before the public, & denounced as not law; & I think the present a fortunate one, because it occupies such a place in public attention. I should be glad, therefore, if, in noticing that case, you could take occasion to express the determination of the executive, that the doctrines of that case were given extrajudicially & against law, and that their reverse will be the

---

262 Washington Irving to Mrs. Hoffman, June 4, 1807. Washington Irving. *The Life and Letters of Washington Irving*. Pierre M. Irving, Editor. Volume I, pp. 155-156.

rule of action with the executive. If this opinion should not be your own, I would wish it be expressed merely as that of the executive. If it is your own also, you would of course give the arguments such a development as a case, incidental only, might render proper....[263]

Several days later, Prosecutor Hay wrote President Jefferson. Hay provided an update on trial proceedings. He informed Jefferson that he requested that the Grand Jury remain embodied since it was thought that Wilkinson would arrive shortly:

> ...We have determined not to present the bills until there is a prospect of a trial before a petit jury. A third ineffectual effort to get a bill found against Burr for treason would excite a sentiment very unfavorable to a fourth, however well supported by evidence. If I could confide in the witnesses, or if the grand jury could know in what manner and as for what facts they ought to be severally examined, I should not hesitate to go on now with the prosecution; but Bollman, Swartwout will never utter a word injurious to Burr, unless it is established by force of public interrogation.

Hay then commented on *Marbury*:

> The case of *Marbury v. Madison* cannot, I conceive, be brought to bear on any jurist worth notice in Burr's case. If it should, I shall readily avail myself of the remark you have been so good as to communicate. I beg leave to add that they are in exact coincidence with the idea which I had already formed on the subject.... The grant of the office is not consummated, until the commission is delivered to the party appointed or to some person for him. In the case of *U.S. v. Hopkins*, who claimed a credit for his salary, until he was notified that his commission was revoked by the appointment of a successor, the court did not seem to adhere very rigidly to the doctrines advanced in *Marbury v. Madison*. But upon this point, I cannot be clear, as the court itself seems to be in some difficulty.[264]

---

263 Thomas Jefferson to George Hay, June 2, 1807. *Works* X, pp. 396-397.
264 George Hay to Thomas Jefferson, June 5, 1807. *The Thomas Jefferson Papers*, Library of Congress digital, American Memory.

9. MARBURY V. MADISON

> It is emphatically the province and duty of the judicial department to say what the law is.
>
> —*Marbury v. Madison*

> I have long wished for a proper occasion to have the gratuitous opinion in Marbury v. Madison brought before the public, & denounced as not law.
>
> —*Thomas Jefferson to George Hay*

Why did President Jefferson request Prosecutor Hay to challenge the *Marbury v. Madison* opinion if provided an opportunity? Republicans and Federalists continued to fiercely debate the role of the Federal judiciary. Republicans believed that the will of the people should prevail, including construction of the Constitution. Federalists believed that the Constitution must be interpreted by independent judges free from politics, even when their opinions conflict with public opinion.

Marbury v. Madison[265] is the first great Constitutional law case decided by the United States Supreme Court. *Marbury* is one of the first cases discussed in Constitutional law textbooks and classes.[266] Supreme Court Justices are constantly reminded of the significance of this decision: pictures of William

---

265 *Marbury v. Madison*, 1 Cranch 137, 5 U.S. 137, 2 L.Ed. 60 (1803).
266 See, for instance, Gerald Gunther and Noel T. Dowling. *Cases and Materials on Constitutional Law*. Mineola, NY: The Foundation Press, 1970, pp. 1-32; Kathleen M. Sullivan and Gerald Gunther, *Constitutional Law*, 2007.

Marbury and Secretary of State James Madison hang side by side in the John Marshall private dining room in the Supreme Court Building in Washington, D.C.[267] The importance of the *Marbury* decision is reflected by its display in the Rotunda of the National Archives Building in Washington, D.C. Upon entering the Rotunda, a number of Charters of Freedom are on exhibit. The first is Magna Carta, followed by the Declaration of Independence, Articles of Confederation, Constitution of the United States and the Bill of Rights. The next Charter is the *Marbury v. Madison* decision. The exhibit reminds visitors that *Marbury* is the cornerstone of our Constitutional system and was the first case to declare an Act of Congress unconstitutional.[268]

In his December 1801 Message to Congress, President Jefferson signaled that changes in the judicial system must be addressed. During the Supreme Court's December 1801 session, the case of *Marbury v. Madison* was filed and an order to show cause issued by the Court, which scheduled the case to be heard at the next session of Court in June 1802. Upon repeal of the Judiciary Act of 1801 and enactment of the Judiciary Act of 1802, the Supreme Court henceforth convened for one annual session in February. With this change, the Supreme Court did not meet again until February 1803, almost fourteen months since its last session. This change in the Court's sessions was considered a deliberate attempt by Republicans to delay a decision *Marbury v. Madison* and to insure that the Supreme Court could not consider Constitutionality of repeal of the Judiciary Act of 1801 until February 1803.

When the Supreme Court finally convened in February 1803, much had happened since its last session: repeal of the Judiciary Act of 1801, enactment of the Judiciary Act of 1802, and resumption of riding circuit by Supreme Court Justices. The Jefferson Administration and its supporters had an additional missile to lob at the judiciary before the Court's term commenced. On February 3, 1803, four days before the Court was scheduled to convene, President Jefferson sent to Congress the following Message: "The enclosed letter and affidavits exhibiting matter of complaint against John Pickering, district judge of New Hampshire, which is not within Executive cognizance, I transmit them to the House of Representatives to whom the Constitution has confided a power of instituting proceedings of redress, if

---

267 Cliff Sloan and David McKean. *The Great Decision: Jefferson, Adams, Marshall and the Battle for the Supreme Court*, pp. 180-181.
268 *The Great Decision,* pp. ix-x; http://archives.gov/exhibits/charters/chartersof freedom.

they shall be of opinion that the case calls for them."[269] President Jefferson's Message referred to only one thing: the Constitutional remedy of Impeachment.[270] President Jefferson and his Republican supporters considered impeachment the most powerful weapon in their toolkit against recalcitrant judges. Impeachment had earlier been used to successfully remove a state judge in Pennsylvania; it would prove successful in removing Federal District Judge Pickering of New Hampshire, but later fall short in removing Supreme Court Associate Justice Samuel Chase.

Shortly after the Supreme Court commenced its February 1803 term and days before the *Marbury* case was decided, Representative Caesar A. Rodney of Delaware, future Jefferson Attorney General, wrote Maryland Representative Joseph H. Nicholson, a House leader:

> ...The Supreme Court will proceed with caution, I should imagine, if the subject be brought before them, which I suspect will be the case. The opposition will try it perhaps in every shape of which this political Proteus is capable. They will wait, I presume, to see what length the Court dare go in the case of the justices and if *encouraged* sufficiently they will appear next on stage. If they (*i.e.* the Judges of the Supreme Court) do assert unconstitutional powers, I confidently trust there will be wisdom and energy enough in the Legislative and Executive branches to resist their encroachments and to arraign them for the abuse of their authority at the proper tribunal. Such monstrous doctrines have been preached and such unlimited powers arrogated for them that I know not what they may possibly do. They should remember, however, that there is a boundary which they cannot pass with impunity. If they cross the Rubicon, they may repent when it will be too late to return. Judicial supremacy may be made to bow before the strong arm of Legislative authority. We shall discover who is master of the ship. Whether men appointed for life or the immediate representatives of the people agreeably to the Constitution are to give laws to the community. The Judges have already undertaken in "evil times" to declare war in violation of that instrument which binds us together. They are hostile to us but they do not possess enough of the old Roman to sacrifice their salaries or even risk them in the contest. They are not sufficiently disinterested.[271]

---

269 President Thomas Jefferson, Message to Congress, February 3, 1803. James D. Richardson, Editor. *A Compilation of the Messages and Papers of the Presidents.* Volume I, p.344.

270 United States Constitution, Article I, Sections 2 and 3; Article II, Section 4.

271 Caesar A. Rodney to Joseph H. Nicholson, February 16, 1803. Warren, pp. 228-229. Warren cites the Joseph H. Nicholson Papers MSS as his source.

The *Marbury v. Madison* case was called February 9th, two days after the Court convened.[272] The *Marbury* case was an original action. In contrast, most cases that come before the Court are appeals from decisions of lower federal courts or the highest court of a state.

Proof necessary to establish Marbury's claim was relatively simple: (1) Nomination of Marbury by President Adams for the position of Justice of the Peace, (2) Advice and consent of the Senate to Marbury's appointment, and (3) A Commission for Marbury's appointment signed by President Adams affixed with the Seal of the United States. There were, however, two problems: First, the actual commission was withheld by the Jefferson Administration from the Court and it was uncertain whether the actual Commission existed. Second, two key witnesses to the events were unavailable. President Adams left Washington in the early morning hours of March 4, 1801 and never returned. The second witness, the Secretary of State, was now the presiding judge. Chief Justice Marshall could not testify unless he removed himself from this case. Recusal was the last thing Attorney Charles Lee or William Marbury wanted; recusal meant that Chief Justice Marshall could not hear the case. Chief Justice Marshall was never requested to recuse himself, even by the government.

THE GREAT DECISION

The Jefferson Administration did nothing to assist the Court. Attorney General Lincoln was present and responded to three of four questions propounded to him; otherwise, the Jefferson Administration was silent. Not only did Secretary of State James Madison fail to appear in Court; the Government never articulated a position to the Court as to why the writ of *mandamus* should not issue. After proofs were closed, the Court was confronted with the two unfavorable prospects: (1) if the Supreme Court ruled in Marbury's favor, the Court would be required to order Secretary of State Madison to deliver the missing commissions. Assuming Madison and the Jefferson Administration refused to comply, the Court had no means to enforce its order; thus, the Court would appear powerless and ineffective. Since the Court was still seeking its voice, a powerless Supreme Court would not enhance its public perception. (2) If the Court ruled against Marbury and

---

272 The case involved four petitioners who sought their commissions as Justices of the Peace: William Marbury, Dennis Ramsey, Robert Townsend Hooe, and William Harper.

denied him his commission, it would appear that the Court caved under pressure from the Jefferson Administration.

The primary issue concerned the writ of *mandamus*. The Constitution provided limited original jurisdiction to the Supreme Court (Article III, Section 2). Section 13 of the Judiciary Act 1789 expanded the Supreme Court's original jurisdiction: "[T]he Supreme Court ... shall have power ... to issue writs of *mandamus*, in cases warranted by the principles and usages of law, to any courts appointed, or persons holding office, under the authority of the United States."[273] Review of Section 13 was the pivotal issue in *Marbury*.

Two weeks after the *Marbury* case was taken under advisement by the Court, Chief Justice Marshall delivered the Court's opinion. With four Associate Justices present, Chief Justice Marshall presented the opinion of the Court in the lobby of Stelle's Hotel in Washington, D.C. (the Court met at this location due to Justice Chase's illness).[274] On February 24, 1803, Chief Justice Marshall read his historic opinion. Marshall began by discussing its background: a rule was issued by the Supreme Court at its last session in December, 1801 for Secretary of State Madison to show cause why a *mandamus* should not issue directing him to deliver William Marbury's commission for Justice of the Peace. After James Madison and the Jefferson Administration presented no evidence, Chief Justice Marshall declared: "No cause has been shown, and the present motion is for a *mandamus*. *The peculiar delicacy of this case, the novelty of some of its circumstances, and the real difficulty attending the points which occur in it, require a complete exposition of the principles, on which the opinion be given by the court, is founded.*"[275] (Emphasis added.)

Chief Justice Marshall identified three questions the Court must address. Marshall chose to address the questions in an atypical order (jurisdictional questions are typically resolved first):

"1st. Has the applicant a right to the commission he demands?

"2[dly.] If he has a right, and that right has been violated, do the laws afford him a remedy?

"3[dly.] If they do afford him a remedy, is it a *mandamus* issuing from this court?"

---

273 Judiciary Act of 1789, Section 13, 1 Stat. 73 (September 24, 1789).
274 Smith, p. 319.
275 This and subsequent quotations are reported in *Marbury v. Madison*, 1 Cranch 137, 5 U.S. 137 (1803). There is no question about the "peculiar delicacy of the case."

The Court first analyzed whether Marbury had been properly appointed to the office of justice of the peace. If so, Marbury had a right to hold the office for five years, in effect being his property. Marshall divided the appointment process into three phases: (1) nomination by the President; (2) appointment by the President with the advice and consent of the Senate; and (3) signing the Commission by the President with the Seal of the United States affixed: "Mr. Marbury, then, since his commission was signed by the President and sealed by the Secretary of State, was appointed; and as the law creating the office gave the officer a right to hold it for five years, independent of the executive, the appointment was not revocable; but vested in the officer legal rights, which are protected by the laws of this country. To withhold his commission, therefore, is an act deemed by the Court not warranted by law, but violative of a vested legal right."

Marshall next resolved whether Marbury was afforded a legal remedy. Here, Marshall upheld the rule of law:

> The very essence of civil liberty certainly consists in the right of every individual to claim the protection of the laws, whenever he receives an injury. One of the first duties of government is to afford that protection…. in all other cases it is a general and indisputable rule, that where there is a legal right, there is also a legal remedy by suit or action at law, whenever that right is invaded…. The government of the United States has been emphatically termed a government of laws, and not of men. It will certainly cease to deserve this high appellation, if the laws furnish no remedy for the violation of a vested legal right.[276] [Emphasis added].

Marshall acknowledged that certain executive decisions are political by nature and are, therefore, not subject to Court review: "But where a *specific duty is assigned by law, and individual rights depend upon the performance of that duty, it seems equally clear that the individual, who considers himself injured, has a right to resort to the laws of his country for a remedy.*" (Emphasis added.)

Concluding his analysis on this issue, Marshall opined:

> 1st. That by signing the commission of Mr. Marbury, the President of the United States appointed him a justice of peace, for the county of Washington in the district of Columbia; and that the seal of the United States, affixed thereto by the secretary of state, is conclusive testimony of the verity of the signature, and the completion of

---

276 The phrase "a government of laws, not of men" is normally attributed to John Adams. "Novanglus Papers," No. 7. *The Works of John Adams,* edited by Charles Francis Adams, Volume 4, p. 106; John Adams also used this phrase when he wrote about the Massachusetts Constitution, Article 30 (1780). *Works of John Adams,* Volume 4, p. 230. Adams attributed this phrase to James Harrington, who, in 1656, used the phrase "the empire of laws and not of men."

the appointment; and that the appointment conferred on him a legal right to the office for the space of five years.

2dly. That, having this legal title to the office he has a consequent right to the commission; a refusal to deliver which, is a plain violation of that right, for which the laws of his country afford him a remedy.

Marbury had prevailed on the first two issues; he had a right to the commission and, in order to secure that right, the law afforded him a remedy. The Marshall Court appeared to be on a collision course with the Jefferson Administration. Resolution of the third and final issue would dispose of the case; was Marbury entitled to the remedy for which he applied. The third question was split by the Court into two parts; the nature of the writ applied for and the power of the Supreme Court.

Marshall discussed the *writ of mandamus*. "Blackstone in his *Commentaries* ... defines a *Mandamus* to be 'a command ... directed to any person, corporation or inferior court ... which appertains to their office and duty ... to be consonant to right and justice.'" The Court assured the parties that it was not about to engage in a political matter and would exercise judicial restraint. Marshall was well aware of the obstacles before him:

> With respect to the officer (Madison) to whom it (writ of *mandamus*) would be directed. The intimate political relation subsisting between the President of the United States and the heads of departments, necessarily renders any legal investigation of the acts of one of those officers particularly irksome, as well as delicate; and excites some hesitation with respect to the propriety of entering into such investigation. *Impressions are often received without much reflection or examination, and it is not wonderful that in such a case as this, the assertion, by an individual, that his legal claims in a court of justice; to which claims it is the duty of that court to attend; should at first be considered by some, as an attempt to intrude into the cabinet, and to intermeddle with the prerogatives of the executive.*

> It is scarcely necessary for the court to disclaim all pretensions to such a jurisdiction. An extravagance, so absurd and excessive, could not have been entertained for a moment. *The province of the court is, solely, to decide on the rights of individuals, not to enquire how the executive, or executive officers, perform duties in which they have a discretion. Questions, in their nature political, or which are, by the Constitution and laws, submitted to the executive, can never be made in this court.* (Emphasis added.)

Chief Justice Marshall determined that neither a discretionary power nor a political question deprived Marbury of his commission; rather, it was the failure of a governmental official to perform an act mandated by law:

> But where he is directed by law to do a certain act affecting the absolute rights of individuals, in the performance of which he is not placed under the particular direction of the President, and the performance of which, the President cannot lawfully forbid, and therefore is never presumed to have forbidden— as for example, to record a commission, or a patent for land, which has received all the legal solemnities; or to give a copy of such record; in such cases, it is not perceived on what ground the courts of the country are further excused from the duty of giving judgment, that right be done to an injured individual, than if the same services were to be performed by a person not the head of a department.

Marshall concluded, "this ... is a plain case for *mandamus*, either to deliver the commission, or a copy of it from the record."

The final and most important question was whether a writ of *mandamus* could issue from the Supreme Court. This was the pivotal issue and the Court's resolution was stunning. Marshall began by citing the authority for the Court to issue a writ of *mandamus* (Section 13 of the Judiciary Act of 1789): "The Secretary of State, being a person holding an office under the authority of the United States, is precisely within the letter of the description; and if this Court is not authorized to issue a writ of *mandamus* to such an officer, it must be because the law is unconstitutional, and therefore absolutely incapable of conferring the authority, and assigning the duties which its words purport to confer and assign." According to Marshall, if the Court found Section 13 of the Judiciary Act of 1789 unconstitutional, it must consider that section of the Judiciary Act of 1789 void and without effect; thus the Court would be without authority to issue a writ of *mandamus.*

Marshall carefully reviewed the Judicial Article of the Constitution (Article III, section 2), which includes both appellate and limited original jurisdiction of the Supreme Court. Article III, Section 2 of the Constitution provides, in pertinent part: "In all cases affecting ambassadors, other public ministers and consuls, and those in which a state shall be a party, the Supreme Court shall have original jurisdiction. *In all other cases* before mentioned, the Supreme Court shall have appellate jurisdiction, both as to law and fact, with such exceptions, and under such regulations as the Congress shall make." (Emphasis added.) Marshall continued:

> The authority, therefore, given to the Supreme Court, by the act establishing the judicial courts of the United States, to issue writs of *mandamus* to public officers, appears not to be warranted by the Constitution; and it becomes necessary to enquire whether a jurisdiction so conferred, can be exercised.

> *The question, whether an act, repugnant to the constitution, can become the law of the land, is a question deeply interesting to the United States; but, happily, not of an intricacy proportioned to its interest. It seems only necessary to recognize certain principles, supposed to have been long and well established to decide it.* (Emphasis added.)

Marshall explained that the Constitution provided limited powers defining the authority of the three branches of government. Since the Constitution is supreme, judicial review is essential:

> *The Constitution is either a superior, paramount law, unchangeable by ordinary means, or it is on a level with ordinary legislative acts, and like other acts, is alterable when the legislature shall please to alter it....*

> *Certainly all those who have framed Constitutions contemplate them as forming the fundamental and paramount law of the nation, and consequently the theory of every such government must be, that an act of the legislature repugnant to the constitution is void....* If an act of the legislature, repugnant to the Constitution, is void, does it, notwithstanding its invalidity, bind the courts, and oblige them to give it effect? Or, in other words, though it be not law, does it constitute a rule as operative as if it was law? This would be to overthrow in fact what was established in theory; and it would seem, at first view, an absurdity too gross to be insisted on. It shall, however, receive a more attentive consideration.

In perhaps the most famous portion of the opinion, Marshall opined:

> *It is emphatically the province and duty of the judicial department to say what the law is. Those who apply the rule to particular cases, must of necessity expound and interpret the rule. If two laws conflict with each other, the courts must decide on the operation of each.*

> *So if a law be in opposition to the Constitution; if both the law and Constitution apply to a particular case, so that the Court must either decide that case conformably to the law, disregarding the Constitution; or conformably to the Constitution, disregarding the law; the Court must determine which of these conflicting rules governs the case. This is the very essence of judicial duty.*

> *If then the courts are to regard the Constitution; and the Constitution is superior to any ordinary act of the legislature; the Constitution, and not such ordinary act, must govern the case to which they both apply.*

> *Those who controvert the principle that the Constitution is to be considered, in court, as a paramount law, are reduced to the necessity of maintaining that courts must close their eyes on the Constitution, and see only the law...*

> *The judicial power of the United States is extended to all cases arising under the constitution.*

> *Could it be the intention of those who gave this power, to say that, in using it, the Constitution should not be looked into? That a case arising under the Constitution should be decided without examining the instrument under which it arises?*
>
> *This is too extravagant to be maintained.*
>
> *In some cases then, the Constitution must be looked into by the judges. And if they can open it at all, what part of it are they forbidden to read, or to obey?* (Emphasis added.)

Chief Justice Marshall offered examples of actions that Congress might take that would be in conflict with the Constitution—if Congress enacted a bill of attainder, an *ex post facto* law or amended the treason law to require that only one witness, rather than two, were necessary to establish an overt act of treason. Marshall reminded the parties that judges take an oath of office that requires them to perform their duties in conformity with the Constitution.

Chief Justice Marshall concluded:

> It is also not entirely unworthy of observation, that in declaring what shall be the *supreme* law of the land, the *Constitution* itself is first mentioned; and not the laws of the United States generally, but those only which shall be made in *pursuance* of the Constitution, have that rank.
>
> *Thus the particular phraseology of the Constitution of the United States confirms and strengthens the principle, supposed to be essential to all written constitutions, that a law repugnant to the constitution is void; and that courts, as well as other departments, are bound by that instrument.*
>
> *The rule is discharged.*[277] (Emphasis added.)

Although Marbury lost his case, the doctrine of judicial review was established by the Supreme Court; at the same time, the Court was able to avoid a direct confrontation with the Jefferson Administration. Resolution of the case was brilliantly conceived. Chief Justice Marshall delivered an opinion to which the Jefferson Administration could not object; at the same time, the decision defined the Supreme Court and established the authority of the Court to review legislation.

In a sense, Chief Justice Marshall fought this battle with President Jefferson using methods similar to those employed by General Washington in his tactical battles during the Revolutionary War. Washington knew that we could never win the war by directly confronting the British in battle;

---

277 *Marbury v. Madison*, 1 Cranch 137-180, 5 U.S. 137 (1803).

in fact, the only way the war could be lost was to try to win it. Marshall observed Washington at Valley Forge and during numerous battles; he later reviewed Washington's papers and correspondence as his biographer. Washington realized that space and time was his ally; this was the only way the War could be won. Chief Justice Marshall viewed his battle with President Jefferson similarly. By avoiding a direct confrontation with Jefferson (space), over (time) he would prevail.[278]

REACTION TO MARBURY V. MADISON

Thomas Jefferson first expressed displeasure with the *Marbury v. Madison* decision in an exchange of letters with Abigail Adams in 1804. Jefferson had not communicated with either John or Abigail Adams for more than three years, since becoming President in 1801. Although they had once been close friends, Jefferson and John and Abigail Adams drifted apart during Jefferson's term as Vice President and, particularly, during the election of 1800. The reason for temporary renewal of communication was precipitated when Abigail Adams learned of the death of Jefferson's youngest daughter, Mary Jefferson Eppes (Polly).[279]

Thomas Jefferson's response to Abigail Adams' letter of condolence was tone deaf. For the most part, he wrote a heartfelt letter to an old friend, regretting political differences that had separated their families. However, Jefferson could not help himself; he reopened old wounds that triggered an incredible exchange of letters:

> ... and I can say with truth that one act of Mr. Adams life, and only one, ever gave me a moment's displeasure. I did consider his last appointments to office as personally unkind. They were among my most ardent political enemies, from whom no faithful cooperation could ever have been expected, and laid me under the embarrassment of acting through men whose views were to defeat mine; or to encounter the odium of putting others in their places. It seemed but common justice to leave a successor free to act by instruments of his own choice. If my respect for him did not permit me to ascribe the whole blame to the influence of others, it left something for friendship to forgive, and after brooding over it for some little time, and not always resisting the expression of it, I forgave him cordially, and

---

278 Washington's space and time theory is described in Joseph Ellis' excellent book, *American Creation: Triumphs and Tragedies at the Founding of the Republic*. New York: Alfred A Knopf, 1996, p.61; John Marshall. *The Life of George Washington*, 5 volumes. Fredricksburg, VA: The Citizen's Guild of Washington's Boyhood Home, 1926.
279 Abigail Adams to Thomas Jefferson, May 20, 1804. Lester J. Cappon. *The Adams-Jefferson Letters*, pp. 265-266, 268-269.

returned to the same state of esteem and respect for him which had so long subsisted....[280]

Jefferson's response opened the floodgates and the two old friends expressed grievances to one another. Five additional letters were written, all without the knowledge or counsel of former President Adams.[281] Although numerous topics were discussed, Jefferson's comments on the judiciary are of particular interest. In Jefferson's final letter to Mrs. Adams, he discussed judicial review:

> You seem to think that it devolved on the judges to decide on the validity of the sedition law. But nothing in the Constitution has given them a right to decide for the executive, more than to the Executive to decide for them. Both magistracies are equally independent in the sphere of action assigned to them. The judges, believing the law to be Constitutional, had a right to pass a sentence of fine and imprisonment, because that power was placed in their hands by the constitution. But the Executive, believing the law to be unconstitutional, was bound to remit the execution of it; because that power has been confided to him in the Constitution. That instrument meant that its coordinate branches should be checks on each other. But that opinion [*Marbury v. Madison*] which gives the judges the right to decide what laws are Constitutional, and what not, not only for themselves in their own sphere of action, but for the legislature and executive also in their spheres, would make the judiciary a despotic branch.[282]

The next reference by President Jefferson to *Marbury v. Madison* is found in his letter to United States Attorney George Hay in 1807.[283] Thomas Jefferson continued his attacks on the *Marbury* decision and Chief Justice Marshall for the remainder of his life.. Three letters are of particular interest. Jefferson wrote W. H. Torrence in 1815:

> The second question, *whether the judges are invested with exclusive authority to decide on the constitutionality of a law, has been heretofore a subject of consideration with me in the exercise of official duties. Certainly there is not a word in the Constitution which has given that power to them more than the executive or legislative branches.... The constitutional validity of the law or laws again prescribing executive action, and to be administered by that branch ultimately and without appeal, the executive must decide for* themselves *also, wheth-*

---

280 Thomas Jefferson to Abigail Adams, June 13, 1804. Cappon, pp. 269-271.
281 Note of November 19, 1804 attached to final letter from Abigail Adams to Thomas Jefferson, October 25, 1804. Cappon, pp. 280-282.
282 Thomas Jefferson to Abigail Adams, September 11, 1804. Cappon, pp. 278-280.
283 Thomas Jefferson to George Hay, June 2, 1807. *Works* X, pp. 396-397.

er, under the constitution, they are valid or not. So also as to laws governing the proceedings of the legislature....²⁸⁴ (Emphasis added.)

In a letter to William Charles Jarvis, Jefferson wrote:

> You seem ... to consider the judges as the ultimate arbiters of all Constitutional questions; a very dangerous doctrine indeed, and one which would place us under the despotism of an oligarchy. Our judges are as honest as other men, and not more so. They have, with others, the same passions of party, for power, and the privilege of their corps. Their maxim is *"boni judicis est anpliare jurisdictionem,"* and their power the more dangerous as they are in office for life, and not responsible, as the other functionaries are, to the elective control.... Betrayed by English example, and unaware, as it should seem, of the control of the our constitution in particular, they have at times overstepped their limit by undertaking to command executive officers in the discharge of their executive duties; but the Constitution, in keeping three departments distinct and independent, restrains the authority of the judges to judiciary organs, as it does the executive and legislative to executive and legislative organs. The judges certainly have more frequent occasion to act on constitutional questions, because the laws of *meum* and *tuum* and of criminal action, forming the great mass of the system of law, constitute their particular department. When the legislative and executive functionaries act unconstitutionally, they are responsible to the people in their elective capacity. The exemption of the judges from that is quite dangerous enough....²⁸⁵

In the third letter, Thomas Jefferson wrote Supreme Court Associate Justice William Johnson (Jefferson's first appointment to the Court):

> *This practice of Judge Marshall, of traveling out of his case to prescribe what the law would be in a moot case not before the court, is very irregular and very censurable.* I recollect another instance, and the more particularly, perhaps, because it in some measures bore on myself. Among the midnight appointments of Mr. Adams, were commissions to some federal justices of the peace for Alexandria.... Yet this case of *Marbury and Madison* is continually cited by bench and bar, as if it were settled law, without any animadversion on its being merely an *obiter* dissertation of the Chief Justice....
>
> But the Chief Justice says, *"there must be an ultimate arbiter somewhere."* True, there must; but does that prove it is either party? The ultimate arbiter is the people of the Union, assembled by their deputies in convention, at the call of Congress, or of two-thirds of the States. Let them decide to which they mean to give an authority claimed by two of their organs. And it has been the peculiar

284 Thomas Jefferson to W. H. Torrence, June 11, 1815. *Works* XI, pp. 471-475.
285 Thomas Jefferson to William Charles Jarvis, September 28, 1820. *Works* XII, pp. 161-164.

wisdom and felicity of our constitution, to have provided this peaceable appeal, where that of other nations is at once to force.... (Emphasis added.)[286]

Former Chief Justice Rehnquist wrote: "One need understand only a few of its cases to understand the Supreme Court's role in our nation's history. But one must assuredly understand the case of *Marbury v. Madison.*"[287] Although Chief Justice Marshall began to define the power and authority of the Supreme Court in *Marbury* by asserting judicial review, the Marshall Court never again declared a Federal act unconstitutional. During the tenure of the Marshall Court (1801–1835), numerous enactments of Congress were examined by the Court; the constitutionality of all federal legislation was upheld. This is in contrast to the Court's judicial review of state laws in conflict with the Constitution: judicial review by the Marshall Court frequently overturned state laws. The first case to overturn federal legislation after the Marbury v. Madison decision was *Scott v. Sandford*, 19 Howard 393, 60 U.S. 393 (1857), the infamous Dred Scott case.

James Madison, Jefferson's closest collaborator, diverged from Jefferson's views on judicial review:

> As the Legislature, Executive, and Judicial Departments of the United States are co-ordinate, and equally bound to support the Constitution...
>
> But notwithstanding this abstract view of the co-ordinate and independent right of the three departments to expound the Constitution, the Judicial Department most familiarizes itself to the public attention as the expositor, by the *order* of its functions in relation to the other departments; and attracts most of the public confidence by the composition of the tribunal.
>
> It is the Judicial Department in which questions of constitutionality, as well as legality, generally find their ultimate discussion and operative decision; and the public deference to and confidence in the judgment of the body are peculiarly inspired by the qualities implied in its members; by the gravity and deliberations of their proceedings; and by the advantage their plurality gives them over the unity of the Executive Department, and their fewness over the multitudinous composition of the Legislative Department.
>
> Without losing sight, therefore, of the co-ordinate relations of the three departments to each other, it may always be expected that the judicial bench, when happily filled, will, for the reasons suggested, most engage the respect and reliance of the public as the

---

286 Thomas Jefferson to William Johnson, June 12, 1823. *Works* XII, pp. 252-259.
287 William H. Rehnquist. *The Supreme Court*. New York: Vintage Books, 2002, p. 21.

surest expositor of the Constitution, as well in questions within its cognizance concerning the boundaries between the several departments of the Government as in those between the Union and its members.[288]

Thomas Jefferson never agreed with judicial review. He believed that the judiciary was unelected and, therefore, unresponsive to the people. He never accepted that the judiciary was an independent branch of government or that the judiciary was to be responsive to the law, not public opinion. In his excellent book about Thomas Jefferson, *American Sphinx*, Joseph Ellis analyzed the *Marbury v. Madison* case:

> The legal genius of Marshall's opinion, which Jefferson described as "sophistry" and later as Marshall's "twistifications," derived from the Chief Justice's rearrangement of the questions presented to the Court, which allowed him to rule against Marbury's petition only after lecturing the President and ruling on the Constitutionality of an Act of Congress, the Judiciary Act of 1789. If he had taken up the questions in the order in which they were presented, there would have been no need to address the broader issues. The political genius of Marshall's opinion was double-barreled: He enhanced the power of the Supreme Court by denying its jurisdiction, and he patronized the President while deciding the case in his favor. It was vintage Marshall at his most maddeningly covert. It also revealed that Marshall, much like Jefferson, preferred to avoid a direct confrontation on the abiding role of the federal judiciary, since he had masked his assertion of judicial review under the veil of impotence and had ruled that Jefferson, though in violation of the law, did not need to appoint Marbury after all. Having sallied forth from his fortress, Marshall had returned quietly to the safety of Gibralter.[289]

---

288 James Madison to Mr. __, 1834. James Madison. *Letters and Other Writings of James Madison, 1829-1836.* Volumes IV. Philadelphia: J. B. Lippincott & Co., 1865, pp. 349-350.

289 Joseph J. Ellis. *American Sphinx: The Character of Thomas Jefferson*, p. 268.

---

10. SUBPOENA *DUCES TECUM*

The court reconvened on June 9; Wilkinson had yet to arrive. The Chief Justice excused the Grand Jury and advised them to return to Court two days hence. Upon discharge of the Grand Jury, Aaron Burr advised the Court that he had a proposition to present. He requested that the court issue a subpoena *duces tecum* to President Jefferson, ordering him to produce all documents referred to in his Special Message to Congress of January 22. Burr specifically requested letters and papers received from General Wilkinson under date of October 21, 1806, together with any other relevant documents.[290] [A subpoena is a writ that commands a person to appear before a court or other tribunal, subject to a penalty for failure to comply.[291] A subpoena *duces tecum,* ("bring with you") is an order to a witness to appear and bring with him specified documents or records. Typically, when the requested documents are produced in a timely manner, the person to whom the subpoena is directed need not appear in court.][292] If this trial was not yet a conflict between the Executive and Judicial Branches, President Jefferson and Chief Justice Marshall in particular, this motion ensured that conflict. After an attempt to resolve Burr's request was unsuccessful, the Court requested legal arguments, specifically on the authority of the Court to issue a subpoena to the President of the United States.

---

290 Robertson I, p. 93; Baker, pp. 476-77; Beveridge, pp. 433-34.
291 Bryan A. Garner, Editor. *West's Law Dictionary,* 7th *Edition,* p. 1440.
292 Ibid., p. 1440.

In an earlier legal proceeding, high ranking members of Jefferson's Cabinet were subpoenaed to appear in Court. President Jefferson and his Cabinet met with General Francisco de Miranda, knowing that Miranda intended to travel to his native Venezuela in an effort to free Venezuela and South America from Spanish rule. Miranda set sail with his supporters from New York on an American owned vessel, the *Leander*. When the Administration learned that an American ship was utilized for this adventure against Spain (a nation with whom we were at peace), Secretary of State James Madison, upon President Jefferson's instructions, requested the United States Attorney in New York to conduct an investigation.[293] Two men were arrested and indicted for violation of the Neutrality Act: Samuel G. Ogden, owner of the *Leander*, and William S. Smith (John Adams' son-in-law), the surveyor of the Port of New York. During preparation for trial, the defense requested subpoenas for the testimony of Jefferson Administration Cabinet members Secretary of State Madison, Secretary of War Dearborn, and Secretary of the Navy Smith.[294] The subpoenas were sought in an effort to establish that the Jefferson Administration approved this filibuster. Although Treasury Secretary Albert Gallatin was never subpoenaed, he wrote to the United States Attorney informing him that forced attendance of department heads would create a dangerous precedent since their required attendance might paralyze the government. He advised him that President Jefferson did not want his Cabinet officers to appear in court.[295] Supreme Court Justice William Paterson, sitting as Circuit Judge, excused attendance of the Cabinet officers, determining that their affidavits would be acceptable. According to Jefferson biographer Dumas Malone, Jefferson privately believed that the defendants and their friends attempted to turn this case into a "government question," making the Judge and the Administration the real culprits.[296]

Although President Jefferson's personal appearance in the Burr trial was never expected, compliance with a subpoena for production of documents was. Hay informed President Jefferson about this most recent development:

> [A]fter the grand jury had been called and adjourned, Mr. Burr moved the court for a *subpoena duces tecum*, directed to the President of the U.S. to enforce the exhibition of *the letter*, mentioned in the

293 Thomas Jefferson to James Madison, February 5, 1806. *Republic of Letters*, Volume 3, p. 1415.

294 James Madison to Thomas Jefferson, May 28, 1806. *Republic of Letters*, Volume 3, pp. 1424-25.

295 Albert Gallatin to Nathan Sandford, July 9, 1806; Malone, Volume 5, p. 87.

296 Malone 5, pp. 81-88.

enclosed, and for such process as would procure *copies* of the orders in relation to himself to the Officers at Orleans, Natchez, and by the secretaries of the War and Navy Departments. The counsel for Burr observed that they wanted the personal attendance of those in whose custody they were.... I told the court that the motion was unnecessary, that I was perfectly convinced that the papers received, especially the orders from the War & Naval departments, had no bearing upon any question that could come before that tribunal, yet I was willing that the accused should have a fair trial, as far as it depended on me he should have a fair one: but it should be fair on both sides, and I had no doubt that the papers wanted would be sent, by the Government, as soon as a request on the subject was communicated. I said that I would on this day, state to the Executive, the application made to the Court. What the results of my communication would be I could not tell, but if the papers were sent, I should retain them in my possession, until the Court decided that they did belong to the question before them. This however was not sufficient, and the motion is to be made in due form tomorrow. I trust, Sir that these papers will be forwarded without delay. The hope of Burr and his counsel is that they will not. The motion is a mere maneuver. They know the papers will not avail them, but the detention of them, will afford some pretext for clamor. This is another circumstance which has aided in bringing on this motion, notwithstanding my declaration that the Government was perfectly disposed to furnish Burr, with any evidence within their power; which it would be proper to communicate. Luther Martin has been here a long time, perfectly inactive. He wants an opportunity of saying something about the administration and the subject is selected to furnish a topic. If this is not a correct supposition, how comes it that the materiality of these papers has escaped notice until this moment?

About the propriety of this motion, I can give no opinion, having had no time to look into the subject. I have no doubt that Burr will swear to the materiality of the documents required. He never scruples about the means of obtaining what he desires. His countenance begins to proclaim this to be true. Hitherto he has manifested some degree of composure; but today, the expression on his face frequently changes. He sometimes looks and spoke as if he was determined to make every effort, however desperate, to save himself from the destiny that seems to await him, and at other times it appears as if he was sinking under the prosecution, and cared not how soon it was brought to a conclusion.

I write in a state of real fatigue, and great precipitation.

Hay added: "The reason why the original letter is said to be required is that Wilkinson may deny any recollection of the letter if only a copy is shown. Before this explanation was given, there was a little explosion in court."[297]

Argument on the motion for subpoena *duces tecum* commenced on June 10. The issues presented required the Court to interpret the Sixth Amendment of the Constitution, in particular the defendant's right to "compulsory process." District Attorney Hay argued that the Court had no authority to issue the subpoena prior to indictment. The defense argued that the Court had authority to issue the subpoena, although that attendance of the President in Court would not be necessary if the documents requested were produced.

Luther Martin, awakened as Hay predicted, argued:

> All that we want is copies of some papers, and the original of another. *This is a peculiar case, sir. The president has undertaken to prejudge my client by declaring, that "Of his guilt there can be no doubt." He has assumed to himself the knowledge of the Supreme Being himself, and pretended to search the heart of my highly respected friend (Burr). He has proclaimed him a traitor in the face of the country which has rewarded him. He has let slip the dogs of war, the hell-hounds of persecution, to hunt down my friend.* And would the president of the United States, who has raised all this absurd clamor, pretend to keep back the papers which are wanted for this trial, where life is at stake? It is a sacred principle, that in all such cases, the accused has a right to all the evidence which is necessary for his defense. And whoever withholds, willfully, information that would save the life of a person charged with a capital offense, is substantially a murderer, and so recorded in the register of heaven."[298] (Emphasis added.)

Emotional argument continued throughout the day. Argument became so heated that Chief Justice Marshall cautioned the attorneys about their inflamed rhetoric. The Court expressed "the wish that counsel for the United States and for Mr. Burr would confine themselves, on every occasion to the point really before the Court; that their own good sense and regard for their characters required them to follow such a course; and it was hoped that they would not hereafter deviate from it."[299]

The next day, Luther Martin continued his argument:

> We have a right to inspect the orders issued from the war and navy departments; because if they were illegal, we have a right to oppose them. If they were unconstitutional and oppressive, it was right to resist them; but this is denied, because we are not trying the presi-

---

297 George Hay to Thomas Jefferson, June 9, 1807. *The Thomas Jefferson Papers*, Library of Congress digital, American Memory.

298 Robertson I, pp. 110-11.

299 Robertson I, pp. 135-36.

dent. God forbid we should. But we are trying if we had a right to resist. If every order, however arbitrary and unjust, is to be obeyed, we are slaves as much as the inhabitants of Turkey. If the presidential edicts are to be the supreme law, and the officers of government have but to register them, as formerly in France (the country once so famed by these gentlemen for its progress and advancement toward liberty) and if we submit to them, however unjust and unconstitutional, we are as subject to despotism as the people of Turkey, the subjects of the former "Grand Monarques" in France, or those of the despot Bonaparte at this day? If this were true where would be our boasted freedom? Where are the superior advantages of our government, or the beneficial effects of our revolutionary struggle?[300]

After the hearing concluded, Hay advised President Jefferson that he believed Wilkinson would arrive soon and then discussed Court proceedings: "Yesterday and this day were consumed in debate as animated as it was frivolous. Everything that was said was intended for the people behind the bar. In this sort of discussion however, our adversaries were fully met, and I doubt whether Mr. Luther Martin ever comes again to Virginia to vindicate a 'persecuted honorable friend.'" [301]

Before the Court ruled on the subpoena *duces tecum*, Jefferson informed Hay that many of the documents sought had earlier been provided to Attorney General Rodney. In his letter, Jefferson, subject to invoking executive privilege, appeared willing to comply with the subpoena *duces tecum*:

> Reserving the right of the President of the U.S. to decide, independently of all other authority, what papers, coming to him as President, the public interests permit to be communicated, & to whom, I assure you of my readiness under that restriction, voluntarily to furnish on all occasions, whatever the purposes of justice may require. But the letter of General Wilkinson, of October 21, requested for the defense of Colonel Burr, with every other paper relating to the charges against him, which were in my possession when the Attorney General went on to Richmond in March, I then delivered to him.... But, as I do not recollect the whole contents of that letter, I must beg leave to devolve on you the exercise of that discretion which it would be my right & duty to exercise, by withholding the communication of any parts of the letter, which are not directly material for the purposes of justice.

> With this application, which is specific, a prompt compliance is practicable. But when the request goes to "copies of the orders issued in relation to Colonel Burr, to the officers at Orleans, Natchez,

300 Robertson I, p. 160.
301 George Hay to Thomas Jefferson, June 11, 1807. *The Thomas Jefferson Papers*, Library of Congress digital, American Memory.

&c., by the Secretaries of the War & Navy departments" it seems to cover a correspondence of many months, with such a variety of officers, civil & military, all over the U.S., as would amount to the laying open the whole executive books. I have desired the Secretary of War to examine his official communications; and on a view of these, we may be able to judge what can & ought to be done, towards a compliance with the request. If the defendant alleges that there was any particular order, which, as a cause, produced any particular act on his part, then he must know what this order was, can specify it, and a prompt answer can be given. If the object had been specified, we might then have some guide for our conjectures, as to what part of the executive records might be useful to him: but, with a perfect willingness to do what is right, we are without the indications which may enable us to do it. If the researches of the Secretary of War should produce anything proper for communication, & pertinent to any point we can perceive in the defense before the court, it shall be forwarded to you....

Jefferson attached a note to his letter indicating that he enclosed two letters received from Secretary of War Dearborn that were sent to the Governors of Mississippi and Louisiana.[302]

The Court reconvened on June 13. Chief Justice Marshall was prepared to rule on the motion for subpoena *duces tecum*. Marshall hoped that the Administration would provide the requested documents to Burr and that the dispute would be amicably resolved. After several days of heated argument, it was obvious that there would be no resolution and that the Court must rule. Once again, Chief Justice Marshall was called upon to rule on an issue of unsettled law. In an earlier case, Thomas Cooper requested a subpoena requiring President John Adams to appear in court, not only to bring requested documents but to testify. Associate Justice Samuel Chase, sitting in the circuit court, refused to issue the subpoena. This case, however, was different. Jefferson's testimony was unnecessary and no one requested that he appear; the defense only wanted the documents.[303] Interestingly, Justice Chase was vigorously attacked by Republicans when he refused to issue the subpoena to President Adams.

In his opinion, Chief Justice Marshall ruled that the Sixth Amendment of the Constitution permitted the defendant the right to compulsory process. The Sixth Amendment requires notice and specificity of charges, so that an accused can adequately prepare his defense. To insure these rights,

---

302 Thomas Jefferson to George Hay, June 12, 1807. *Works* X, pp. 398-400.
303 Jane Shaffer Elsmere. *Justice Samuel Chase*. Muncie, IN: Janevar Publishing Co., pp. 315-316.

an accused is entitled to compulsory process for witnesses. Chief Justice Marshall determined that an accused is entitled to Court process as soon as he is charged with a crime and brought under Court control. Although Burr had yet to be indicted, he had been formally charged with a criminal complaint for violation of the Neutrality Act.

After the Court ruled that the defendant was entitled to a subpoena *duces tecum* for production of documents, the Court next addressed the issue of whether a subpoena *duces tecum* could be issued to the President of the United States. Marshall noted that the Constitution and a statute enacted for criminal cases (United States Statutes at Large, I, 188-119, section 29) provided for compulsory process. Chief Justice Marshall contrasted American law with British law and found a major difference: the King. Marshall noted two differences between the King and the President. Under British law, the King could do no wrong; under the Constitution, the President could be impeached and removed from office upon conviction for high crimes and misdemeanors. Under British law, the crown was hereditary, since the King was never a subject; under the Constitution, the President is elected by the mass of the people and, upon expiration of his term, returns to the mass of people. The Chief Justice found no law that prohibited issuance of a subpoena to a President (no such law was cited by the prosecution or the defense). One objection raised by the prosecution was that the President is required to spend his whole time as President. Chief Justice Marshall suggested that the demand of time on the President was not 'unremitting.'

Chief Justice Marshall next responded to three objections offered by the prosecution, particularly production of a letter from General Wilkinson. First, was production of the document material to the defense? Marshall determined that since it appeared that Wilkinson was the key witness against Burr, Burr should be provided with all relevant documents relating to the General. Burr was entitled to any documents that would assist him during cross-examination of prosecution witnesses. Second, what if the requested letters contained confidential information that should not be publicly disclosed? Marshall acknowledged that this argument related to confidential communications and executive privilege. Marshall opined that such determination, if necessary, would be made by the Court upon return of the subpoena with the requested documents. The Court could examine the documents and resolve confidentiality and executive privilege issues. Third, may a copy of the document be received instead of the original? The

Court determined that the original was necessary for questioning the author of the letter. Marshall held that the President was not above the law; the law did not discriminate between a President and a private citizen as to issuance of a subpoena.

One portion of Chief Justice Marshall's opinion received criticism from the prosecution and Jefferson's supporters:

> It is not for the court to anticipate the event of the present prosecution. Should it terminate as is *expected/wished* on the part of the United States, all those who are concerned in it should certainly regret that a paper which the accused believed to be essential to his defense, which may, for aught that now appears, be essential, has been withheld from him. I will not say that this circumstance would in any degree tarnish the reputation of the government, but I will say that it would justly tarnish the reputation of the court which had given its sanction to its being withheld. Might I be permitted to utter one sentiment with respect to myself, it would be to deplore most earnestly, the occasion which should compel me to look back on any part of my official conduct with so much self-reproach as I should feel, could I declare on the information now possessed, that the accused is not entitled to the letter in question, if it should be really important to him.[304] (Emphasis added.)

Immediately after the Chief Justice concluded his opinion, Prosecutor Alexander MacRae objected:

> I hope, sir, that I have misunderstood an expression which has just escaped from your honor.... Your honor has declared, if I mistake not that "if the present prosecution terminates as is wished on the part of the United States." I hope, sir, that nothing has appeared in my conduct, nothing in the conduct of the gentlemen who are associated with me on the present occasion, and nothing in the conduct of the government, to produce such a conviction in the breast of the court. Permit me, sir, to assure this court, if we feel any sentiment at all, that it is one of a very different description. The impression that has been conveyed by the court, that we wished to convict him, is completely abhorrent to our feelings. We trust, that it has rather accidentally fallen from the pen of your honor, than that it is your deliberate opinion. We wish for nothing, sir, but a fair and competent investigation of this case. It is far from our wishes that Aaron Burr should be convicted but upon the most satisfactory evidence. And let me assure this court, that nothing more would severely wound my feelings, that if you or any other man would suppose it possible, that I myself, or the gentlemen with whom I am associated, or the

---

304 *PJM* VII, pp. 37-49. (The Opinion of Chief Justice Marshall)

government which we have the honor to represent, should at all events, desire the conviction of the prisoner.[305]

The Chief Justice replied that it had not been his intention to insinuate that attorneys for the prosecution, or the Administration for that matter, wished the conviction of Colonel Burr, whether he was guilty or innocent: "Gentlemen had so often, and so uniformly asserted, that Colonel Burr was guilty, and they had so often repeated it before the testimony was perceived, on which that guilt could alone be substantiated, that it appeared to him probable that they were not indifferent on the subject." Marshall rephrased his wording: he intended to use the word "expected" rather than "wished" in his opinion. He expunged the offending word from his written opinion.[306]

Marshall's opinion was favorably received by most, with the exception of Jefferson and his prosecution team. That no man is above the law, no matter how high the governmental official, is a cornerstone of our legal system. Even the pro-Republican *Richmond Enquirer*, published by Jefferson friend Thomas Ritchie, did not criticize this opinion.[307] Marshall re-affirmed the Court's obligation to protect an accused, particularly with rights found within the first Ten Amendments of the Constitution. This was the second most important ruling in the Burr case; it was later quoted extensively by Chief Justice Warren Burger in the Watergate tapes case, *United States v. Nixon*, 418 U.S. 683 (1974) and by the Court in the more recent case of *Clinton v. Jones*, 117 S. Ct. 1636, 1649 (1997).

The rule of law, as protected by Chief Justice Marshall throughout the Burr trial, prevailed. Although the doctrine of executive privilege was recognized by the Court, it was for the Court rather than the Executive to determine the extent of the privilege and whether documents will be produced. Harvard Law Professor Paul Freund, writing in the *Harvard Law Review*, suggested that Chief Justice Marshall's opinion established four legal principles that were later applied in the Nixon Watergate tapes cases:

There is no absolute privilege in a criminal case for communications to which the President is a party.

---

305 Robertson I, p. 187.
306 Robertson I, pp. 187, 196; *PJM* VII, p. 50, note 15.
307 Beveridge III, p. 450.

Upon a particularized claim of privilege by the President, the court, giving due respect to the President's judgment, will weigh the claim against the materiality of the evidence and the need of the accused for its production.

For purposes of determining whether disclosure is required, the material sought may be produced for *in camera* inspection by the court, with the participation of counsel and the accused.

In lieu of such production, the court may direct that inferences shall be drawn in favor of the accused, or that the prosecution be dismissed.[308]

---

308 Paul Freund. "Forward: On Executive Privilege," pp. 30-31; Smith, pp.364-65.

11. INDICTMENT

George Hay, on June 14th, informed President Jefferson that Wilkinson had finally arrived:

> I have had an interview with Wilkinson. We conversed yesterday morning for about an hour. I will confess to you that my impressions concerning him have undergone a great change. His erect attitude, the serenity of his countenance, the composure of his manners, the mild but determined expression of his eye; all conspired to make me think that he has been most grossly calumniated. I trust in God that the ordeal which Burr and Martin are preparing for him will be passed this with safety and honor. Burr is obviously depressed by his arrival, and his friends manifest their sympathy and chagrin, by being less conspicuous and less clamorous. General Jackson of Tennessee has been here ever since the 22nd denouncing Wilkinson in the coarsest terms in every company. The latter showed me a paper which at once explained the motive of this incessant hostility. His own character depends on the prostration of Wilkinson's. Enclosed is a note from G.W. which will exhibit to you the state of his feelings....

Hay then discussed the earlier defense challenge to the Grand Jury and a letter received from Attorney General Rodney:

> [Rodney] admits the propriety of an exception to a grand jury. I confess that I do not feel satisfied on this subject. The more I think about it, the more I am convinced that the law does not warrant such a procedure. Still however I am content with the course that has been pursued on the part of the prosecution. I have no doubt that the grand jury who are now examining the witnesses will find the bills, and if they do, the waiver of any objection on the part of

the U.S. to the withdrawing of two of the grand jurors will be only an additional evidence of that fairness which has been steadily and carefully observed.[309]

Hay next updated President Jefferson about Chief Justice Marshall's ruling that granted Burr's motion for a subpoena *duces tecum*:

> The Judge yesterday established Burr's right to the papers wanted. In the course of his opinion, which does not state correctly the conduct or positions of the Counsel for the U.S., he said, "if this prosecution terminates as wished and expected on the part of the U.S." This expression produced a very strong general sensation. The friends of the Judge, both personal and political condemned it. Alexander McRae rose as soon as he had finished, and in terms mild yet determined, demanded an explanation of it. The Judge actually blushed. He did attempt an explanation. He said that he had made the remark in consequence of the very strong and repeated declarations of the Attorney of the U.S., of his belief of Mr. Burr's guilt and I observed, with an indifference which was not assumed, that I had endeavored to do my duty, according to my own judgment and feelings, that I regretted nothing that I had said or done, that I should pursue the same Course throughout, and that it was a truth that I cared not what any man said or thought about it.
>
> Almost three hours afterwards, when the crowd was the thinnest, the Judge acknowledged the impropriety of the expression objected to, informed us from the Bench that he has erased it. After he had adjourned the court, he descended from the Bench, and told me that he regretted the remark, and then by way of apology said that he had been so pressed for time, that he had never read the opinion, after he had written it. An observation from me that I did not perceive any connection between my declarations and his remark or how the former could regularly be the Cause of the latter, closed the conversation.—...

Hay complained to Jefferson about the trial and Bollman:

> There never was such a trial from the beginning of the world to this day. I expect to be employed for twenty days to come.
>
> Bollman resolutely refuses his pardon and is determined not to utter a word if he can avoid it. The pardon lies on the Clerk's table. The Court are to decide, whether he is really pardoned or not. Martin says he is not pardoned. Such are the questions with which we are worried. If the Judge says he is not pardoned, I will take the pardon back, what shall I then do with him?

---

309 George Hay to Thomas Jefferson, June 14, 1807. *The Thomas Jefferson Papers*, Library of Congress digital, American Memory.

Excuse this almost illegible letter. Like the C.J. I am so pressed for time that I cannot read what I write....

Hay concluded: "Since writing the above, I have had another interview with Gen. Wilkinson and read many of his reports, particularly Armstrong's statement. I am now convinced that Burr himself is the man, who occasioned the constant association of his name with Wilkinson for the vilest purposes and that Wilkinson could not have acted better than he has done - in relation to the conspirator's and their schemes."[310] United States Attorney Hay's opinion about General Wilkinson would later change.

WILKINSON'S ARRIVAL

Upon his arrival in Court, General Wilkinson was sworn and directed to appear before the Grand Jury.[311] Washington Irving humorously described General Wilkinson's initial appearance in Court:

> Wilkinson you will observe has arrived; the bets were against Burr that he would abscond, should Wilkinson come to Richmond; but he still maintains his ground, and still enters the Court every morning with the same serene and placid air that he would show were he brought to plead another man's cause, and not his own.

> Wilkinson is now before the grand jury, and has such a mighty mass of words to deliver himself of, that he claims at least two days more to discharge the wondrous cargo. The jury are tired enough of verbosity. The first interview between him and Burr was highly interesting, and I secured a good place to witness it. Burr was seated with his back to the entrance, facing the judge, and conversing with one of his counsel. Wilkinson strutted into Court, and took his stand in parallel line with Burr on his right hand. Here he stood for a moment like a turkey-cock, and bracing himself up for the encounter with Burr's eye. The latter did not take any notice of him until the judge directed the clerk to swear General Wilkinson; at the mention of his name Burr turned his head, looked him full in the face with one of his piercing regards, swept his eye over his whole person from head to foot, as if to scan its dimensions, and then coolly resumed his former position, and went on conversing with his counsel as tranquilly as ever. The whole look was over in an instant; but it was an admirable one. There was no appearance of study or constraint to it; no affectation of disdain or defiance; a slight expression of contempt played over his countenance, such as you would show on regarding any person you were indifferent, but whom you con-

---

310 George Hay to Thomas Jefferson, June 14, 1807, *The Thomas Jefferson Papers*, Library of Congress digital, American Memory.
311 Robertson I, p. 196.

sidered mean and contemptible. Wilkinson did not remain in Court many minutes....[312]

Wilkinson, in a letter to President Jefferson, offered a contrasting description of his appearance in court:

> I saluted the Bench & in spite of myself my Eyes darted a flash of indignation at the little Traitor, on whom they continued fixed until I was called to the Book—here Sir I found my expectations verified—The Lyon hearted Eagle Eyed Hero, sinking under the weight of conscious guilt, with haggard Eye, made an Effort to meet the indignant salutation of outraged Honor, but it was in vain, his audacity failed Him. He averted his face, grew pale & affected passion to conceal his perturbation.[313]

Jefferson and Hay exchanged letters on June 17. Hay wrote:

> In a former letter you stated that you had directed several blank pardons be prepared and sent to me. I received but one in addition to that sent for Bollman. This I believe I shall give to Dunbaugh: but he is not the only man who ought to be placed in a state of entire confidence and security. There are about three others, whose evidence would be very important, if they did not shelter themselves under the plea of not accusing themselves.
>
> The grand jury are still engaged and certainly attend to that part of their oath which enjoins them to keep their own and their fellow counsel secret.–No time should be lost in forwarding the pardons.[314]

Jefferson once again provided legal advice to Hay, this time on the subpoenaed documents:

> In answering your letter of the 9th, which desired a communication of one to me from General Wilkinson, specified by it's date, I informed you in mine of the 12th that I had delivered it, with all other papers respecting the charges against Aaron Burr, to the Attorney General, when he went to Richmond; that I had supposed he had left them in your possession, but would immediately write to him, if he had not, to forward that particular letter without delay.... The receipt of these papers had, I presume, so far anticipated, and others this day forwarded will have substantially fulfilled the object of the subpoena from the District Court of Richmond, requiring that those officers & myself shall attend the Court in Richmond, with the letter of General Wilkinson, the answer to that letter & the orders of the departments of War & the Navy, therein generally de-

---

312 Washington Irving to James K. Paulding, June 22, 1807. Irving, p. 157-159.

313 General William Wilkinson to Thomas Jefferson, June 17, 1807. *The Thomas Jefferson Papers*, Library of Congress digital; Beveridge III, pp. 456-57.

314 George Hay to Thomas Jefferson, June 17, 1807. *The Thomas Jefferson Papers*, Library of Congress digital, American Memory.

scribed. No answer to General Wilkinson's letter, other than a mere acknowledgement of its receipt, in a letter written for a different purpose, was ever written by myself or any other. To these communications of papers, I will add, that if the defendant supposes there are any facts within the knowledge of the Heads of departments, or of myself, which can be useful for his defense, from a desire of doing anything our situation will permit in furtherance of justice, we shall be ready to give him the benefit of it, by way of deposition, through any persons the Court shall authorize to take our testimony at this place. I know, indeed, that this cannot be done but by the consent of the parties; & I therefore authorize you to give consent on the part of the U.S. Mr. Burr's consent will be given of course, if he supposes the testimony useful.

As to our personal attendance at Richmond, I am persuaded the Court is sensible, that paramount duties to the nation at large control the obligation of compliance with their summons in this case; as they would, should we receive a similar one, to attend the trials of Blennerhassett and others, in the Mississippi territory, those instituted at St. Louis and other places on the western waters, or at any place, other than the seat of government. To comply with such calls would leave the nation without an executive branch, whose agency, nevertheless, is understood to be so constantly necessary, that it is the sole branch which the constitution requires to be always in function. It could not mean that it should be withdrawn from its station by any co-ordinate authority.

With respect to papers, there is certainly a public & private side to our offices. To the former belong grants of land, patents for inventions, certain commissions, proclamations, & other papers patent in their nature. To the other belong mere executive proceedings. All nations have found it necessary, that for the advantageous conduct of their affairs, some of these proceedings, at least, should remain known to their executive functionary only. He, of course, from the nature of the case, must be the sole judge of which of them the public interests will permit publication. Hence, under our Constitution, in requests of papers, from the legislative to the executive branch, an exception is carefully expressed, as to those which he may deem the public welfare may require not to be disclosed; as you will see in the enclosed resolution of the House of Representatives, which produced the message of Jan 22, respecting this case. The respect mutually due between the constituted authorities, in their official intercourse, as well as sincere dispositions to do for every one what is just, will always insure from the executive, in exercising the duty of discrimination confided to him, the same candor & integrity to which the nation has in like manner trusted in the disposal of it's judiciary authorities. Considering you as the organ for communicating these sentiments to the Court, I address them to you for that purpose....[315]

RULING ON SELF-INCRIMINATION

On June 18, the Court delivered an opinion on the materiality of the cipher letter and whether a witness called to answer questions about the document but who refused to answer could claim the privilege against self-incrimination guaranteed by the Fifth Amendment. On this important question, the Court found:

> It is the province of the court to judge, whether any direct answer to the question, which may be proposed, will furnish evidence against the witness.
>
> If such answer may disclose a fact, which forms a necessary and essential link in the chain of testimony, which would be sufficient to convict him of any crime, he is not bound to answer it so as to furnish matter for that conviction.
>
> In such a case, the witness must himself judge, what his answer will be, and if he says on oath that he cannot answer without accusing himself, he cannot be compelled to answer.[316]

Chief Justice Marshall's ruling on self-incrimination was later cited by Justice Potter Stewart in *United States v. Hoffa*, 385 U.S. 293, 303-4 (1966): "...since at least as long ago as 1807, when Chief Justice Marshall gave attention to the matter in the trial of Aaron Burr, all have agreed that a necessary element of compulsory self-incrimination is some kind of compulsion." Justice Potter Stewart wrote, in a footnote: "Many links frequently compose that chain of testimony which is necessary to convict any individual of a crime. It appears to the Court to be the true sense of the rule that no witness is compelled to furnish any one of them against himself...."

JEFFERSON PLAYS TOUGH

President Jefferson, on June 19, addressed Hay's earlier question about blank pardons and provided legal direction:

> Three blank pardons have been (as I expect) made up & forwarded by the mail of yesterday, and I have desired 3 others to go by that

---

315 Thomas Jefferson to George Hay, June 17, 1807. *Works* X, pp. 400-402.
316 *PJM* VII, 50-53; Robertson I, 251-55. (During argument on this issue, Judge Griffin offered a comment, apparently the only time that he spoke during the entire Burr proceedings. Griffin specifically commented on the case of *United States v. Goosely* (1796), a case he decided with Justice Iredell in Virginia).

---

of this evening. *You ask what is to be done if Bollman finally rejects his pardon & the Judge decides it to have no effect? Move to commit him immediately for treason or misdemeanor, as you think the evidence will support.* Let the Court decide where he shall be sent for trial; and on application, I will have the Marshal aided in his transportation, with the executive means. And we think it proper, further, that when Burr shall have been convicted of treason or the misdemeanor, you should immediately have committed all those persons against whom you should find evidence sufficient, whose agency has been so prominent as to mark them as proper objects of punishment, & especially where their boldness has betrayed an inveteracy of criminal disposition. As to obscure offenders & repenting ones, let them lie for consideration. (Emphasis added.)

Jefferson then exhibited his ability to play hardball:

I enclose you a copy of a letter received last night, and giving singular information. I have inquired into the character of Graybell. He was an old revolutionary captain, is now a flour merchant in Baltimore, of the most respectable character, & whose word would be taken as implicitly as any man's for whatever he affirms. The letter writer, also, is a man of entire respectability. *I am well informed that for more than a twelvemonth it has been believed in Baltimore, generally, that Burr was engaged in some criminal enterprise, & that Luther Martin knew about it.* We think you should immediately dispatch a subpoena for Graybell & while that is on the road, you will have time to consider in what form you will use his testimony; e.g. *shall Luther Martin be summoned as a witness against Burr, & Graybell held ready to confront him?* It may be doubted whether we could examine a witness to discredit our own witness. Besides, the lawyers say they are privileged from being forced to breaches of confidence, and that no others are. *Shall we move to commit Luther Martin, as particeps criminis with Burr?* Graybell will fix upon him misprision of treason at least. *And at any rate, his evidence will put down this unprincipled & impudent federal bull-dog, and add another proof that the most clamorous defenders of Burr are all his accomplices. It will explain why Luther Martin flew so hastily to the aid of his "honorable friend," abandoning his clients & their property during a session of a principal court in Maryland, now filled, I am told, with the clamors & ruin of his clients.* I believe we shall send on Latrobe as a witness. He will prove that AB (Burr) endeavored to get him to engage several thousand men, chiefly Irish emigrants, whom he had been in the habit of employing in the works he directs, under pretence of a canal opposite Louisville, or of the Washita, in which, had he succeeded, he could with that force alone have carried everything before him, and would not have been where he now is. He knows, too, of certain meetings of Burr, Bollman, Yrujo, & one other whom we have never named yet, but have him not the less in our view..." [317] (Emphasis added.)

---

317 Thomas Jefferson to George Hay, June 19, 1807. *Works* X, pp. 402-403.

What an incredible letter. First, President Jefferson reneged on his promise to Bollman. Second, he suggested prosecution of one of Burr's defense attorneys, Luther Martin. Jefferson was exhibiting his "dark side," so brilliantly described by historian Leonard Levy. [318]

President Jefferson wrote Attorney General Rodney, acknowledging receipt of an earlier letter that included a letter from Wilkinson dated October 21, 1806. Unfortunately, the letter Rodney sent was not the one Jefferson needed. Jefferson requested Rodney to send the other letter of that date. Jefferson next informed Rodney about his information about Graybell earlier mentioned in his letter to Prosecutor Hay. Jefferson requested Rodney to determine whether he should converse with Graybell and conduct an interview with him as secretly as possible so that his [Jefferson's] name would remain confidential. Jefferson advised Rodney: "I think it material to break down this bull-dog of Federalism (Martin) and to break down the imprudent supporters of Burr by showing to the world that they are his accomplices." [319]

In an another letter to Hay, President Jefferson informed him that he had not seen, until the night before, Marshall's opinion on the issuance of the subpoena *duces tecum*: "Considering the question there as *coram non judice*, I did not read his argument with much attention. Yet I saw readily enough, that, as is usual where an opinion is to be supported, right or wrong, he dwells much on smaller objections, and passes over those which are solid. Laying down the position generally, that all persons owe obedience to subpoenas, he admits no exception unless it can be produced in the law books."

President Jefferson railed about the possibility that he might be required to appear in Court. He advised Hay that he was always "on duty" and worked as hard, if not harder, when he was absent from Washington and home at Monticello. [320]

President Jefferson wrote General Wilkinson upon his arrival Richmond:

> I ... sincerely congratulate you on your safe arrival at Richmond, against the impudent surmises and hopes of the band of conspirators, who, because they are as yet permitted to walk abroad, and even to be in the character of witnesses until such a measure of evidence shall be collected as will place them securely at the bar of justice, attempt to cover their crimes under noise and insolence. You

---

318 Leonard W. Levy. *Jefferson and Civil Liberties: The Darker Side.*

319 Thomas Jefferson to Caesar Rodney, June 19, 1807. *The Thomas Jefferson Papers,* Library of Congress digital, American Memory.

320 Thomas Jefferson to George Hay, June 20, 1807. *Works X*, pp. 403-405.

have indeed had a fiery trial at New Orleans, but it was soon apparent that the clamorous were only the criminal, endeavoring to turn the public attention from themselves & their leader upon any other object...Your enemies have filled the public ear with slanders, & your mind will trouble on that account. The establishment of their guilt will let the world see what they ought to think of their clamors; it will dissipate the doubts of those who doubted for want of knowledge, and will place you on higher ground in the public estimate and public confidence. No one is more sensible than myself of the injustice which has been aimed at you....[321]

President Jefferson wrote Hay about providing the requested documents to the Court:

> ...These papers have been recurred to so often, on so many occasions, and some of them delivered out for particular purposes, that we find several missing, without being able to recollect what has been done with them. Some of them were delivered to the Attorney of this district, to be used on the occasions which arose in the District Court, & a part of them were filed, as is said, in their office. The Attorney General will examine their office to day, and has written to the District Attorney to know whether he retained any of them. No researches shall be spared to recover this letter, & if recovered, it shall immediately be sent on to you. Compiling the message from a great mass of papers, and pressed in time, the date of the peculiar paper may have been mistaken, but we all perfectly remember the one referred to in the message, & that its substance is there correctly stated. General Wilkinson probably has copies of all the letters he wrote me, & having expressed a willingness to furnish the one desired by the Court, the defendant can still have the benefit of it. Or should he not have the particular one on which the passage in the message is founded, I trust that his memory would enable him to affirm that it is substantially correct....[322]

MOTION FOR WRIT OF ATTACHMENT AGAINST WILKINSON/INDICTMENTS RETURNED

On June 17, Aaron Burr and his attorneys informed the Court that they intended to bring a motion for a Writ of Attachment against General Wilkinson for illegally forcing witnesses in Louisiana to appear in court and depriving them of their Constitutional rights. The defense requested that General Wilkinson be ordered to show cause why a Writ of Attachment should not issue against him for using coercive means and abusing process against a witness, James Knox, part of Burr's expedition. The Writ was ar-

---

321 Thomas Jefferson to General James Wilkinson, June 21, 1807. *Works* X, pp. 336-37.

322 Thomas Jefferson to George Hay, June 23, 1807. *Works* X, pp. 405-406.

gued on June 19, 1807, and continued intermittingly until June 27 when the Court ruled. The motion was primarily an effort by the defense to discredit Wilkinson for his attempt to "obstruct the free administration of justice." Chief Justice Marshall denied the motion, ruling that Wilkinson did not control or influence the conduct of the civil magistrate and, therefore, a Writ of Attachment should not issue. Further, the Court indicated that there were other legal remedies available to the affected parties to challenge General Wilkinson's actions.[323]

The Grand Jury returned true bills of Indictment against Burr and Blennerhassett, among others, for treason and violation of the Neutrality Act. The indictment against Burr charged him, in pertinent part, with: "... not having the fear of God before his eyes ... but being moved and seduced by the instigation of the devil, wickedly devising and intending the peace and tranquility of the United States to disturb; and to stir, move, and excite insurrection, rebellion, and war ... with a great multitude of persons ... did falsely and traitorously assemble and join themselves together ... and then and there with force and arms did falsely and traitorously and in a warlike manner, array and dispose themselves against the said United States...." The indictment alleged that Burr "in order to fulfill and bring into effect the said traitorous compassings ... with a great number of persons ... to wit the number of thirty persons and upwards, armed and arrayed in a warlike manner ... with guns, swords, and dirks ... being them and the traitorously assembled ... did ... array and dispose themselves against the said United States."[324]

The day the Indictment was returned; Chief Justice Marshall committed Burr to custody. The next day, the Grand Jury returned five additional indictments against Jonathon Dayton, former United States Senator from New Jersey; Senator John S. Brown, Ohio; and Comfort Tyler, Israel Smith, and Davis Floyd. The Grand Jury was discharged on June 25 and the Court ordered that Burr's trial was to commence August 3; the Court directed forty-eight petit jurors be called, twelve from Wood County, Virginia, the physical location of Blennerhassett's Island.[325]

General Wilkinson narrowly escaped indictment. Representative John Randolph, foreman of the Grand Jury, described General Wilkinson's appearance before the Grand Jury to former Congressman and now Judge,

323 *PJM* VII, pp. 56-59; Robertson I, pp. 390-93.
324 Burr Indictment, Robertson I, pp. 482-484.
325 Robertson I, pp. 329-338.

Joseph H. Nicholson of Maryland: "Yesterday the grand jury found bills of treason and misdemeanor against Burr and Blennerhassett ... for treason. But the mammoth of iniquity escaped; not that any man pretended to think him *innocent*, but upon certain wiredrawn distinctions that I will not pester you with. Wilkinson is the only man that I ever saw who was from the bark to the very core a villain." Several days later, he again wrote Nicholson: "W. is the most finished scoundrel that ever lived; a ream of paper would not contain all the proofs; but what of that? Perhaps you never saw human nature in so degraded a situation as in the person of Wilkinson before the grand jury, and yet this man stands on the very summit and pinnacle of executive favor. He is 'the man whom the king delights to honor!'"[326]

On June 24, 1807, Hay had good news to report to President Jefferson:

> The jury have returned with the indictments against Burr and Blennerhassett and have found the two pled in each true bill. The motion to commit was followed by a motion to bail which the court rejected for the present; saying that they would permit bail, if they could be satisfied that a person against whom an indictment for treason has been found, could according to the usages of law be bailed. Burr is therefore now in the custody of the Marshal.

> In the desperate state to which the accused is now reduced, I expect that every impediment will be thrown in the way of the trial, which motion upon motion can produce. We shall however with as much patience as possible, do our duty. The first effort was, to commence an examination of the evidence to show that the indictment was founded on perjury. This however proved abortive, the Court in considering the question of bail, would not permit any such innovation. We have been engaged from 11 o'clock until this moment 7 o'clock on the question about the attachment re: Wilkinson, & that about bail. The first is not yet argued, the latter I presume will be suspended.[327]

The next day, Hay wrote again to President Jefferson:

> ...An occurrence took place today, which convinced me that in the morning the grand jury had not dismissed all their suspicions of Wilkinson, and that these apprehensions are not perhaps totally removed.–They came into court, and their foreman J. Randolph stated to the court, that they had been informed that the prisoner was in

326 John Randolph to Joseph H. Nicholson, June 25, 1807 and June 28, 1807. Henry Adams. *John Randolph*, pp. 219-220; . Nathan Schachner, *Aaron Burr*, p. 422; MSS, Library of Congress

327 George Hay to Thomas Jefferson, June 24, 1807. *The Thomas Jefferson Papers*, Library of Congress digital, American Memory.

possession of a letter from General Wilkinson to himself of ___ date which they wished to obtain, if they could legally obtain it. Burr immediately declared that no consideration, no extremity, no desperation, should induce him to betray a letter confidentially written.... The Judge said that he saw no legal objection to sending Mr. B. as a witness before the G. Jury. The foreman solemnly and emphatically remarked that their application was not understood. The Grand Jury did not want A.B. as a witness. Their object was the letter. If that could not be obtained, their function in court was unnecessary, the Grand Jury would retire: and they did retire. The attitude and tone assumed by Burr struck everybody. There was an appearance of honor and magnanimity which brightened the countenances of the phalanx who daily attend, for his encouragement & support. Acting as the Attorney of the United States, I felt it my duty to be silent: but MacRae, who is convinced of Wilkinson's integrity immediately quitted the Court, consulted Wilkinson and got from him an authority to absolve Mr. Burr from all such affront or confidence, and to demand the production of all his letters. This demand was emphatically announced. Burr then said that he did not have Wilkinson's letters—that he had delivered them to a friend, and that Wilkinson knew that he could not produce them. This evasion coming after much embarrassment and humiliation was perceived by everybody, and excited a sentiment as injurious to Burr's understanding, as it was favorable to the G's integrity. MacRae entreated the Judge to certify to the Grand Jury, his proposition on the part of Wilkinson and the reply of the accused. The Judge did certify them. In a short time the Grand Jury returned with the presentments stated before, declaring that they had no further presentments to make.[328]

CHIEF JUSTICE MARSHALL'S REQUEST FOR ASSISTANCE

After the indictments were returned, it was painfully apparent to Chief Justice Marshall that a portion of his opinion in *United States v. Bollman and Swartwout* was the basis for the indictment against Burr and that the opinion had been mistakenly construed by the prosecution and the Grand Jury. The doctrine of constructive treason had mistakenly been understood to have been adopted by the Court in *Bollman and Swartwout*. Constructive treason did not apply to the American law of treason, since treason was so tightly defined in the Constitution. Marshall realized that his earlier opinion had been misinterpreted, misapplied and needed clarification. Chief Justice Marshall turned to his fellow Supreme Court Justices for advice. Although only one letter is extant (Chief Justice Marshall to Associate Justice William Cushing dated June 29, 1807), it is believed that Marshall consulted

---

328 George Hay to Thomas Jefferson, June 25, 1807. Ibid.

with all or most of his colleagues. Marshall posed several questions, the most important involving constructive treason and whether the earlier *Boll-man and Swartwout* decision needed revision. Although there are no existing letters written by any Justices in response to Marshall's request, we must assume that Chief Justice Marshall heard from some or all of them. This is confirmed in Chief Justice Marshall's seminal decision in the Burr case on August 31, 1807. The letter Chief Justice Marshall sent to Justice Cushing dispels any notion that Marshall was arrogant or intended to embarrass President Jefferson. Typical of the Chief Justice, he sought advice from his colleagues, not only for protection of the judiciary, but to maintain consistency in Court opinions.[329]

Chief Justice Marshall wrote Justice Cushing:

> It has been my fate to be engaged in the trial of a person whose case presents real intrinsic difficulties which are infinitely multiplied by extrinsic circumstances. It would have been my earnest wish to consult with all my brethren of the bench on the various intricate points that occur, on which a contrariety of opinion ought not to prevail in the different circuits, but which cannot easily be carried before the Supreme Court. Sincerely do I lament that this wish cannot be completely indulged.

> ... Many points of difficulty will arise before the petty jury which cannot be foreseen & on which I must decide according to the best lights I possess. But there are some which will certainly occur, respecting which considerable doubts may be entertained, & on which I most anxiously desire the aid of all the Judges. One of these respects the doctrine of constructive treasons. How far is this doctrine to be carried in the United States? If a body of men assembles for a treasonable purpose, does this implicate all those who are concerned in the conspiracy whether acquainted with the assemblage or not? Does it implicate those who advised or approved it? Or does it implicate those only who were present and within the district?

> ... The opinion of the Supreme Court in the case of *Bollman & Swart-wout* certainly adopts the doctrine of constructive treasons. How far does that case carry this doctrine? Ought the expressions in that opinion be revised?

> A second question of much importance is, how far may the declarations or confessions of one person be given in evidence against another who is proved to be connected with him in the same conspiracy? Is there a distinction between written & verbal declarations?

---

329 John Marshall to William Cushing, June, 1807. *PJM* VII, pp. 60-62.

... A third question which I shall certainly be compelled to decide & on which I feel some doubt is whether an overt act of treason committed out of the district & consequently not laid in the indict-ment, can be given in evidence?

... I am aware of the unwillingness with which a Judge will com-mit himself by an opinion on a case not before him & on which he has heard no argument. Could this case be readily carried into the Supreme Court I would not ask an opinion in its present stage. But these questions must be decided by the Judges separately on their respective circuits, & I am sure there would be strong & general re-pugnance to giving contradictory decisions on the same points. Such a circumstance would be disreputable to the Judges themselves as well as to our judicial system. This consideration considers the pro-priety of a consultation on new & difficult subjects & will I trust apologize for this letter.

In a postscript, Chief Justice Marshall wrote:

My letter to Judge Washington (Justice Bushrod Washington) may perhaps not find him. Should you see him, be so obliging as to show him this & ask him to consider it as addressed also to himself.

Since writing the above another question has occurred to my mind which I will also take the liberty to state.

Must all the circumstances which tend to prove the treason—as for example declarations made by the prisoner of his intentions, be proved by two witnesses, or is it only necessary that the military as-semblage should be proved by two witnesses?[330]

MARTIN LETTER/POST INDICTMENT

After the Indictment against Burr was returned, Luther Martin wrote to Joseph Alston, husband of Burr's beloved daughter Theodosia:

I have the painful task to inform you that my esteemed friend, Col. Burr, was yesterday committed to Prison in consequence of a Bill for Treason being found by the Grand Jury against him. I arrived here the evening of May twenty-seventh, and have been with Colo-nel Burr ever since. Nor shall I leave him until his trial is at an end. Never, I believe, did any Government thirst more for the Blood of a victim of our enlightened, philosophic, mild, philanthropic govern-ment for the Blood of my friend. Two Gentlemen, considered here of the first talents, are employed to assist in the prosecution, or, as it may be truly said, the persecution—and the unfeeling, the savage manner each of these three George Hay, William Wirt, and Alexan-der MacRae have adopted, in the course of the prosecution, would

---

330 Ibid.

dishonor any beings but Demons from Hell. That Colonel Burr is as innocent of everything of a treasonable nature as the child unborn I remain fully convinced, that he never had any object in view, but what did honor to himself, and would have been greatly useful to the United States, and to all Europe, except France and Spain I am fully convinced. That a Bill has found, has been owing to the jury not being informed what facts constitute Treason, and to gross perjury in swearing to facts not true. We feel the utmost confidence that he will be acquitted upon his Trial, and that he will ultimately Triumph over that malignant jealousy and inveterate hatred by which he is now persecuted. The Government ardently desires to destroy Colonel Burr, that it would feel no more compunction in taking his life, than that which a philosopher views a rat expiring, with convulsions, at the bottom [of] an exhausted receiver, I have not a doubt. And I am confident that Government does not believe him to have been guilty of a treasonable act or design....[331]

A few weeks after the indictments were returned, President Jefferson received a letter from John Smith, an associate of several businessmen in New Orleans who opposed Wilkinson. Smith warned Jefferson that Wilkinson worked for and was paid by the Spanish government:

Although I am the friend of General Wilkinson, I think it my duty to inform you, that it has been confidentially asserted to me by one of your friends and mine, since I arrived in the city only two or three days ago that General Wilkinson has been in Spanish pay for many years. Of that the most unequivocal proofs are in the hands of a few designing Federalists, who are waiting with anxious hope for the time when you may have committed your reputation with the General and then publish the evidence of his guilt.

I confess, Sir that I hope better things of the General, yet I deem it advisable to give you this information, for I am proud in uniting my wishes with millions, that when you are pleased to retire to private life, it may be with an undiminished as well as with unprecedented glory....[332]

Jefferson had received numerous warnings about Wilkinson's duplicity for well over a year but continued to express confidence in General Wilkinson and relied upon his advice. Jefferson, for whatever reason, was blinded by Wilkinson's questionable activities.

Washington Irving left Richmond after the indictments were returned. He wrote a friend about Burr's incarceration:

---

331 Luther Martin to Joseph Alston, June 26, 1807. Clarkson, pp. 254-55.
332 John Smith to Thomas Jefferson, July 6, 1807. The Papers of Thomas Jefferson, Library of Congress digital.

... like the illustrious Jefferson, who, after toiling all day in deciding the fates of the nation, retires to his closet and amuses himself with impaling a tadpole...

... The last time I saw Burr was the day before I left Richmond. He was then in the Penitentiary, a kind of State prison. The only reason given for immuring him in this abode of thieves, cut-throats, and incendiaries, was that it would save the United States a couple hundred dollars, (the charge of guarding him at this lodgings), and it would insure the security of his person. This building stands about a mile and a half from town, situated in a solitary place among the hills. It will prevent his counsel from being as much with him as they deemed necessary. I found great difficulty in gaining admission to him, for a few moments. The keeper had orders to admit none but his counsel and witnesses—strange measures these! That it is not sufficient that a man against whom no certainty of crime is proved, should be confined by bolts, and bars, and mossy walls in a criminal prison; but he is likewise to be cut off from all intercourse with society, deprived of all the kind offices of friendship, and made to suffer all the penalties and deprivations of a condemned criminal. I was permitted to enter for a few moments, as a special favor, contrary to orders. Burr seemed in lower spirits than formerly; he was composed and collected as usual; but there was not the same cheerfulness that I have hitherto remarked. He said it was with difficulty that his servant was allowed to occasionally see him; he had a bad cold, which I suppose was occasioned by the dampness of his chamber, which had been whitewashed. I bid him farewell with a heavy heart, and he expressed his peculiar warmth and feeling his sense of the interest I had taken in his fate. I never felt in a more melancholy mood than when I rode from his solitary prison. Such is the last interview I had with poor Burr, and I shall never forget it.[333]

The penitentiary in Richmond was designed by Jefferson, among his numerous plans for public buildings in Richmond.[334] Benjamin Latrobe completed the design of the prison which was placed "on a steep gravelly knoll which overlooked the James River and was inhabited by snakes and cows." It opened in 1800 and embodied Jeffersonian concepts of penology. The prison existed until 1928; it was intended to house hardened criminals while the city jail housed minor offenders.[335]

Irving never forgot his trip to Richmond; he formed strong opinions about Jefferson and Wilkinson. In Irving's *History of New York by Diedrich Knickerbocher*, both men were satirized. The pompous Dutch general Ja-

333 Washington Irving to Miss Mary Fairlie, July 7, 1807. Irving, pp. 165.
334 Thomas Jefferson to James Wood, March 31, 1797. *PTJ* 29, pp. 335-338
335 Virginius Dabney. *Richmond: The Story of a City.* Garden City, NY: Doubleday, 1976.

cobus Von Poffenburgh was based upon Wilkinson. This character was described as "a huge, full-bodied man, with a ruddy face that glowed like a fiery furnace." Von Poffenburgh "strutted about," was a "bitter looking man of war," and "swelled and strutted like a vainglorious cock pigeon." The Dutch governor, patterned after Jefferson, was Wilhelmus Kieft, also known as "William the Testy." The portrayal of Jefferson was not complimentary, describing him as a dreamer. Kieft opined that his relations with Von Poffenburgh were such that he "tries to pass official his brass and copper upon the Governor, who was no judge of base coin, as pure and genuine as gold."[336]

During the five week interlude between indictment and trial, President Jefferson wrote to two foreign friends. In a letter to Du Pont de Nemours, he wrote:

> Burr's conspiracy has been one of the most flagitious of which history will ever furnish an example. He had combined the objects of separating the western States from us, of adding Mexico to them, and of placing himself at their head. But he who could expect to effect such objects by the aid of American citizens, must be perfectly ripe for Bedlam. Yet although there is not a man in the U.S. who is not satisfied of the depth of his guilt, such are the jealous provisions of our laws in favor of the accused, & against the accuser, that I question if he can be convicted. Out of the 48 jurors who are to be summoned, he has a right to choose 12 who are to try him, and if any one of the 12 refuses to concur in finding him guilty, he escapes. This affair has been a great confirmation in my mind of the innate strength of the form of our government. He had probably induced near a thousand men to engage with him, by making them believe the government connived at it. A proclamation alone, by undeceiving them, so completely disarmed him that he had not above 30 men left, ready to go all lengths with him. The first enterprise was to have been the seizure of New Orleans, which he supposed would powerfully bridle the country above, & place him at the door of Mexico. It has given me infinite satisfaction that not a single native Creole of Louisiana, and but one American, settled there before the delivery of the country to us, were in his interest. His partisans were made up of fugitives from justice, or from their debts, who had flocked there from other parts of the U.S., after the delivery of the country, and of adventurers & speculators of all descriptions....[337]

---

336 George Tremaine McDowell. "General James Wilkinson in the Knickerbocker History of New York." *The Johns Hopkins University Press-Modern Language Notes*, Vol. 41, No. 6 (June 1926),pp. 353-359.

337 Thomas Jefferson to Dupont de Nemoirs, July 14, 1807. *Works* X, pp. 460-462.

Jefferson wrote to old friend the Marquis De Lafayette on Bastille Day (July 14) and employed much the same information contained in the Dupont de Nemours letter. Jefferson discussed Bollman, who had earlier attempted to rescue Lafayette:

> I am sorry to tell you that Bollman was Burr's right hand man in his guilty schemes. On being brought to prison here, he communicated to Mr. Madison & myself the whole of the plans, always, however, apologetically for Burr, as far as they would bear. But his subsequent tergiversations have proved him conspicuously base. I gave him a pardon, however, which covers him from anything but infamy. I was the more astonished at his engaging in this business, from the peculiar motives he should have felt for fidelity. When I came into the government, I sought him out on account of the services he had rendered you, cherished him, offered him two different appointments of value, which, after keeping them long under consideration, he declined for commercial views, and would have given him anything for which he was fit. Be assured he is unworthy of ever occupying again the care of any honest man.[338]

On August 7, 1807 President Jefferson wrote Hay from Monticello:

> I inclose you a letter received yesterday on the subject of General Presley Nevil. With respect to both him & his son I believe there is no doubt of a participation in Burr's designs but I suppose that after the issue of the principal trial will be the proper time to decide what subordinate offenders may be laid hold of.
>
> I learn by the newspapers that I am to have another *subpoena duces tecum* for Eaton's declaration. With respect to my personal attendance higher duties keep me here. During the present & ensuing months I am here to avoid the diseases of tide water situations and all communications on the business of my office, will be daily received and transacted here. With respect to the paper in question it was delivered to the Attorney General with all other papers relating to Burr. I have therefore neither that nor any of the others in my possession. Possibly the Attorney General may have delivered it to you. If not, he has it, & he is the person to whom a subpoena to bring that or any others into court, may at once be addressed.[339]

A letter, possibly never sent, is extant and provides a glimpse into Jefferson's state of mind, particularly his opinions about the judiciary, Chief Justice Marshall, and his fear of being served with a subpoena *duces tecum*:

> The enclosed letter is written in a spirit of conciliation & with the desire to avoid conflicts of authority between the high branches of

---

338 Thomas Jefferson to Marquis de LaFayette, July 14, 1807. *Works* X, pp. 462-466.
339 Thomas Jefferson to George Hay, August 7, 1807. *Works* X, Volume 10, pp. 406-407.

the government which would discredit it equally at home & abroad. That Burr & his counsel should wish to [struck out "divert the public attention from him to this battle of giants was to be"] convert his Trial into a contest between the judiciary & Executive Authorities was to be expected. But that the Chief Justice should lend himself to it, and take the first step to bring it on, was not expected. Nor can it be now believed that his prudence or good sense will permit him to press it. But should he contrary to expectation, proceed to issue any process which should involve any act of force to be committed in the persons of the Executive or heads of departments, I must desire you to give me instant notice, & by express if you find that it can done quicker than post; and that moreover you will advise the marshal on his conduct, as he will be critically placed between us. His safest way will be to take no part in the exercise of any act of force ordered in this case. The powers given the Executive by the constitution are sufficient to protect the other branches from judiciary usurpation of preeminence, & every individual also from judiciary vengeance, and the marshal may be assured if it's effective exercise to cover him. I hope however that the discretion of the Chief Justice will suffer this question to lie over for the present, and at the ensuing session of the legislature he may have means provided for giving to individuals the benefit of the testimony of the Executive functionaries in proper cases, without breaking up the government. Will not the associate judge [Judge Griffin] assume to divide his court and procure a truce at least in so critical a conjecture?[340]

---

340 Thomas Jefferson to George Hay, without date. *Works* X, Volume 10, pp. 406-407.

12. The Trial of the Century

The Burr trial would take place in the Virginia State Capitol in Richmond. In 1779 the Virginia Legislature decided to move the Capitol from Williamsburg to Richmond. The State Capitol building, designed by Thomas Jefferson, was first occupied by the Virginia General Assembly in 1788. Although the new Capitol was occupied in 1788, it was not prepared in time to house the Virginia Constitutional Ratification Convention. The original structure is now the middle portion the present-day capitol building. After the state capital was transferred from Williamsburg in 1779, the City of Richmond grew rapidly. The British attacked Richmond in 1781 and burned a portion of the city. However, the city was sufficiently rebuilt by 1788 when Richmond hosted the Ratification Convention for the Constitution. Later in 1798–99, the Virginia Resolutions opposing the Alien and Sedition Acts were debated in the state capitol.

The population of Richmond increased from approximately 1,500 residents in 1790 to more than 5,300 by 1800. In comparison, only five cities in the United States had a population of at least 10,000 residents—New York, Philadelphia, Boston, Charleston, and Baltimore. By 1810, Richmond's population was approximately 10,000 residents and swelled to over 20,000 by 1820.[341] During the Burr trial, Richmond's population swelled; taverns were full and accommodations scarce.

---

341 Chadwick, pp. 10-11.

In the early 1800s, federal trials in Richmond were held in the State Capitol building, usually in a medium-sized room on the third floor. Since additional space was needed for the Burr trial, the trial was convened in the larger House of Delegates Chamber on the second floor of the State Capitol.

The Old Hall of the House of Delegates, as it is known today, is located in the north end of the Capitol next to the Rotunda. It was the largest room in the original Capitol: 76 feet long and 30 feet 8 inches in width. It has a cove ceiling with rounded corners. The wooden cornice resembles the exterior eaves of a classical building with fluted Doric pilasters on the walls. The windows in the Old Hall today are in the same location as they were at the time of the trial in 1807 (this may be the only part of the Old Hall that has not changed). Although we are not certain about the exact configuration of the Old House at the time of the Burr trial, most likely it resembled a painting that depicted the Virginia State Constitutional Convention in 1829–30 by George Catlin. There were four walls with an upper gallery at the east end of the room (today there is a second upper gallery on the west wall). The entrance to the Hall at the time of trial was at the southeast corner of the room. Today, there are double doors in the middle of the south wall which serve as the entrance to the Hall; at the time of the trial, those doors did not exist. Instead there were three niches along the south wall. It is thought that the Speaker's Chair, most probably used by Chief Justice Marshall, backed up to the wall with the niches or, possibly, was located in the west end of the room. Overflow crowds filled the Old Hall.

The Old Hall was the meeting place of the Virginia House of Delegates from 1788 to 1904. It served as the site for several state Constitutional Conventions, including the 1829–1830 Convention that included former Presidents James Madison and James Monroe and Chief Justice John Marshall. The Old Hall would be the site for one of the greatest trials in American history—the trial of Aaron Burr.[342]

The Aaron Burr trial began on August 3, 1807. Prosecutor Hay called over 100 subpoenaed witnesses. Many witnesses had yet to arrive. Hay, as Prosecutor, was required to provide the defense with a list of names and

---

342 Information about the State Capitol and the Old Hall was provided by Mark Greenough in an interview conducted on May 5, 2009. Mr. Greenough is the Supervisor and Historian for tours of the Virginia State Capitol. In his spare time, Mr. Greenough does an excellent job interpreting John Marshall at historical events at the Marshall home in Richmond and at various locations throughout Virginia and other states.

addresses of the government's prospective witnesses, a requirement not yet met. Further, he had yet to provide the required list of prospective jurors. Both notice requirements were mandated by the Judiciary Act of 1789. President Jefferson expended $11,000 from the continuing fund of the government to enable United States Attorney Hay to hire additional prosecutors William Wirt and Alexander MacRae. The government transported, housed, and fed approximately 140 witnesses, subpoenaed throughout the country. It is estimated that the government spent almost $100,000 for this prosecution, an enormous amount of money in 1807, all without specific Congressional appropriation. Today, this expenditure would equate to more than $2 million.[343]

While awaiting the arrival of witnesses, Burr renewed his request for a subpoena *duces tecum*. Certain documents had yet to be produced pursuant to his earlier request; in particular Wilkinson's letter to President Jefferson of October 21, 1806. Burr additionally requested a letter from General Eaton to President Jefferson. Since witnesses were not present and requisite lists not provided, the Court adjourned for several days.

A number of interesting personalities attended all or a portion of the trial proceedings. Future President Andrew Jackson, who had been subpoenaed, was present. Already a military and political hero in his home state of Tennessee, Jackson was a vociferous Burr supporter; in contrast, Jackson was an avowed enemy of General Wilkinson and, to a degree, President Jefferson. After the prosecution realized that Jackson would not assist their case, Jackson was never called as a witness. Before trial commenced, Jackson wrote, "this thing ... has assumed the shape of a political persecution." Jackson placed much of the blame for Burr's predicament squarely on President Jefferson.[344]

Another interested spectator was Winfield Scott, a young Richmond attorney who later became General of the Army and, ironically, would lead American troops into Mexico. Scott wrote in his *Memoirs*: "It was President Jefferson who directed and animated the prosecution. Hence, every Republican clamored for Burr's execution. Of course, the Federalists ... comported themselves on the other side."[345] Scott continued: "But the interest of the

---

343 Isenberg, pp. 338-339; Beveridge III, pp.390-393.
344 Andrew Jackson to W. Patten Anderson, June 16, 1807. James Parton, *The Life of Andrew Jackson* Volume I. New York: Harper Brothers, 1861, p. 334.
345 Winfield Scott, *Memoirs of Lieutenant-General Scott*. Volume I. New York: Sheldon, 1864, pp. 13, 16.

trial, eminent as was the standing of the defendant; eminent as was the forensic talent engaged; brilliant as were the surroundings, and great as were
the passions excited—the hatreds, hopes, and fears of party—the interest
would have been less than half, but that the majesty of the law was, on the
great occasion, nobly represented by John Marshall, Chief Justice of the
United States. He was the master spirit of the scene."[346]

Jury Selection

Court re-convened on August 5 and 7 without action, primarily due to
absence of witnesses. The trial finally commenced on August 10 with selection of the jury. During jury selection, Chief Justice Marshall delivered two
rulings. The first was delivered after the defense propounded a question to
a prospective juror as to whether he had "expressed and formed an opinion
about Burr's guilt." The prosecution immediately objected to the form of the
question. A Constitutional issue was before the Court: what is the meaning
of the term "impartial jury" within the Sixth Amendment of the Constitution? Chief Justice Marshall suggested that the proper question to be posed
to the prospective juror was: "have you formed, or delivered, an opinion on
the case of Col. Burr?" Marshall opined that the question should "ascertain,
whether he has any opinion, formed or not, on the case, as it is.... Every man
might have formed an opinion as to the treasonable nature of certain acts; it
is the application of that treason to the individual that makes the opinions
of the juror objectionable."[347] After the Court ruled, the prospective juror
was discharged from the petit jury. The parties continued questioning the
remaining jurors. Of forty-eight prospective jurors, four were selected; nine
were suspended for further questioning, and thirty-five were discharged.

The next day, counsel questioned the nine petit jurors suspended the
day before. After extensive argument by the parties, Chief Justice Marshall
delivered a second opinion:

> [T]he jury should enter upon the trial, with minds open to those
> impressions, which the testimony and the law of the case ought
> to make, not with those preconceived opinions, which will resist
> those impressions.... The question now to be decided is, whether an
> opinion formed and delivered, not upon the full case, but upon an
> essential part of it, not that the prisoner is absolutely guilty of the
> whole crime charged in the indictment, but that he is guilty in some
> of those great points, which constitute it, do also disqualify a man in

---

346 Winfield Scott, p. 16
347 *PJM* VII, pp. 63-64; Robertson I, pp. 408-409.

the sense of the law and of the Constitution from being an impartial juror?... The opinion of the court is, that to have made up and delivered the opinion, that the prisoner entertained the treasonable designs with which he is charged, and that he retained those designs, and was prosecuting them when the act charged in the indictment is alleged to have been committed, is a good cause of challenge."

In short, a prospective juror must be capable of fairly hearing the testimony presented at trial.[348] After the Court delivered its opinions, all suspended jurors were excused. Prosecutor Hay requested that the Court call an additional forty-eight venire men, which the court agreed to do.[349]

On August 11, 1807, Prosecutor Hay updated President Jefferson on events in Richmond:

> Your letter of the 7th inclosing a representation from Pittsburg, relating to General Neville has been received. If Burr should be acquitted, it can hardly be expected that his agents will be found guilty....
>
> The panel was yesterday called. Out of 48, four only were selected.... The completion of the jury will probably occupy two or three days more. The bias of Judge Marshall is as obvious, as if it was stamped upon his forehead. I may do him injustice, but I do not believe that I am when I say, that endeavoring to work himself up to a state of ___, which will enable him to aid Burr throughout the trial without appearing to be conscious of doing wrong. He seems to think that his reputation is irretrievably gone, and that he has now nothing to lose by doing as he pleases.—His concern for Mr. Burr is wonderful. He told me many years ago, when Burr was rising in the estimation of the republican party, that he was as profligate in principle, as he was desperate in fortune. I remember his words. They astonished me. Yet when the Grand Jury brought in their bill, the Chief Justice gazed at him, for a long time, without appearing conscious that he was doing so, with an expression of sympathy and sorrow, as strong, as the human countenance can exhibit without palpable emotion.
>
> If Mr. Burr has any feeling left yesterday it must have been a day of agonizing humiliation. The answers of the jurors, as to the opinions they had formed or expressed were subsequently addressed to him, and to this effect. "I have no doubt of your intention to commit treason. I have had a bad opinion of your principles for many years: it is now more unfavorable than ever ___ by the Prisoner". "Have you not said that Colonel Burr ought to be hung? Answer—No. I said hanging was too good for him." Another answer—"I have no doubt that Colonel Burr intended to commit treason: but I doubt whether he has committed it. I have taken it for granted that he has left a hole

---

348 *PJM* VII, pp. 65-70; Robertson I, pp. 464-470.
349 *PJM* VII, p. 70, n. 6.

to creep out of." "I doubt Sir whether I ought to be a juryman. The idea that any man should commit treason in such a country as ours has produced feelings and expressions, which I hope will disqualify me."—In short every man on the panel except David Lambert, acknowledged that his impressions were unfavorable to the accused. He said that he had never given any opinion whatever. If the jury should be hung, this man will be the hanger.—But I cannot believe that a doubt will exist. The evidence here is in my estimation irresistible. There is but one chance for the accused, and that is good one because it rests with the Chief Justice. It is already hinted, but not by himself, that the decision of the Supreme Court will not be deemed binding. If the assembly of men on an island can be pronounced "not an overt act," let it be so pronounced.[350]

When the additional petit jurors were presented, Aaron Burr accepted the next eight jurors without objection, even though most indicated that they had formed an opinion about his guilt. Burr concluded that it would be impossible to find anyone who had not formed an opinion about his case; Burr was tired of delay.

On another front, President Jefferson wrote a curious letter to indicted co-defendant Jonathon Dayton. Dayton, a former United States Senator, had earlier written to Jefferson requesting that he be released on bail:

I received your letter of the 6th inst requesting my interference to have you admitted to bail, and I have considered it with a sincere disposition to administer every relief from unnecessary suffering, which lies within the limits of my regular authority. But when a person charged with an offence is placed in the possession of the judiciary authority, the laws commit to that solely the whole direction of the case; and any interference with it on the part of the Executive would be an encroachment on their independence, and open to censure. And still more censurable would this be in a case originating, as yours does, not with the Executive, but an independent authority. I am persuaded therefore, that on reconsideration, you will be sensible that, in declining to interpose in the present case, I do but obey the vigorous prescriptions of duty. [I do it however with the less regret as I presume that the same provisions of the law that have given to the principal defendant the accommodation of common apartments, give the same right to yourself and every other defendant, in a country where the application of equal law to every condition of man is a fundamental principal].

I salute you with every wish that the appearances which may have excited the attentions of one inquest towards you, may be so

---

350 George Hay to Thomas Jefferson, August 11/12, 1807. *The Thomas Jefferson Papers*, Library of Congress digital. American Memory.

explained as to establish your innocence to the satisfaction of the other.[351]

The portion in brackets was struck by President Jefferson after consultation with Secretary of State Madison and Prosecutor Hay.[352] Interestingly, President Jefferson wrote that it would be wrong for him to interfere with judicial actions and process, when, in fact, he had been doing so for months. President Jefferson was disingenuous when he suggested that it was not his government that brought the present action against Burr and the other men. Since the United States Attorney worked for President Jefferson, he could have advised Hay that he (the government) had no objection to Dayton's admission to bail. Hay could present the government's position to the Court; based upon the Administration's recommendation, the Court would then make its determination as to whether Dayton should be admitted to bail. It is unlikely that the Court would disregard the government's recommendation.

During trial, Jefferson wrote two other letters of note. The first was to Treasury Secretary Gallatin: "Burr's trial goes on to the astonishment of all, as to the manner of conducting it."[353] The second was to Hay: "Before an impartial jury, Burr's conduct would convict himself, were not one word of testimony to be offered against him. But to what state will our law be reduced by party feelings in those who administer it?"[354]

TRIAL TESTIMONY

The trial commenced on August 17th. The jury was sworn and the Indictment against Aaron Burr read. United States Attorney George Hay, in his opening statement, admitted that Burr had not been physically present on Blennerhassett's Island at the time the charged conspiracy took place. Since the prosecution relied upon a portion of the opinion in *United States v. Bollman and Swartwout*, Hay argued that Burr's physical presence on Blennerhassett's Island on the date charged was unnecessary.[355] After Hay concluded his opening statement, he called the government's first witness, General Wil-

---

351 Thomas Jefferson to Jonathon Dayton, August 17, 1807. *Works* X, pp. 478-479.
352 Thomas Jefferson to James Madison, August 20, 1807. *Republic of Letters*, 3, pp. 1489-1490.
353 Thomas Jefferson to Albert Gallatin, August 20, 1807. *The Thomas Jefferson Papers*, Library of Congress digital. American Memory.
354 Thomas Jefferson to George Hay, August 20, 1807. *Works* X, pp. 407-408.
355 Robertson I, pp. 484-507.

---

liam Eaton. Aaron Burr immediately objected to the prosecution's proposed order of proof and submitted to the Court that an overt act of treason must first be proved before any testimony on Burr's intent could be offered.[356] Resolution of this question would be the seminal legal issue in this case.

After considering legal arguments, Chief Justice Marshall ruled. Marshall opined that it was proper to first present evidence of an overt act and, then, after the overt act was established, evidence of criminal intent could be presented. Marshall, however, permitted the prosecution to proceed with its evidence in whatever order it preferred, as long as the testimony was relevant. The defense argued that the *corpus delecti* of the crime must first be established before other testimony could be introduced. Regarding Eaton's testimony, Marshall determined that if his testimony related to facts charged within the Indictment, specifically levying of war on Blennerhassett's Island, the design to seize New Orleans, or the separation of the Western States from the Atlantic States by force, Eaton's testimony would be relevant. Marshall opined that any evidence of plans formulated in locations other than the specific location charged within the Indictment (Blennerhassett's Island) was irrelevant and inadmissible.[357]

GENERAL WILLIAM EATON

The star witness, General James Wilkinson, was never called as a witness during either the treason trial or subsequent misdemeanor trial. One can only conclude that the prosecution determined that Wilkinson's credibility had been irreparably damaged after his disastrous Grand Jury appearance and his admission that he altered the cipher letter (the cipher letter was never offered into evidence). Since no one knew Burr's intentions better than Wilkinson, the prosecution's case was fatally flawed from its inception.

After the Court ruled on Burr's motion to restrict the order of proof, General William Eaton resumed the witness stand. General William Eaton, 43, had been American Consul to Algiers, appointed by President John Adams. President Jefferson later appointed him United States Naval Agent to the Barbary States. In 1805, Eaton led an expedition, consisting of a handful of marines and a few Egyptian soldiers overland to Derna, which was captured by Eaton and his expedition. Eaton's actions resulted in peace

---

356 Robertson I, pp. 508-531.
357 Robertson I, pp. 531-35; *PJM* VII, pp. 70-74.

with the Barbary pirates. Although General Eaton won initial praise for his efforts against the Barbary pirates, upon his return to the United States, Eaton grew increasingly disturbed with the manner in which the government handled his dramatic victory. More importantly, since Eaton spent a substantial portion of his own money on assignment for the government, he felt that he was entitled to reimbursement. When the government was not forthcoming with reimbursement, Eaton grew increasingly bitter. It was around this time that Eaton met Burr. Burr sympathized with Eaton's unhappiness with the government. Burr informed Eaton about his plans for the Spanish territories and Mexico and offered Eaton a command. Eaton later informed President Jefferson that Burr not only planned to invade Mexico, but intended to break up the western states, assassinate the President, and take over the government. No other witness testified to such outrageous plans by Burr, particularly the takeover of the Federal government and assassination of the President. Commodore Truxton and General Wilkinson, both of whom Burr knew far better than Eaton, never testified to such plans. The first time Eaton discussed Burr's activities with President Jefferson, around March, 1806, he failed to mention the outrageous plans of Burr that he would later allege. Although Eaton advised Jefferson about potential actions that Burr might take in the West, he never discussed Burr's intent to takeover the government, assassination plan, and break up of the western states. Incredibly, during the first meeting with the President, Eaton recommended that President Jefferson appoint Burr ambassador to a European country: Spain, Great Britain, or perhaps France. Eaton suggested that it would be beneficial to remove Burr from the United States, opining that Burr was a patriot and would serve his country honorably and faithfully if given such an assignment.[358] When Congressman William Ely of Massachusetts heard about Eaton's more elaborate version of Burr's plans, including the possible assassination of the President, he immediately advised Postmaster General Gideon Granger, who then advised President Jefferson by letter in October, 1806. After receiving Granger's letter, Jefferson, for the first time, took affirmative action. This was after receiving letters, hearing rumors, and receiving other information for more than ten months.[359]

---

358 Adams *History of the United States*, pp. 770-71.
359 Louis B. Wright and Julia H. Macleod. "William Eaton's Relations with Aaron Burr," pp. 523-536; Beveridge III, pp. 302-7; Baker pp. 497-99.

President Jefferson obtained the affidavit from General Eaton about the information Eaton provided to Jefferson months earlier. It was less than coincidental that three days before Eaton prepared an affidavit for President Jefferson, Eaton's monetary claim for reimbursement was referred to a House Committee for action. A month later, Congress passed a bill authorizing payment for Eaton's claims. Representative John Randolph, a House leader, suggested the bill was passed by surprise. After the legislation was enacted, Eaton received $10,000 from the United States government.[360] John Quincy Adams described Eaton's payment: "A bill for settling the accounts of William Eaton passed the third reading; opposed by Mr. Giles, Mr. Sumter, and myself.... It was a transaction which I so strongly disapproved that I had resolved to expose the nature of the claims which are thus to be passed; But Mr. Giles this day, after the question was taken, told me the business was settled *out of doors*...."[361]

Eaton, dressed in his military uniform and with pompous mannerisms, made quite an appearance in Richmond. Blennerhassett described Eaton's look: "the once redoubted Eaton has dwindled down in the eyes of this sarcastic town into a ridiculous mountebank, strutting about the streets under a tremendous hat, with a Turkish sash over colored clothes, when he is not tippling in the taverns, where he offers up with his libations the bitter effusions of his sorrows, in audibly bewailing to the sympathies of the bystanders—that he is despised by the Federalists, mistrusted by the Democrats...." Blennerhassett described Eaton's appearance in court: "he strutted more in bushkin than usual on that occasion, and the effect was as diverting to the whole court as it probably was beneficial to the defense."[362]

When Eaton resumed his testimony, he requested the Court's permission to refer to notes, some made by him, some by others. The Court ruled that he could not refer to notes during his testimony. Following this ruling but before his testimony commenced, Eaton informed the Court that he knew nothing about any overt acts of treason that might prove Burr's guilt. Eaton further advised the Court that he was unaware of any actions Burr had taken on Blennerhassett's Island or other overt actions by Burr. Eaton testified that he was aware of Burr's treasonable intentions. According to Eaton, he first met Burr during the winter of 1805–06 in Washington. Burr

---

360 Beveridge III, p. 345.
361 *Memoirs of John Quincy Adams*, pp. 464-465
362 Harmon Blennerhassett,. *The Blennerhassett Papers*. Edited by William Safford. Cincinnati: Moore Wilstach & Baldwin, 1864, pp. 315-316; 343.

informed Eaton that he was organizing a military expedition against the Spanish provinces in the southwest; Eaton initially understood that Burr's actions were taken with authority of the Federal government. Eaton further believed that war with Spain was inevitable. As their conversations progressed, Eaton concluded that Burr was as disaffected with the Federal government as he was, although their reasons differed. As he heard more about Burr's plans, Eaton suspected the plans were unlawful. Burr offered Eaton a military command under General Wilkinson. Burr advised Eaton that Wilkinson was actively a part of his plans. According to Eaton, Burr spoke about revolution in the western states, west of the Allegheny's.

Eaton testified that he concluded that the best way to terminate Burr's adventures would be to remove him from the country. To do so, he sought a meeting with President Jefferson. According to Eaton, he advised the President about Burr's plans and recommended that the President appoint Burr ambassador to a European country. President Jefferson, according to Eaton, was unreceptive, doubting Burr's integrity. Eaton stated that he went to the President after he concluded that Burr's plans could result in disaster for the United States. After his meetings with Burr and the President, Eaton returned to his native state of Massachusetts. When he learned that Burr was moving forward with his plans, he informed Congressman Ely.

Aaron Burr cross-examined Eaton about the money he claimed the government owed him. The defense argued that payment of $10,000 was made simultaneously with Eaton's cooperation with the government. Eaton was questioned why he recommended that President Jefferson appoint Burr to such a high and important governmental post if, in fact, Burr was such a dangerous and bad person. Although Eaton's testimony describing Burr's plans was damaging, the defense strategically attacked Eaton's credibility and motives for cooperating with the government. Eaton's testimony was discredited. Thomas Jefferson's historian, Dumas Malone, described Eaton as an intemperate and vainglorious person whose credibility was undermined by Burr's clever attorneys at trial.[363]

COMMODORE THOMAS TRUXTON

Commodore Thomas Truxton, a 52 year old former naval officer, was the next witness. In 1794, Truxton was one of six captains commissioned in the newly authorized United States Navy. During the Quasi-War with France

---

363 Malone 5, p. 241; Robertson I, pp. 535-48.

in the late 1790s, Truxton was commander of the frigate *Constellation* and became a national hero when he captured several French ships. Although Truxton's name was mentioned in the cipher letter, his testimony failed to assist the government's case. Truxton testified that he was aware of no overt acts or treasonable designs by Burr; they had no such conversations. Truxton testified that Burr first spoke to him about speculation in the western lands, particularly building canals and a bridge. Burr never spoke to him about separation of the western states or claimed that the United States government sanctioned an excursion into Mexico. Truxton claimed that in July, 1806 Burr spoke to him about an expedition into Mexico, but only in the event war was declared against Spain. Burr, according to Truxton, was confident that war with Spain was inevitable. After Burr informed him that President Jefferson did not know about or authorize his expedition, Truxton advised Burr that he could not join his enterprise as a naval officer. Truxton informed Burr that, in his opinion, there would be no war with Spain. According to Truxton, Burr had decided to peaceably settle lands along the Washita in the event there was no war with Spain; all his conversations with Burr related to actions that might take place in the event of war with Spain. Truxton and Burr talked intimately and without reservation; Burr never spoke about dividing the union. Truxton was astonished to read in the newspapers that Burr may have had different views than those they had discussed.[364] Truxton's testimony did Burr no damage.

Peter Taylor

The third witness was Blennerhassett's gardener, Peter Taylor. The prosecution attempted, without success, to establish an overt act through this witness. Taylor's testimony involved his actions after Mrs. Blennerhassett sent him to warn Mr. Blennerhassett and Joseph Alston, Burr's son-in-law, that Burr could not safely return to the Island. Mrs. Blennerhassett was concerned for Burr's safety since many people in the vicinity of her home were agitated due to numerous rumors. Taylor offered no evidence that Burr either intended to levy war or was present on the Island. Taylor successfully located Burr in Lexington, Kentucky and informed him about events on Blennerhassett's Island and Mrs. Blennerhassett's warnings. Before this meeting, Taylor had never met Burr. Taylor informed Burr that if he returned to the Island, people might shoot him. Burr was surprised that

---

364 Robertson I, pp. 548-55.

people would contemplate such action against him. Although Taylor understood that Burr visited the Island three times, Taylor never observed him.

Taylor testified that he later found Mr. Blennerhassett and made preparations to return to the Island. Blennerhassett advised Taylor about the Washita lands that he purchased with Burr and invited Taylor to join them there. During subsequent conversations, Blennerhassett informed Taylor that they were "going to take Mexico; one of the finest and richest places in the whole world." Blennerhassett told Taylor that Burr would become King of Mexico and Theodosia, Burr's daughter, would become Queen upon Burr's death. Taylor warned Blennerhassett that he heard that Burr and his followers intended to divide the union. Blennerhassett assured him that he and Burr would not do this; such decision could only be made by the people. Taylor observed four boats with thirty men that later left the Island. The men possessed a few weapons, primarily for hunting and self-defense. Taylor provided no direct testimony that implicated Burr.[365]

GENERAL JOHN MORGAN

General John Morgan was the first prosecution witness when Court re-convened the next day. Morgan described a dinner with Burr at his father's house, known as "Morganza," near Pittsburgh, Pennsylvania in late August, 1806. Morgan and his brother met Burr and escorted him to their father's home. According to Morgan, Burr told them that, in his opinion, separation of the Union would occur within the next several years. Burr mentioned that he admired workmen in the area and suggested that these men would be useful to him. At dinner, Burr reiterated his earlier statements. Morgan testified that Burr speculated that with 200 men, he could drive the President and Congress into the Potomac—with 400–500 men, he could take the City of New York. Burr advised that he could use their help. Morgan warned his father, Colonel Morgan, about Burr's suggestions and recommended that his father advise President Jefferson about Burr's plans. Upon cross-examination by Aaron Burr, Morgan described their conversation with Burr as having been presented in a "lively or careless manner."[366] President Jefferson and others expressed similar comments about possible

---

365 Robertson I, pp. 555-61; Wheelan, pp. 201-2.
366 Robertson I, pp. 561-64; Clarkson, p. 266; Baker, p. 500.

separation of the union.[367] Such expression of opinions did not constitute the crime of treason.

COLONEL GEORGE MORGAN

The next witness was Colonel George Morgan, 63. Morgan, in earlier days, had himself been a western adventurer, received financial assistance from Spain, and helped to found present day New Madrid, Missouri. Colonel Morgan expressed affection for Burr, opining that Burr had been persecuted as Vice President and for the fatal duel with Hamilton. Colonel Morgan testified that Burr, after dinner, suggested that the country would be divided in five years or less. Morgan informed Burr that he hoped that such a thing would never happen. Burr, according to Morgan, complained about the weakness and stupidity of the government. Colonel Morgan confirmed the earlier testimony of his son that Burr suggested that with 200 men, he could drive Congress and the President into the Potomac. Shortly after his conversation, Burr left the dining room and requested that Colonel Morgan's son, Thomas, join him. Morgan later was warned that Burr requested the assistance of his son. The next day, Colonel Morgan concluded that he should apprise the President of his conversations with Burr.

After Colonel Morgan's testimony concluded, General John Morgan was recalled as a witness. He testified that when he met with Burr, there was discussion about war with Spain.[368]

THOMAS MORGAN

Thomas Morgan, Colonel Morgan's youngest son, was the next witness. He recalled that Burr spoke about the eventual separation of western states and territories. Burr suggested that quality leadership was more important than the number of men involved when executing a military plan. Thomas Morgan had a private conversation with Burr after dinner; Burr asked young Morgan about his plans. After Thomas informed Burr that he was studying law, Burr told him that employment would be difficult in this part of the country and that there was no encouragement for talent. Burr related a comment by Representative John Randolph of Virginia that men of talent were dangerous to the government. Burr asked Morgan whether he would

---

367 Thomas Jefferson to John Breckinridge, August 12, 1803, Library of Congress digital.
368 Robertson I, pp. 569.

consider being part of a military expedition or enterprise. Morgan advised that his answer depended on its object or cause.[369]

Jacob Allbright

So far, an overt act had not been established by the prosecution. Jacob Allbright would potentially represent the prosecution's best opportunity to establish an overt act of treason. Allbright was hired to build a kiln for drying corn on Blennerhassett's estate. Mrs. Blennerhassett informed Allbright that her husband and Burr needed provisions for an army for a year. Mrs. Blennerhassett invited Allbright to travel with Burr and her husband down the Ohio River and asked Allbright to secure additional Dutchmen for the trip. When boats started to arrive at the Island, several men stated that they worked for Burr and showed Allbright their rifles. Allbright observed four boats and several boatmen running bullets. He observed General Tupper of the Ohio militia attempt to arrest Blennerhassett. (Tupper, present at trial, was identified by Allbright). According to Allbright, when seven or eight men immediately pointed their muskets at Tupper, Tupper withdrew. Allbright observed twenty to thirty men depart the Island in boats with weapons, although the weapons may not have been raised in earnest. Allbright observed rifles and short guns; none had bayonets. On one occasion he observed Burr on the Island, approximately six weeks before departure of boats. Burr earlier admitted that he had visited the Island around the latter part of August and early part of September, 1806.[370]

Allbright was, potentially, the most important witness for the prosecution. His testimony came closest to establishing an overt act of treason—Blennerhassett's men pointed muskets at a military officer, General Tupper. However, as required by the Constitution, two witnesses are necessary to prove an overt act of treason. Since General Tupper was present in the Courtroom, he could have been called as a witness to corroborate Allbright's testimony; if he had done so and affirmed Allbright's testimony, the two witness requirement for treason would have been met. Incredibly, Tupper, although present in the Courtroom, was never called as a witness. When discovered years later, the reason for Tupper's silence was clear; Tupper signed an affidavit refuting Allbright's trial testimony. In his affidavit, Tupper swore that he was not present on Blennerhassett's Island to

---

369 Robertson I, pp. 569-571.
370 Robertson I, pp. 571-579; Wheelan, pp. 202-203; Baker, pp. 500-502.

arrest Blennerhassett; rather, he had been invited to the Island, was never molested, and no one pointed a weapon at him. If his affidavit was true, he directly refuted Allbright's testimony. The prosecution must have known Tupper would refute Allbright's testimony if called as a witness. If the prosecution knew this, it had an affirmative duty to disclose this evidence to the defense. In a criminal case, the prosecution must disclose exculpatory evidence in its possession or within its knowledge, to the defense. The prosecution surely must have known how Tupper would testify; why else was he not called as a witness. If the prosecution was aware that Tupper would refute Allbright's testimony, they permitted Allbright to perjure himself.[371]

WILLIAM LOVE

William Love, Blennerhassett's groom, was the next witness. Love testified that he was among approximately twenty to twenty-five men with four boats and a few weapons and his group was the last to depart Blennerhassett's Island. At the time he left the Island, General Tupper was in the greatest friendship with them. Love never saw Burr on the Island, although he met him at Natchez several years earlier. The defense objected to portions of his testimony that related to events that occurred outside Virginia. Love testified that the men on the Island were not in an offensive posture, but rather were only attempting to defend themselves. Love advised that Blennerhassett informed him that if he traveled to the Washita lands with them, he would be given land; if he chose not to go, Blennerhassett would recommend him for a job. He testified that they left the Island because they were afraid they would be arrested by the Governor of Ohio. Love understood the purpose of the trip was to settle the Washita lands.[372]

DUDLEY WOODBRIDGE

Dudley Woodbridge, once a partner of Harmon Blennerhassett's, lived in Marietta, Ohio. He testified that he was on the Island the evening the boats departed. He observed four boats with about twenty men and two pistols. He previously met Burr in August or September 1806, when Burr and Blennerhassett came to his place of business to order fifteen boats (similar to those utilized on the Mohawk River and depicted in James Fennimore Cooper's *Leatherstocking Tales*) and supplies, mainly food. Woodbridge

---

371 Baker, pp. 501-502.
372 Robertson I, pp. 579-582.

inferred from Blennerhassett that his intent was to take the boats and supplies to Mexico. Woodbridge knew Blennerhassett and knew that he was not a military man. He testified that Blennerhassett was well educated, talented, and that he had every kind of sense except common sense. Woodbridge's understood that Burr would, at some point, return to the Island.[373]

The prosecution now stipulated that Burr was in Kentucky during the time the acts charged in the indictment were allegedly committed on Blennerhassett's Island.[374] This was a crucial admission. At the time the alleged "assembly of men" met in Virginia, Burr was not present. When Court resumed the next day, Burr again insisted that the prosecution must first present all evidence relative to an overt act of treason before other testimony could be introduced, specifically evidence that related to intent. The court determined that after the prosecution offered all its evidence to prove an overt act, the defense could then present legal arguments to the Court.

SIMEON POOLE

Simeon Poole was sent by the Governor of Ohio to arrest Blennerhassett. Poole testified that he observed the Island while standing across the River in Ohio; he saw boats and activity on December 10, 1806. He thought he observed armed men, but could not be certain since his observations were at nighttime and he was some distance away. He did observe several boats come and go from the Island.[375]

MAURICE P. BELKNAP

Maurice P Belknap, an Ohio businessman, was the next witness. On December 10, 1806, he observed two or three boats and approximately 20 men on the Island and two or three men cleaning their rifles. [376]

EDWARD P. DANA

Edward P. Dana testified that he never observed Burr on the Island the night of December 10. He believed that he did observe approximately fifteen to sixteen men that night.[377]

---

373 Robertson I, pp. 582-590; Wheelan, p. 204.
374 Robertson I, pp. 595.
375 Robertson I, pp. 590-592.
376 Robertson I, pp. 592-593.
377 Robertson I, p. 593.

Twelve witnesses had been called by the prosecution, including General Eaton; none could establish an overt act of treason. The anticipated star witness, General James Wilkinson was not called to testify, and the key piece of evidence, the cipher letter, thought to be the smoking gun, was never offered. Burr and his attorneys renewed their objection to admission of evidence of intent before an overt act of treason was established. Chief Justice Marshall opined that a motion to exclude evidence may be appropriate, but suggested it be postponed. Hay informed the Court that he had two additional witnesses who could describe conditions on Blennerhassett's Island. Following receipt of this additional testimony, Chief Justice Marshall permitted the defense to renew its motion to restrict further testimony. The Court would now hear arguments from counsel, argument uncommonly eloquent and powerful. Arguments presented by John Wickham and Luther Martin for the defense and William Wirt for the prosecution were particularly brilliant. The arguments lasted almost six days. The defining moment in the Burr trial had now arrived.

13. Legal Arguments on the Law of Treason and Order of Proof

John Wickham was the first to be heard on the Defense Motion to Limit Testimony. Wickham's argument was described by local attorney Littleton Tazewell as "the greatest forensic effort of the American Bar."[378] Wickham submitted that the prosecution must first prove an overt act of treason before evidence can be introduced about anything said or done at a location not charged in the indictment. He contended that no person can be convicted of treason by levying war when not personally present during commission of the act. In other words, in order to convict Burr under the Indictment, Burr must have been physically present on Blennerhassett's Island on the charged date. [379] The prosecution earlier stipulated that Burr had not been present at the scene of the crime charged in the Indictment at the time and date alleged.

Wickham tackled the prosecution's fatal reliance on the doctrine of constructive treason; the prosecution's misinterpretation of *United States v. Bollman and Swartwout*. Wickham suggested that the constructive treason discussion in the earlier opinion was unnecessary— it was dictum:

> I will admit that in the case of Messrs. Bollmann and Swartwout, which was only a question of commitment, decided by the Supreme Court, there is dictum, which is reported to have fallen from the Chief Justice in delivering the opinion of the Court, that is in oppo-

378 Lomask, p. 270; Smith, p. 369.
379 Robertson, p. 598.

187

sition to the doctrine I have been contending for; but the decision of the Court did not turn on that point; a determination of that question, one way or the other, would have no effect on the judgment; it was therefore extrajudicial. Your honor can set me right if I be mistaken; but I believe the point now relied on by the prosecution, either did not come before the Court, or was very slightly touched on by the bar: it was a mere dictum of the judges stated *arguendo*, *obiter* opinion delivered without argument, and not necessary to have been decided....[380]

Wickham explained the consequences that would ensue if the prosecution's interpretation of the law of treason prevailed:

If the principles for which I have contended be correct, this prosecution can not succeed; it appears to my judgment, that if they be disregarded, and the doctrines supported by the gentlemen on the other side prevail, there will be these consequences:

First. If a man can be indicted as being present, for overt acts committed by others, when he was absent in a different state and district, the Constitution of the United States, which was so ably and carefully drawn up in order to secure and perpetuate the freedom of the people of the country, will be a dead letter. A citizen may be seized by military force, dragged from one end of the continent to the other, tried far away from his family and friends, where he is a stranger, at a place where he never was, and among people whom he never saw; nay more.

Second. He is to be tried without any notice in the indictment of the real nature of the charge against him, or where the war was which he is accused of levying. The indictment against him states that he did the act himself, when in truth he was hundreds of miles distant from the scene of the action, and the act charged against him done by others.

Third. The doctrine of the cruel Jeffries [the infamous English hanging judge] is to be applied against him. He is to be tried for an act done by another, without producing a record of the conviction of that other, for whose alleged guilt he is to suffer.

Fourth. The law of treason, and the rules concerning it, as heretofore universally considered, are totally misunderstood. A new definition of treason is adopted. The levying of war may be secret, without arms, without force, without any overt act.

All these arguments will apply not to this case only, but to every case that may happen in any part of the United States. There will be certain consequences of the doctrines contended for by the gentle-

---

380 Robertson, pp. 626-627.

men on the other side, if sanctioned by this Court. Will they seriously contend for doctrines that will expose all the people of this country more to the dangers of constructive treason, to greater oppression and hardships, than to the people of any other country have been subjected to? Certainly they will not. The records of this trial will be a monument to an attempt to establish principles that must infallibly introduce slavery. The attempt cannot succeed. But while I thus speak of the principles themselves, God forbid that I should make the smallest reference to the conduct of the government, or the motives of the gentlemen on the other side. I disclaim all personal allusions, which must be without reference to the merits at all times, and frequently tend to substitute invective for argument. I believe the government will disclaim all agency in the business, and that if they wish the accused to be convicted, still they only wish him to be convicted according to law.

Will gentlemen advance doctrines which the government will disclaim? If, indeed, it were possible that they wished to conduct the prosecution on principles that would destroy the liberties of their country, those which they advocated would certainly produce that dreadful effect; for it is obvious they have a direct tendency to root out and destroy every principle of freedom; but I trust they will never be sanctioned in this country.[381]

DEFENSE ATTORNEY EDMUND RANDOLPH

Defense Attorney Edmund Randolph continued the defense argument in support of its motion to limit testimony.[382] Randolph asked four questions. First, can there be treason in levying war without force? Second, under the United States Constitution, can a person who may be considered an accessory in the commission of a felony, be a principal in levying war against the United States? Third, when the Indictment charged Colonel Burr with committing an act personally, can evidence of a derivative or accessorial nature be admitted? Fourth, if such derivative or accessorial evidence treason is to be considered, shouldn't the real principal first be convicted? Randolph submitted that it was of utmost importance that the law of treason be clearly understood and that its rules and regulations well-defined. Randolph cited Montesquieu for the proposition that "if the doctrine of treason be indeterminate in any country, however free its form of government, it is sufficient to make it degenerate into tyranny."[383]

---

381 Robertson, pp. 675-76; Wheelan, pp. 209-211; Baker, p. 502; Beveridge III, pp. 491-494; Isenberg, 359-360.

382 Robertson II, pp. 2-29.

383 Robertson II, p. 3.

Randolph directly challenged Chief Justice Marshall to reconsider the problematic language in *United States v. Bollman and Swartwout*:

> If the law of treason ought not to be left unfixed or uncertain, there ought to be no treason in levying war without the employment of force; for if force be dispensed with, it will be extremely uncertain and dependent on the will of the government. It was intimated the other day by the gentlemen on the other side, that we had a definition of treason in levying war by the Supreme Court, in the case of *Bollman and Swartwout*; and that it consisted in enlisting and assembling men without the exertion of any force.

> I should yield to the decided and still acknowledged good sense of the judiciary; because that corps is, in my estimation, the palladium of individual safety. I should do so with the greater cheerfulness because those who compose it are individuals who are studious to avoid, averse to repeat, and never unwilling to recant error.

> Sir, may I be indulged with one remark, which may perhaps seem too strong: *I should be deceived for more than twenty years with respect to him who delivered that opinion, if he would hazard a stain on the sword of justice by such a construction of the law of treason as has been given by the gentleman on the other side. Yes, sir. I do say that this cannot be the language and sentiment of the Supreme Court....*[384] (Emphasis added.)

PROSECUTOR ALEXANDER MACRAE

On August 24, 1807, Alexander MacRae presented the prosecution's initial argument. MacRae, in his usual fiery and sarcastic manner, submitted that Burr's absence from the Island did not absolve him of responsibility: "The prisoner has never been regarded as an accessory before the fact. He is the first mover of the plot; he planned it, he matured it; he contrived the doing of the overt acts which others have done. He was the Alpha and Omega of this treasonable scheme, the very body and soul, the very life of this treason...."[385]

PROSECUTOR WILLIAM WIRT

William Wirt, the most gifted and powerful orator for the prosecution, presented the next prosecution argument. The most famous portion of Wirt's argument answered the rhetorical question: "Who is Blennerhassett?" Years after the Burr trial, school-children read and memorized this portion of Wirt's argument in rhetoric classes. By studying and reciting

---

384 Robertson II, pp. 4-5.
385 Robertson II, p. 45.

Wirt's argument, the universal belief that Burr was guilty of treason must have been confirmed. In a recent book, Joseph Wheelan referred to this part of Wirt's argument as a "metaphorical trip to Eden and the Fall."[386]

Wirt rhetorically asked:

> Who is Blennerhassett? A native of Ireland, a man of letters, who fled from the storms of his own country to find quiet in ours. His history shows that war is not the natural element of his mind; if it had been, he would never have exchanged Ireland for America. So far is an army from furnishing the society natural and proper to Mr. Blennerhassett's character, that on his arrival in America, he retired even from the population of the Atlantic states, and sought quiet and solitude in the bosom in our western forests. But he carried with him taste and science and wealth; and, lo! the desert smiled. Possessing himself of a beautiful island in the Ohio, he rears upon it a palace, and decorates it with every romantic embellishment of fancy.... And to crown the enchantment of the scene, a wife who is said to be lovely beyond her sex, and graced with every accomplishment that can render it irresistible, had blessed him with her love, and made him a father of several children. The evidence would convince you that this is but a faint picture of his life.

Wirt then argued that the Devil, Burr, arrived at this idyllic setting:

> In the midst of all this peace, this innocent simplicity, and this tranquility, this feast of the mind, this pure banquet of the heart, the destroyer comes; he comes to change this paradise into a hell.... A stranger presents himself. Introduced to their civilities by the high rank which he had lately held in his country, he soon finds his way to their hearts by the dignity and elegance of his demeanor, the light and beauty of his conversation, and the seductive and fascinating powers of his address. The conquest was not difficult. Innocence is ever simple and credulous. Conscious of no design itself, it suspects none in others. It wears no guard before its breast. Every door and portal and avenue of the heart is thrown open, and all who choose it enter. Such was the state in Eden when the serpent entered its bowers. The prisoner, in a more engaging form, winding himself into the open and unpracticed heart of the unfortunate Blennerhassett, found but little difficulty in changing the native character of that heart and the objects of its affection.

Wirt next suggested that Burr poisoned, changed, and ruined Blennerhassett:

> ...Yet this unfortunate man, thus deluded from his interest and his happiness, thus seduced from the paths of innocence and peace, thus confounded in the toils that were deliberately spread for him, and overwhelmed by the mastering spirit and genius of another—this

---

386 Wheelan, p. 216; Beveridge, pp. 495-497.

man, thus ruined and undone, and made to play a subordinate part in this grand drama of guilt and treason, this man is to be called the principal offender, while he, by whom he was thus plunged in misery, is comparatively innocent, a mere accessory! Is this reason? Is it law? Is it humanity? Sir, neither the human heart nor the human understanding will bear a perversion so monstrous and absurd, so shocking in the soul, so revolting to reason! Let Aaron Burr, then, not shrink from high destination which he has courted; and having already ruined Blennerhassett in fortune, character, and happiness forever, let him not attempt to finish the tragedy by thrusting that ill-fated man between himself and punishment.[387]

Wirt concluded by addressing the law of treason and the doctrine of constructive treason:

> In America the crime is defined by the Constitution. It consists of levying war against the United States. In England it consists in an opposition to the king's authority and prerogative. Here it is against the Constitution and government. In England, when it is intended against the life of the prince, it may consist in mere imagination, in the mere design or intent of the mind. But in this country the offence is against the government, the political person only; and it is actual war. As it is against the government, not against a natural person, it may be said to be constructive. But constructive interpretations of treason, which produced so much terror and alarm formerly in England, and against the abuses of which gentlemen have declaimed so pathetically, cannot take place in this country. They are expressly excluded by the Constitution. Upon the whole, I contend that the meeting on Blennerhassett's Island, the intention of which is proven to be traitorous, was an act of treason; that the assemblage with such intention was sufficient for that purpose. And if it were not sufficient, this Court cannot stop the proceedings. The jury must proceed with the inquiry.[388]

Defense Attorney Benjamin Botts

Defense Attorney Benjamin Botts had the unenviable task of following Wirt's eloquent argument; he was more than up to the challenge. Botts, employing both sarcasm and eloquence, directly addressed Wirt's argument:

> I cannot promise you, sir, a speech manufactured out of tropes and figures. Instead of the magnificent image of Bonaparte ascending to quench the stars, so fitted for the dry law question in debate, my humble efforts will be altogether below the clouds. Instead of the introduction of a sleeping Venus, with all the luxury of voluptuous and wanton nakedness to charm the reason through the refined medium of sensuality, and to convince us that the law of treason is with

---

387 Robertson II, pp. 118-120.
388 Robertson II, pp. 151-52.

---

the prosecution by leading our imaginations to the fascinating rich-
ness and symmetry of a heaving bosom and luscious waist, I am compelled to plod heavily and meekly through the dull discussions of
Hale and Foster [legal commentators]. So far, though, from reprov-
ing the gentleman's excitement of the boiling blood of such of us as
are in the heyday of youth, without the previous caution of clearing
the hall of those whose once panting desires have been chilled with
age, and upon whom the forced ecstasy sat unnaturally and uneasily,
I only lament my utter incapacity to elicit topics of legal science by
an imitation of so novel and tempting an example. Nothing but the
impossibility of success would prevent me also from grasping at the
fame and glory on this grave occasion, and at this time of pleasure, of
enriching the leering lasciviousness of a like bewildering thought, to
transport anew the old and the young.[389]

Botts' satirical response to Wirt's argument produced laughter from
the audience: attorneys, spectators, witnesses, jurors, and, reportedly, even
from the Chief Justice.[390]

Later Botts reminded the Court that grand juries in Kentucky and Mississippi failed to indict Burr:

The Mississippi territory and Kentucky, as we are informed, were
the seat of the war. But the simpletons of that state and territory
hunted, but could not find the war. They were so stupid as not to
perceive in a collection of men without arms, without any possible
means of annoyance, without any hostile disposition, and without
the possibility of getting away their women and families, anything
criminal, much less any aptitude to overturn two mighty empires. It
remained for us, the members of the Virginia bar, to come out and
astonish the world with the profundity of our learning in matters of
war. They have ascertained that there was a terrible war. I ask you,
what manner of war was it? We have had a much more serious war
here than was on the island. We have had here carnage of breaths,
sour looks, and hard words, and the roaring of vocal cannon. We
have had a battle with the laws and the Constitution, fought cou-
rageously and furiously by our enemy. Is it not a mockery to speak
of the war on Blennerhassetts Island? Shall we not be the sport of
Europe and the world by such a discussion? We are gravely deliberating whether acts eminently characterized by peace and good order
were war or not. Sir, there was nothing on the island that was not
directly opposite in all its parts to war. If saying a great deal, if vo-
ciferation, if a great deal of vocal roaring may be war, then we have
had a war....[391]

---

389 Robertson II, p. 152
390 Beveridge III, pp. 497-498; Baker, p. 506.
391 Robertson II, pp. 166-167.

Botts concluded by warning about the potential for abuse if the doctrine of constructive treason became American law. He spoke directly to President Jefferson:

> What may they (Presidents) not do if the doctrine of constructive treason be left to their guidance? This is a power that may be exercised by either a virtuous or vicious president. But though it may be exercised, it is improper for any president to do so. But I do not mean to admit that the president is bound, or has even a right, to interfere in any prosecution whatever. On the contrary, I insist that the president's interference with the prosecution is improper, illegal, and unconstitutional. From the very moment that a case enters into the pale of the judiciary, he ought to avoid all interference with it.... He is therefore to suppress insurrections; but the very moment that an insurgent is taken before the judiciary, the two departments become distinct, and he has no right to interfere. If he do interfere, he violates the constitution.... I have no doubt that the President acted from good motive, without sufficiently reflecting on the subject, and that he has inadvertently followed one of the very worst British examples in the most arbitrary reigns. I wish Mr. Jefferson were here by your side, and could hear what could be said on the subject. I am confident that he would determine that he had done wrong.[392]

Prosecutor George Hay

Chief Prosecutor George Hay continued the prosecution's argument. Hay was Jefferson's prosecutor and many Jeffersonian thoughts may be found in Hay's argument. Hay suggested that Chief Justice Marshall intended to rule in the same manner that led to the impeachment of Associate Justice Samuel Chase: Chase had not permitted the jury to hear all the evidence in several cases. Chase's actions in the *Fries* case, one of the grounds for his impeachment, were cited by Hay:

> *To wrest from the jury the decision of facts in a criminal prosecution is a most dangerous proposition. It is replete with incalculable mischief.* I feel infinitely more solicitude about the preservation of this principle in all its purity, than for the correct construction of the doctrine of Constitutional treason as contradistinguished from constructive or oppressive treason. I consider this principle of trial by jury, preserved in its utmost purity and independence, as connected with the best principles of the human heart. *It ought to be viewed and approached with the utmost reverence and caution; and when a judge is called on to do what may lead him to encroach on this principle, he will advance with the utmost circumspection and awe.* I will take the liberty to say, that it will be far more safe and correct to remain a thousand miles on this side of the line which separates the rights of the jury from those of the court, than

---

392 Robertson II, pp. 208-209.

to go a hair's breadth beyond it; and if he should approach, he ought for no human consideration to touch it. If ever he do, he undermines civil liberty. The principle has for so long been held, not only in the highest estimation, but even regarded as sacred, in England. It is to the reverence with which it has been regarded that we are to ascribe that portion of civil liberty which the people there enjoy. It is for these reasons that no such case as this has ever happened....[393] (Emphasis added.)

Hay concluded: "They say that the question whether this was an act of treason or not must be decided by this Court. The principle that the Court is to supersede the jury in the decision of questions of facts is monstrous...."[394]

Hay had directly threatened the Court. This was not a subtle threat. He reminded Chief Justice Marshall about Justice Chase's impeachment and threatened the Court with similar action if the Court ruled against the prosecution.

DEFENSE ATTORNEY CHARLES LEE

Charles Lee responded to Hay's reference to the Chase impeachment and the veiled threat made against the Chief Justice. The following colloquy then took place:

"Mr. Lee: the gentleman then said, that in substance there was no difference between the opinion which we desire you to give and that for which Judge Chase was impeached. It was very kind in the gentleman to remind the Court of the danger of a decision of the motion in favor of the prisoner; a decision like that which had already produced the impeachment of another judge."

Mr. Hay: "The cases are different. What I said was only said to put Mr. Botts right in his representation. It was innocently said and compatible with the highest respect for the Court; not with the design which the gentleman (I will say not very candidly) insinuates."

Chief Justice: "I did not consider you as making any personal allusion, but as merely referring to the law."

Mr. Lee: *"The gentleman plainly insinuated the possibility of danger to the Court, from a favorable opinion to the prisoner; because he said that the opinion which we claimed for him was the same in substance as had occasioned the impeachment of one judge already. It certainly would not be unfair to infer that it was intended to show that the same cause might again produce the same effect. The idea, then, of danger to the Court from a decision in our favor, when there was*

---

393 Robertson II, pp. 246-247.
394 Robertson II, p. 288.

no danger, we were bound to repel, whatever might have been the intention with which the observation was made...."[395] (Emphasis added.)

DEFENSE ATTORNEY LUTHER MARTIN

The final argument was presented by Luther Martin. Martin's argument would take two full days and part of a third to complete. Martin noted that if all prosecution witnesses were called, the length of the trial would be greatly expanded. So far, the prosecution had called twelve witnesses. However, the prosecution had more than 140 witnesses under subpoena waiting to testify in Richmond. The defense, according to Martin, was prepared to call an additional thirty witnesses, which would greatly add to the length of the trial and to his client's confinement. In addition, the Court, jury, and witnesses would be further inconvenienced. Martin suggested that he was personally disposed to proceed with all testimony so that he could establish the innocence of his client. However, Martin was persuaded that to continue the examination of witnesses would permit the receipt of inadmissible evidence.[396]

Martin first distinguished the Supreme Court's *United States v. Bollman and Swartwout* decision:

> An opinion given in court, if not necessary for the judgment given of record, but that it might have been as well given, if no such or a contrary opinion had been broached, is no judicial opinion, no more than a gratis dictum.... The particular circumstances attending the judges of the Supreme Court strengthen this argument. When the opinion was given, only four of six judges could sit. One of them was sick; and another, a gentleman of highly distinguished talents in the law (Justice Henry Brockholst Livingston) was obliged to go home on account of the sickness of his family. Would four judges, in an extrajudicial manner, have undertaken to settle the construction of a law so infinitely important to the United States? Would they have decided so important a question in a collateral, irregular manner, on a point not immediately before them, and that also without the aid of the other two judges? ... *As a binding judicial opinion, it ought to have no more weight than the ballad or song of Chevy Chase.*[397] (Emphasis added.)

Martin continued:

> We have had two insurrections in Pennsylvania: the one named the *Whiskey Insurrection,* and the other the *hot* water insurrection. *If I were to name this, I would call it the Will-o'-the wisp treason. For though it is*

395 Robertson II, p. 294.
396 Robertson II, pp. 322-323.
397 Robertson II, pp. 410-412.

said to be here and there and everywhere, yet it is no-where. It exists only in the newspapers, and in the mouths of the enemies of the gentleman for whom I appear, who get it put into the newspapers.[398] (Emphasis added.)

Martin responded to Prosecutor Hay's impeachment threat to Chief Justice Marshall. Martin knew well the impeachment of Justice Chase; he had represented him. During the impeachment trial, Martin argued that Chase was correct in his legal rulings; the problem was that Congress and the President did not like or agree with those rulings. Martin argued that it was entirely proper for a judge to rule on admissibility of evidence. Ironically, in this case, Martin argued that Chief Justice Marshall was now being criticized for protecting the rights of the accused, precisely what Justice Chase was accused of ignoring.[399]

Martin concluded by speaking directly from the heart to Chief Justice Marshall, not only on behalf of his client, but urging Marshall to ignore threats and to do what was right:

> Before concluding, let me observe that it has been my intention to argue the cause correctly, without hurting the feelings of any person in the world. We are unfortunately situated. We labor against great prejudices against my client, which tend to prevent him from having a fair trial. I have with pain heard it said that such are the public prejudices against Colonel Burr, that a jury, even should they be satisfied of his innocence, must have considerable firmness of mind to pronounce him not guilty. I have heard it not without horror. God of heaven! Have we already under our form of government (which we have so often been told is best calculated of all governments to secure all our rights) arrived at a period when a trial in a court of justice, where life is at stake, shall be but a solemn mockery, a mere idle form and ceremony to transfer innocence from the jail to the gibbet, to gratify popular indignation excited by bloodthirsty enemies! But if it require in such situation firmness in a jury, so does it equally require fortitude in judges to perform their duty. And here permit me again most solemnly and at the same time most respectfully to observe that in the case of life or death, where there remains one single doubt in the minds of the jury as to the facts, or of the court as to law, it is their duty to decide in favor of life. If they do not, and the prisoner fall a victim, they are guilty of murder in *foro coeli*, whatever their guilt may be in *foro legis*.
>
> *When the sun mildly shines upon us, when the gentle zephyrs play around us, we can easily proceed forward in the straight path of our duty; but when black clouds enshroud the sky with darkness, when the tempest rages, the winds howl, and the waves break over us,—when the thunders awfully roar over our heads, and the*

398 Robertson II, pp. 414-415.
399 Robertson II, pp. 455-456.

lightnings of heaven blaze around us,—it is then that all the energies of the human soul are called into action. It is then that the truly brave man stands firm at this post. It is then that, by an unshaken performance of his duty, man approaches the nearest possible to the Divinity. Nor is there any object in the creation on which the Supreme Being can look down with more delight and approbation than on a human being in such a situation and thus acting. May that God who now looks down upon us, who has in his infinite wisdom called you into existence, and placed you in that seat to dispense justice to your fellow citizens, to preserve and protect innocence against persecution—may that god so illuminate your understanding that you may know what is right; and may he nerve your souls with the firmness and fortitude to act according to that knowledge.[400] (Emphasis added.)

Arguments had concluded. The arguments of Wickham, Wirt, and Martin were eloquent, masterful, and powerful. It was now time for Chief Justice Marshall to deliver his opinion.

---

400 Robertson II, pp. 465-466.

14. Impeachment

> *A removal by impeachment was nothing more than a declaration by Congress to this effect: You hold dangerous opinions, and if you are suffered to carry them into effect you will work the destruction of the nation. We want your offices; for the purpose of giving them to men who will fill them better.*
> —*William Branch Giles*

Before explaining Chief Justice Marshall's opinion, the significance of Prosecutor Hay's impeachment threat must be explained. Impeachment, as employed by Jefferson's supporters, was a threat to a free and independent judiciary and represented the third major confrontation between President Jefferson and the judiciary during his Administration. The Election of 1800 brought seismic changes to the political system. Republicans, led by Thomas Jefferson and James Madison, gained control of two branches of government: the Executive and Legislative. The third branch, the Judicial, remained a Federalist stronghold. President Jefferson became increasingly frustrated with limited options available to him for remaking the judiciary. Jefferson's efforts to replace or remove Federalist judges and appoint Republican judges in their stead met with limited success. Federalist judges, in his opinion, were not dying quickly enough and too few were resigning. Without a Constitutional Amendment to limit judicial terms and narrow judicial authority, the only option for Jefferson and his supporters was impeachment. If impeachment proved successful, Jefferson could remove Federalist judges, including those on the Supreme Court, who did not agree with his political views.

When the Republican Administration assumed office on March 4, 1801, the Federalist judiciary was in the crosshairs of President Jefferson and his lieutenants. Republican disgust with the Federalist judiciary was expressed in a letter from Virginia Governor James Monroe to Jefferson: "...This party (Federalist) has retired into the judiciary in a strong body where it lives in the treasury, & therefore cannot be starved out. While in possession of that ground it can check the popular current which runs against them, & seize the favorable occasion to promote reaction, which it does not despair of. It is a desperate party because it knows it has lost the public confidence...."[401]

The first direct evidence of Jefferson's intent to challenge the judiciary is found in a letter written to Archibald Stuart, a Virginia state judge: "The judge of course stands till the law is repealed, which we trust will be at the next Congress. But as to all others, I made it immediately known, that I should consider them as nullities, and appoint others: as I think I have a preferable right to name agents for my own administration, at least to the vacancies falling after it was known that Mr. Adams was not naming for himself...."[402]

When the newly elected Republican Congress met for the first time in December, 1801, President Jefferson delivered this Message to Congress: "The judiciary system of the United States, and especially that portion of it recently erected, will of course present itself to the contemplation of Congress."[403] A few days later, Jefferson wrote: "On their part they have retired into the judiciary as a stronghold. There the remains of federalism are to be preserved and fed from the treasury and from that battery all the works of republicanism are to be beaten down and erased. By a fraudulent use of the Constitution, which has made judges irremovable, they have multiplied useless judges merely to strengthen their phalanx."[404]

---

401 James Monroe to Thomas Jefferson, March 3, 1801. *PTJ* 33, pp. 126-127.
402 Thomas Jefferson to Archibald Stuart, April 8, 1801. *PTJ* 33, p. 555.
403 Jefferson's First Annual Message to Congress, December 8, 1801. *PTJ* 36, pp. 58-65; the portion of that Presidential Message that President Jefferson crossed-out represented Jefferson's true feelings about the judiciary.
404 Thomas Jefferson to John Dickinson, December 19, 1801. *PTJ* 36, pp. 165-166.

CONSTITUTIONAL AUTHORITY FOR IMPEACHMENT

The impeachment arrow in the Republicans' quiver was used for the first time when President Jefferson sent a Message to Congress on February 3, 1803, days before the Supreme Court convened for the first time in fourteen months. The message detailed erratic behavior of Federal District Judge John Pickering of New Hampshire. President Jefferson's Message could mean only one thing: impeachment. The timing of the Message was not accidental. Two cases of great importance to the Administration were on the docket of the Court: one challenged the failure of the Jefferson Administration to proceed with the appointment of four justice of the peace appointees (*Marbury v. Madison*); the other challenged constitutionality of repeal of the Judiciary Act of 1801 (*Stuart v. Laird*).

Impeachment is the Constitutional method for removal of civil officers of the government, including judges. Impeachment authorizes a legislative body to remove a public official from office. Congress' impeachment authority is one of its most powerful weapons. Impeachment consists of: (1) an accusation (bill of impeachment) brought by a majority of the House of Representatives, acting, in effect, as prosecutor and Grand Jury and (2) trial in the Senate, with the entire Senate acting as judge and jury with a two-thirds majority required for conviction. Impeachment is found within the United States Constitution (Article I–Sections 2 and 3, Article II–Sections 1 and 2, and Article III–Sections 1 and 2).

Although impeachment, as defined in the Constitution, followed British law, there were differences:

Conviction by impeachment requires a two-thirds majority vote of the Senate; the British required a simple majority of the House of Lords.

Punishment for impeachment under the Constitution can only extend to removal from office and disqualification from holding future offices. In Britain, punishment for impeachment was discretionary with the House of Lords; conviction could include imprisonment and punishment by death.

In Britain, all the King's subjects were potentially liable for impeachment; under the Constitution, only "officers" of the government are liable.

In Britain, the Lords are not sworn before trying the impeachment; under the Constitution, Senators are sworn before proceedings commence.

In Britain, the King cannot be impeached; in the United States, the President may be impeached.

In Britain, impeachment is considered a method to punish criminal behavior; in the United States, impeachment is used solely to remove an offender from office—although the impeached offender may also be subject to criminal indictment, trial, and punishment in a separate legal proceeding.[405]

Alexander Hamilton, in *Federalist* Nos. 65 and 66, discussed impeachment, particularly the role of the Senate. In *Federalist* Nos. 78 and 79 Hamilton discussed independence of the judiciary and removal of judges by impeachment:

> The precautions for the responsibility are comprised in the article respecting impeachments. They (Judges) are liable to be impeached for malconduct by the House of Representatives and tried by the Senate; and, if convicted, may be dismissed from office and disqualified from office and disqualified for holding any other. This is the only provision on the point which is consistent with the necessary independence of the judicial character, and the only one which we find in our own Constitution in respect to our own judges.

> The want of provision for removing judges on account of inability has been a subject of complaint. But all considerate men will be sensible that such a provision would either not be practiced upon or would be more liable to abuse than calculated to answer any good purpose...The result, except in the case of insanity, must for the most part be arbitrary; and insanity, without any formal or express provision, may be safely pronounced to be a virtual disqualification."[406]

The first attempt by Republicans to remove a judge by the impeachment was at the state level; Republicans in Pennsylvania removed a Federalist state judge, Alexander Addison, branded the "transmontane Goliath of Federalism" by Pennsylvania Governor Thomas McKean.[407]

The impeachment of Judge Addison served as a roadmap for Republicans in Congress. Although Addison had not committed a crime, he was impeached under the doctrine "dangerous tendency," a theory later relied upon for the impeachments of Federal District Judge John Pickering and Supreme Court Justice Samuel Chase. The theory of "dangerous tendency"

---

405 Judge William Lawrence. "The Law of Impeachment," *American Law Register*, Vol. 15, No. 11, New Series Vol. 6 (September 1867), pp. 643-644.

406 *The Federalist Papers*. Rossiter, pp. 396-407; 464-475.

407 Thomas McKean to Thomas Jefferson, February 4, 1803. *The Thomas Jefferson Papers*, Library of Congress digital, American Memory; Richard E. Ellis. *The Jeffersonian Crisis: Courts and Politics in the Young Republic*, p. 164.

expanded the definition of "high crimes and misdemeanors" to include po-litical offenses committed by judges, particularly in cases where the judge went too far in the opinion of the opposing political party.[408]

By 1803, the power of President Jefferson and his supporters was at its apex. Congressional elections in 1802 added to Republican majorities in both Houses of Congress. The Judiciary Act of 1801 had been repealed, Federal offices (with the exception of the judiciary) were filled with sym-pathetic supporters of the Administration, and Jefferson was never more popular. Jefferson, however, was distressed with his inability to appoint Republicans to the Federal bench. After the successful removal of Judge Ad-dison in Pennsylvania under the "dangerous tendency" doctrine, impeach-ment of Federal judges was now in play. Over the course of our history, impeachment of Federal judges has been rare. Congress has inquired into the behavior of approximately seventy-eight federal judges; fourteen were impeached and eight convicted and removed from office. [409]

IMPEACHMENT OF JUDGE PICKERING

The first effort to remove a Federal Judge by impeachment involved an unusual and sad case. Federal District Judge John Pickering of New Hamp-shire was one of that state's most distinguished and honored citizens. Pick-ering was an author of the New Hampshire state constitution, a patriot during the Revolution, and a state legislator and attorney general. He was active in New Hampshire's ratification of the Constitution and later ap-pointed Chief Justice of the New Hampshire State Supreme Court. How-ever, by 1794 Pickering began exhibiting erratic behavior that suggested mental illness; his condition was later exacerbated by excessive drinking. When a vacancy occurred on the Federal District Court in New Hampshire, he was appointed by President Washington. Unfortunately, Pickering's condition further deteriorated after his appointment. His bizarre behavior warranted investigation, the results of which were reported to President Jefferson by Secretary of the Treasury Albert Gallatin.[410] President Jefferson

---

408 Peter Charles Hoffer and N.E.H. Hull *Impeachment in America, 1635-1805*, pp. 195-205.

409 "In a Rare Occurrence, House Weighs Impeachment of Judge." *Wall Street Jour-nal*, December 1, 2009.

410 An excellent treatment of Judge Pickering's impeachment is found in an article written by Lynn W. Turner, "The Impeachment of John Pickering," pp. 485-507); see also, *Impeachment in America*, pp. 207-208.

forwarded Gallatin's findings to Congress, together with this message: "The enclosed letter and affidavits exhibiting matter of complaint against John Pickering, district judge of New Hampshire, which is not within Executive cognizance, I transmit them to the House of Representatives, to whom the Constitution has confided a power of instituting proceedings of redress, if they shall be of opinion that the case calls for them."[411] The "power of instituting proceedings of redress" meant impeachment.

The Constitution is silent on how a Federal Judge, unable to perform duties due to incapacity, can be removed. Under the Constitution, a Federal judge holds office "during good behavior."[412] Removal of a Federal Judge may only be by impeachment. In Pickering's case, he did not commit treason, bribery or other high crimes or misdemeanors; his behavior was bizarre and irrational. Judge Pickering could only be impeached if the term "high crimes and misdemeanors" had a broader meaning than commission of a crime. Republicans, therefore, employed the doctrine of "dangerous tendency."

Although the Judiciary Act of 1801 was much hated by Republicans, it included several necessary and important changes to the federal judicial system. When the Act was repealed, Supreme Court Justices resumed circuit court responsibilities, resulting in Chief Justice Marshall presiding in the Burr trial. Another meritorious provision that was eliminated after repeal specifically addressed the Judge Pickering issue. Section 25 of that Act provided:

> ... That in case of the inability of the district judge of either of the districts of the United States, to perform the duties of his office, and satisfactory evidence thereof being shown to the circuit court, in and for such district, it shall be the duty of such circuit court, from time to time, as occasion may require, to direct one of the judges of said circuit court, to perform the duties of such district judge, within and for said district, for and during the period of the inability of the district judge shall continue. And it shall be the duty of the circuit judge, to whom the duties of the district judge shall be assigned in manner aforesaid, and he is hereby authorized to perform the duties of said district judge, during the continuance of his disability.[413]

This provision was suggested to John Marshall, then Secretary of State, during debate on the Judiciary Act of 1801, by Jeremiah Smith. Smith, a former Representative from New Hampshire who later became a Federal Judge,

---

411 President Jefferson's Message to the House of Representatives, February 3, 1803. Richardson, Editor, Volume I, p. 344.

412 U.S. Constitution, Article III, Section 1.

413 Judiciary Act of 1801, 2 Stat. 89, February 13, 1801.

Governor, and state judge in New Hampshire, recommended this provision to address incapacitation of federal judges, specifically Judge Pickering:

> If any Act respecting the judiciary should pass during the present session of Congress I take the liberty to suggest to you the propriety of a clause which would remedy an evil under which we labor in this State—The district Judge has been deranged in his mind for the year past & his malady has every Appearance of continuing through life.... In the bill now before Congress which I have seen it would be easy to insert a clause providing for the appointment of a Circuit Judge & giving during Mr. Pickering's disability administrative jurisdiction to the Circuit Judge...[414]

After enactment of the Judiciary Act of 1801, Judge Pickering's disability was considered by newly appointed circuit court judges in New Hampshire; a circuit judge assumed Judge Pickering's duties. When the Judiciary Act of 1801 was repealed, Pickering was forced to resume judicial responsibilities; not long thereafter Republican's sought to remove him from office.[415]

In late 1802, a case came before Judge Pickering that provided Republicans with the means to take action. Judge Pickering appeared at a trial thoroughly intoxicated and irrational. His behavior throughout—at one point, he felt lonely and directed a marshal to sit next to him; later he advised the prosecutor that he would decide the case in four minutes and said that he would give him until all eternity to present his case. The next day, Judge Pickering changed his mind and rendered an instant decision against the prosecution. When the prosecution objected, Judge Pickering advised the parties that he would hear all testimony, but even if the testimony took four thousand years to present, he would still rule the same way.[416]

After President Jefferson submitted his Message to Congress in early 1803, the House voted to impeach Judge Pickering. Senators who sat in judgment of Judge Pickering were uncomfortable with the propriety of trying an insane man. Rather than vote to convict Pickering for "high crimes and misdemeanors," the Senate chose to convict him "as charged." Judge Pickering was removed from office.[417]

---

414 Jeremiah Smith to John Marshall, January 21, 1801. Marcus, *The Documentary History of the Supreme Court of the United States*, Volume 4, pp. 698-699. This letter, although addressed to Secretary of State Marshall, may be found in the Adams' Papers housed in the Massachusetts Historical Society. The Society graciously provided a copy of the letter.

415 "The Impeachment of John Pickering, " pp. 488-489.

416 Ibid., pp. 489-490.

417 Ibid., pp. 504-505.

Diaries of two United States senators who participated in the impeachment trial provide fascinating perspectives. The diarists, both Federalists, were Senators William Plumer of New Hampshire and John Quincy Adams of Massachusetts. Plumer described a dinner with President Jefferson:

> I dined this day with President Jefferson—I was at his house near an hour before the other gentlemen—Speaking of the impeachment of Pickering, I observed I had no doubt that the judge was *insane*, & asked him whether insanity was good cause for impeachment & removal from office. He replied, "If the facts of denying an appeal & of his intoxication, as stated in the impeachment are proven, that will be sufficient cause of removal without further enquiry."[418]

Two days later, Plumer wrote:

> The removal of the Judges, & the destruction of the independence of the judicial department, has been an object on which Mr. Jefferson has been long resolved, at least ever since he has been in office. In his first message to Congress, Dec. 8, 1801, he insinuated, *That the state legislatures had the principle care of our persons, property, & reputation*—He was explicit, *That the Judiciary of the United States was too expensive & that it required reform.* To prove that there were too many Judges he had previously required from the Clerk of each District the number of actions that had been entered on their dockets—these he communicated to Congress. In the same session, Congress passed the Act repealing the Law that established the Circuit Court—by this single operation all those Judges, without the slightest accusation were removed from office—an office which the Constitution expressly guaranteed to them *during good behavior. At the last session Mr. Jefferson told me that the Constitution ought to be so altered as that the President, on application of Congress should have authority to remove any Judge from office.* This business of *amending* the Constitution is found to be a tedious process—the good work of *reform* cannot be delayed—The President & his Cabinet agree that impeachment conviction & removal from office is necessary—A triumphant majority in each House are devoted to their views & will carry them into effect.

> The doctrine is now established in the House that a specific charge against a Judge is not necessary to institute an enquiry into his official conduct. A committee of enquiry is said to be a harmless measure—some vote for it, who are not prepared to vote for impeachment—not perceiving that when the Committee have collected *ex parte* testimony & reported an impeachment—that then they will be under a kind of necessity to impeach...

> When the Judges of the Circuit Court were removed by the repeal of the law in 1802, then was the time for the Judges of the Supreme

---

418 William Plumer. *William Plumer's Memorandum of Proceedings in the United States Senate,* January 5, 1804, pp. 100-101.

Court, to have taken their stand against the encroachments of Congress & of the Executive. That Court ought to have declared the repealing law unconstitutional—they ought to have refused to have held Circuit Courts—& the Judges of the Circuits ought to have continued to have held their Courts the repeal notwithstanding. But unfortunately there was then a diversity of opinion in the Supreme Court upon this subject—[419] (Emphasis added.)

Senator John Quincy Adams of Massachusetts was the son of John Adams (second president) and Abigail Smith Adams. Adams recorded in his *Memoirs*:

Senate sat until four o'clock—almost the whole day deliberating with closed doors on the question whether evidence and counsel in support of the petition of Jacob S. Pickering (son of John Pickering) should be heard...The dispositions and the principles advanced on this occasion are painful to reflect upon. The most persevering and determined opposition is made against hearing evidence and counsel to prove the man *insane*—only from the fear, that if the insanity should be proved, he cannot be convicted of *high crimes and misdemeanors* by acts of decisive madness. Motions were made to assign him counsel, who, upon the plea of *not guilty*, should give in evidence insanity by way of mitigation; as if a madman could either plead *guilty* or *not guilty*. Mr. Jackson was for hearing none of these pretenses of insanity; because they might prevent us from getting rid of the man. He said that the House of Representatives were at this moment debating whether they should impeach another Judge, and by-and-by we should have Judge Chase's friends come and pretend he was mad.... The dilemma is, between the determination to remove the man on IMPEACHMENT *for high crimes and misdemeanors*, though he be insane, and the fear that the evidence of this insanity, and the argument of counsel on its legal operation, will affect the popularity of the measure.[420]

John Quincy Adams later wrote to his father after the Chase impeachment trial and referenced the Pickering case:

The attack by *impeachment* upon the judicial department of our national government began two years ago, and has been conducted with great address as well as with persevering violence. The impeachment and conviction of Mr. Pickering, of a man notoriously and confessedly insane, for acts committed in that state, and during the whole course of the impeachment remaining in it, was but a preparatory step to the assault upon Judge Chase, as this in its turn was unquestionably intended to pave the way for another prosecution, which would have swept the supreme judicial bench clean at a stroke.... I can, indeed, never reflect upon the proceedings and judg-

---

419 *Memorandum of Proceedings,* January 7, 1804, pp. 101-103.
420 John Quincy Adams. *Memoirs of John Quincy Adams,* March 3, 1804, pp. 299-300.

ments in that cruel affair without dejection of heart and humiliation of spirit. I felt the honor of the body to which I belong, and for the honor of my country, sullied as they are by a sentence of *guilt*, inflicted upon a man for being among the most miserable of the human race, for being bereft by the hand of heaven of that attribute, which by rendering man rational would render him accountable...[421]

ASSOCIATE JUSTICE SAMUEL CHASE

The impeachment of Supreme Court Associate Justice Samuel Chase's was wholly different from Judge Pickering's removal. Although a burr in the side of Republicans, the legal competence and acumen of Justice Chase was beyond question. Justice Chase's problem was his judicial temperament, together with legal rulings and opinions with which Republicans disagreed. The impeachment of Justice Chase involved little law and much politics. If Justice Chase had been convicted, a free and independent judiciary would have been in jeopardy. Charles Warren, in his *The Supreme Court in United States History*, wrote: "The profound effect produced upon the course of American legal history by the failure of the Chase impeachment can hardly be overestimated; for it is an undoubted fact that, had the effort been successful, it was the intention of the Republicans to institute impeachment proceedings against all the Judges of the Court."[422] It is difficult to imagine a trial in American history that had greater political overtones than the Chase impeachment. If Justice Chase had been removed, Chief Justice Marshall and his Supreme Court brethren would have been next.

No judge was more hated than Chase. The *Philadelphia Aurora* wrote: "his [Chase] disposition was so arbitrary and his temper so ferocious and disregardful of decorum that few men, perhaps, had a humbler estimation among his fellow citizens."[423] No formal action was taken against Chase until he delivered a jury charge to a Maryland Federal Circuit Court jury in 1803. Chase's charge provided Republicans with the ammunition to pursue his impeachment.

Samuel Chase, born in 1741, was admitted to the Bar at age twenty. He was a member of the Maryland Assembly for twenty years and was a delegate to the First Continental Congress. A signer of the Declaration of Inde-

---

421 John Quincy Adams to John Adams, March 8, 1805. *John Quincy Adams* edited by Worthington Chauncey Ford, pp. 106-114.
422 Warren, Volume I, pp. 292-293.
423 *Philadelphia Aurora*, January 15, 1801.

pendence, together with fellow Marylander Luther Martin, Chase initially opposed the new federal Constitution. He believed that it inadequately protected the right to trial by jury or freedom of the press; Chase was later accused of denying these rights on the Bench. Over time, Chase became a strong supporter of the Constitution and the Washington Administration. President Washington appointed him to the Supreme Court. Upon learning of the appointment of Samuel Chase, Vice President John Adams wrote his wife Abigail: "...Mr. Chase is a new Judge, but although a good 1774 Man, his Character has a Mist about it of suspicion and Imperity which gives occasion to the enemy to censure. He has been a warm Party Man, and has made many Enemies. His Corpulency, which has increased very much since I saw him last in England, is against his riding Circuits very long..."[424]

As a Supreme Court Justice, Chase's abilities were beyond question. His actions as circuit judge were another matter. Justice Chase had self-destructive tendencies. While sitting as Circuit Judge, three Sedition Act cases (prosecutions of Thomas Cooper, James Callender, and John Fries) drew the ire of Republicans.[425] Judge Richard Peters, a District Judge from Pennsylvania who often sat with Justice Chase on the circuit court, lamented that Chase sought controversy whenever he could: "... of all the others, I like the least to be coupled with him. I never sat with him without pain, as he was forever getting into some intemperate and unnecessary squabble."[426] In appearance, Chase was six feet tall, with thick, broad, burly shoulders. He had more than adequate girth. His face was broad and massive, with a brownish red complexion—leading to the nickname "bacon face."[427] Future Supreme Court Justice Joseph Story described Chase three years after his impeachment trial:

> [T]he elements of his mind are of the very first excellence; age and infirmity have in some degree impaired them. His manners are coarse, and in appearance harsh; but in reality he abounds with good humor....In person, in manners, in unwieldy strength, in severity of reproof, in real tendencies of heart; and above all in intellect, he is the living, I had almost said the exact, image of Samuel Johnson. To use a provincial expression, I like him hugely.[428]

424 John Adams to Abigail Adams, February 6, 1796. *Adams Family Papers*, The Massachusetts Historical Society Digital.
425 Richard B. Lillach. "The Chase Impeachment," pp. 49-72.
426 Richard Peters to Timothy Pickering, January 24, 1804. Warren, p. 281.
427 Beveridge III, p. 184.
428 Joseph Story to Samuel F.P. Fay, February 25, 1808. Joseph Story. *Life and Letters of Joseph Story,* Edited by William W. Story. Volume I. Boston: Charles C. Little

Chase disagreed with repeal of the Judiciary Act of 1801. When his brethren avoided challenging the President and Congress over repeal, Justice Chase went along. Although he concurred in the later *Stuart v. Laird* opinion that upheld repeal of the Judiciary Act of 1801, Chase strongly opposed Jefferson and Republicans. Using the Federal bench in Maryland as a political platform, Chase, while charging the grand jury, directly attacked President Jefferson and his Republican followers on a number of issues, including repeal of the Judiciary Act:

> Where law is uncertain, partial, or arbitrary; where justice is not impartially administered to all; where property is insecure, and the person is liable to insult and violence without redress by law, the people are not free whatever may be their form of government. To this situation I greatly fear we are fast approaching!
>
> You know, gentlemen, that our State and national institutions were framed to secure to every member of the society equal liberty and equal rights; but the late alteration of the Federal Judiciary by the abolition of the office of the sixteen circuit judges, and the recent change in our State constitution by the establishing of universal suffrage, and the further alteration that is contemplated in our State judiciary (if adopted) will, in my judgment, take away all security for property and personal liberty. The independence of the national Judiciary is already shaken to its foundation, and the virtue of the people alone can restore it.... and the modern doctrines by our late reformers, that all men in a state of society are entitled to enjoy equal liberty and equal rights, have brought this mighty mischief upon us [thought to be an attack on President Jefferson]and I fear that it will rapidly progress, until peace and order, freedom and property, shall be destroyed. Our people are taught as a political creed, that men living under an established Government, are, nevertheless, entitled to exercise certain rights which they are possessed in a state of nature; and, also, that every member of this Government is entitled to enjoy an equality of liberty and rights....
>
> ... Any other interpretation of these terms is, in my judgment, destructive of all government and all laws. If I am substantially correct in these sentiments, it is unnecessary to make any application of them, and I will only ask two questions. Will justice be impartially administered by judges dependent on the Legislature for their continuance in office, and also for their support? Will liberty or property be protected or secured, by laws made by representatives chosen by electors, who have no property in, a common interest with, or attachment to the community?[429] (Emphasis added.)

---

and James Brown, 1851, pp. 166-168.
429 Library of Congress digital, Annals of Congress, Senate, 8th Congress, 2nd Session, pp. 673-676.

Jefferson referred Justice Chase's jury charge to one of his Congressional lieutenants, Joseph H. Nicholson of Maryland, a House manager in the earlier Pickering impeachment trial: "You must have heard of the extraordinary charge of Chase to the Grand Jury at Baltimore. Ought this seditious and official attack on the principles of our Constitution, and on the proceedings of a State, to go unpunished? And to whom so pointedly as yourself will the public look for the necessary measures? I ask these questions for your consideration; for myself it is better that I should not interfere."[430]

In January 1804, impeachment proceedings in the House of Representatives against Justice Chase commenced. On March 11, 1804, the same day the Senate convicted Judge Pickering, a House Committee recommended impeachment of Justice Chase; the House approved by a vote of 73–32.[431]

The Articles of Impeachment against Justice Chase involved four events, none of which related to his duties as Justice of the Supreme Court. The first Article involved the Sedition Act trial of John Fries. Chase was charged with announcing an opinion before counsel were provided an opportunity to argue the law, restricting counsel from citing legal authority, and restricting counsel from addressing the jury on questions of law.

The next five Articles related to the James Thompson Callender trial in Richmond Circuit Court. Callender was a muckraking journalist who, at the time of his trial, was a Jefferson supporter (he later opposed Jefferson and alleged that Jefferson had relations with a female slave, among other allegations). Chase was charged in these Articles with improperly permitting a juror to serve on the jury, refusing to permit John Taylor to appear as a witness, rude and intemperate conduct for requiring written questions be submitted by counsel before counsel were permitted to question a witness, refusing to postpone the trial due to the absence of a witness, insulting defense counsel, repeated and vexatious interruptions of defense counsel that resulted in withdrawal from the case, indecent solicitude for the conviction

---

430 Thomas Jefferson to Congressman Joseph H. Nicholson, May 13, 1803. *The Writings of Thomas Jefferson*, Vol. X, pp. 387-390.

431 Beveridge III, 169; Samuel Chase. *Trial of Samuel Chase.* Taken in short-hand by Samuel H. Smith and Thomas Lloyd. Volumes I & II, pp. 1-8. On January 5, 1804, the House adopted a Resolution that "a committee be appointed to inquire into the official conduct of Samuel Chase, one of the Associate Justices of the Supreme Court of the United States, and to report their opinion whether the said Samuel Chase hath so acted in his judicial capacity as to require the interposition of the Constitutional power of this House." 13 *Annals of Congress* 806.

of the defendant, misconduct for issuing a bench warrant instead of a summons, and misconduct for failing to grant a continuance .

The seventh Article involved Chase's actions before a grand jury in Delaware. After the grand jury failed to return an indictment involving allegations related to the Sedition Act, Chase addressed the grand jury. Although the grand jury wished to be discharged, Chase refused and ordered that United States Attorney to search for additional evidence. The grand jury was dismissed the next day after the prosecutor informed the Court that he could find no Seditious behavior.[432]

The final Article involved Chase's charge to the jury in Baltimore, Maryland, the charge President Jefferson reported to Representative Nicholson on May 13, 1803.[433]

Senator John Quincy Adams wrote about Chase's impeachment:

> This Mr. Giles has long been one of the most inveterate enemies of Judge Chase in the United States, and while a member of the House of Representatives, two years ago, declared he would himself impeach him were he not compelled by the state of his health to relinquish his seat in Congress. He has now become one of the judges to try him, and what chance of impartiality is to be expected from him may easily be imagined. But the issue of the prosecution, like that of Judge Pickering last winter, must be settled *out of doors*. And for this purpose, Mr. John Randolph, the prosecutor, and Mr. Giles, the judge, are in daily conference together.[434]

Adams commented about Senator William Branch Giles' opinion on impeachment: "According to him [Giles], impeachment is nothing more than enquiry, by the two Houses of Congress, whether the office of any public man might not be filled by another. This is undoubtedly the source and object of Mr. Chase's impeachment, and on the same principle any officer may easily be removed at any time."[435]

On December 21, 1804, Senator Adams described Giles' efforts to convince Senators to support Chase's impeachment:

> Sitting by the fireside afterwards, I witnessed a conversation between Mr. Giles and Mr. Israel Smith [Senator], on the subject of impeachment; during which Mr. John Randolph came in and took part in the discussion. Giles labored with excessive earnestness to con-

---

432 Ellis, *The Jeffersonian Crisis*, p. 78.
433 The Articles of Impeachment may be found in the Library of Congress Digital, Annals of Congress, 8th Congress, 2d Session; Thomas Jefferson to J.H. Nicholson, May 13, 1803. *Writings X*, pp. 387-390.
434 *Memoirs of John Quincy Adams*, p. 318.
435 *Memoirs of John Quincy Adams*, p. 321.

vince Smith of certain principles, upon which not only Mr. Chase, but all other Judges of the Supreme Court, excepting the last one appointed [Justice William Johnson appointed by President Jefferson], must be impeached and removed. He treated with the utmost contempt the idea of an *independent* judiciary—said there was not a word about such independence in the Constitution, and that their pretensions to it were nothing more or less than an attempt to establish an aristocratic despotism in themselves. The power of impeachment was given without limitation to the House of Representatives; *the power of trying impeachments was given equally without limitation to the Senate; and if the Judges of the Supreme Court should dare, AS THEY HAD DONE, to declare an act of Congress unconstitutional, or to send a mandamus to the Secretary of State, AS THEY HAD DONE, it was the undoubted right of the House of Representatives to impeach them, and of the Senate to remove them, for giving such opinions,* however honest or sincere they may have been in entertaining them. *Impeachment was not a criminal prosecution; it was no prosecution at all.* The Senate sitting for the trial of impeachments was not a court, and ought to discard and reject all process of analogy to a court of justice. A trial and removal of a judge upon impeachment need not imply any criminality or corruption in him.... *And a removal by impeachment was nothing more than a declaration by Congress to this effect: You hold dangerous opinions, and if you are suffered to carry them into effect you will work the destruction of the nation. We want your offices; for the purpose of giving them to men who will fill them better....* So that Smith and Giles were really trying the judge over the fireside. Old Mathers, the doorkeeper, saw this so plainly that after they were gone he said to me, "If all were of Mr. Giles opinion, they never need trouble themselves to bring Judge Chase here." I perceive, also, that the impeachment system is to be pursued, and the whole bench of the Supreme Court swept away, because *their offices are wanted.* And in the present state of things I am convinced it is easy for Mr. John Randolph and Mr. Giles to do this as to say it.[436] [Emphasis added.]

Senator Plumer described Justice Chase's first appearance on his Impeachment charges before the Senate on January 2, 1805:

> [I]t is indeed a humiliating scene to behold an *aged man, a Judge,* of the Supreme Court of the United States—A man who from 1796 has held very high responsible offices in the nation—discharged the duties of them with integrity—brought to trial as a criminal—Arraigned before a Court, the president of which is a fugitive from Justice—& stands indicted as MURDERER!
>
> The Judge was affected—tears suspended his voice for a moment or two—he soon recovered...
>
> The conduct of Mr. Burr to Judge Chase during the proceedings of the day has been very rude and highly reprehensible. These violent

---

436 *Memoirs of John Quincy Adams,* pp. 321-323.

> measures in Mr. Burr may, & I believe are, adopted with a view to ingratiate himself with the Administration....[437]

Throughout the trial of Justice Chase, Senator Plumer expected Chase to be found guilty and anticipated that Jefferson and his followers would attempt to remove all Federalist judges, particularly those on the Supreme Court. In a letter to Jeremiah Mason on January 14, 1805, Plumer wrote: "The judges of the Supreme Court must fall. They are denounced by the Executive as well as the House.... Men of more flexible nerves can be found to succeed them."[438]

The Impeachment trial convened on February 4, 1805. Justice Samuel Chase provided a lengthy and well-prepared answer to each Article of Impeachment. He denied that any actions charged in the Articles of Impeachment rose to a violation of law or common law (high crimes or misdemeanors), a requirement that Chase and his attorney's insisted upon.[439] More than fifty witnesses presented testimony during the impeachment trial. Testimony commenced on February 9, 1805, and concluded on February 20, 1805.[440]

The Senate reconvened on March 1, 1805 to decide Justice Chase's fate. All thirty-four Senators were present. To emphasize the importance of the impeachment trial, Senator Uriah Tracy of Connecticut was present; he was so ill that it was necessary to carry him into the Senate Chamber on a couch. He was barely able to move from the couch to seats assigned for Senators.[441]

Vice President Burr, as President of the Senate, commenced the vote on each Article of Impeachment: two-thirds majority vote (twenty-three votes) was necessary to convict for impeachment:

Article I: sixteen guilty, eighteen not guilty.

Article II: ten guilty, twenty-four not guilty.

Article III: eighteen guilty, sixteen not guilty.

Article IV: eighteen guilty, sixteen not guilty.

Article V: Zero guilty, thirty-four not guilty.

Article VI: four guilty, thirty not guilty.

Article VII: ten guilty, twenty-four not guilty.

---

437 *Memorandum of Proceedings,* January 2, 1805, pp. 238-239.
438 Turner. *William Plumer of New Hampshire, 1759-1850,* p. 155.
439 Trial transcript, pp. 23-103.
440 Beveridge III, pp. 189-196; Chase trial, Volume 1, pp. 127—319.
441 *Memorandum of Proceedings,* March 1, 1805, p. 308; Beveridge III, p. 217.

Article VIII: nineteen guilty, fifteen not guilty.[442]

Vice President Burr, after announcing the vote, stated: "It appears there is not a constitutional majority of votes finding Samuel Chase, Esquire, guilty, on any one Article. It therefore becomes my duty to declare that Samuel Chase, Esquire, stands acquitted of all the Articles exhibited by the House of Representatives against him." The impeachment trial concluded.[443] John Randolph, incensed after Justice Chase was acquitted, immediately returned to the House of Representatives and offered a Constitutional Amendment authorizing removal of Federal judges by the President on joint address of both Houses of Congress. Representative Nicholson later moved that the House amend the Constitution so that state legislatures could recall Senators from office. Both measures went nowhere.[444]

CONCLUSION

What was the result of the failed attempt to impeach Justice Chase? First, attacks on Federalist judges subsided and impeachment was never again attempted. Federalist judges did receive a message; they were less opinionated in Court proceedings, counsel and witnesses were treated with greater respect, and judges avoided political activity outside the courtroom. Most importantly, the frontal attack on the judiciary had been repelled; the war against the judiciary was lost.

Following trial, Senator John Quincy Adams wrote:

> As I was coming home, Mr. Cocke [Senator from Tennessee], walked with me part of the way and spoke with much severity of Mr. Randolph and his conduct upon this impeachment, and various other subjects; charged him with excessive vanity, ambition, insolence, and even dishonesty, which he exemplified by the mis-recital of Virginia law referred to in the fifth article of the impeachment, which he said must have been intentional. He told me that he had always been very sorry that this impeachment was brought forward, and though, when compelled to vote, his judgment had been as un-

---

442 President Jefferson was interested in the outcome of Justice Chase's impeachment trial. *The Thomas Jefferson Papers*, Library of Congress, digital. A list found in the Thomas Jefferson Papers indicates how Senator's voted on each of the eight Articles of Impeachment. In addition, there is a list showing the number of "yes" and "no" votes cast by each Senator. For example, Senator Breckinridge voted "yes" on seven of the eight Articles; Senator Giles "yes" on four of eight Articles; Senators Adams and Plumer voted "no" on all eight Articles.
443 Trial Transcript, pp. 492-493.
444 Beveridge III, pp. 220-221.

favorable to Mr. Chase as that of any member of the court, he was heartily glad of his acquittal, which it appeared to him would have a tendency to mitigate the irritation of party spirit. He said that Mr. Randolph had boasted with great exultation that this was *his* impeachment—that every article was drawn by *his* hand, and that *he* was to have the whole merit of it; though, if the facts were so, it was not a very glorious feat for a young man to plume himself upon; for the undertaking to ruin the reputation and fortune of an old public servant, who had long possessed the confidence of his country, might be excusable, but was no subject to boast of.[445]

Senator Plumer opined:

"The removal of Judge Chase was deemed an imprudent measure—public opinion so far as it could be collected was decidedly opposed to the measure. In this case a great point is gained in favor of the Constitution. A prosecution commenced with the rage of party has been arrested—& to the honor of the Accused his political foes, his enemies have acquitted him."[446] Years later, Plumer had not changed his opinion about impeachment: "Though I considered Judge Chase as having, in a few instances, been guilty of intemperate feelings & language, & if imprudence not becoming the character of a judge, yet I did not in any instance consider them of such a nature as ought to have prevented me from voting for his appointment as a judge, much less to remove him on impeachment, & being satisfied he was not guilty of high crimes & misdemeanors as charged, my vote on each article was *not guilty*. The propriety of these votes I have never seen cause to question."[447]

Senator Adams recorded his thoughts about this session of Congress:

Thus has terminated the second session of the Eighth Congress; the most remarkable transaction of which has been the trial of the impeachment of against Samuel Chase. This is a subject fruitful of reflections, but their place is not here. I shall only remark that this was a party prosecution, and has issued in the unexpected and total disappointment of those by whom it was brought forward. It has exhibited the Senate of the United States fulfilling the most important purpose of its institution, by putting a check upon the impetuous violence of the House of Representatives. It has proved that a sense of justice is yet strong enough to overpower the furies of faction; but it has, at the same time, shown the wisdom and necessity of that provision of the Constitution which requires the concurrence

---

445 *Memoirs of John Quincy Adams*, March 1, 1805, p. 364.

446 *Memorandum of Proceedings*, March 2, 1805, pp. 311-312.

447 Plumer's *Autobiography*, p.146; Lynn W. Turner. *William Plumer of New Hampshire, 1759-1850*, pp. 156-157.

of two-thirds for conviction upon impeachments. The attack upon Mr. Chase was a systematic attempt upon the independence and powers of the Judicial Department, and at the same time an attempt to prostrate the authority of the National Government before those of individual states. The principles first started in the case of Judge Pickering, at the last session, have on the present occasion widened and improved upon to an extent for which the party itself was not prepared. Hence, besides the federal members, six of the twenty-five devoted to the present administration voted for the acquittal of Judge Chase on all the charges, and have for a time arrested the career of political frenzy....[448]

Historian Henry Adams later opined about Judge Chase's acquittal:

> [I]mpeachment was a scarecrow; but its effect on impeachment as a principle of law was less evident. No point was decided ... but although the acquittal of Chase decided no point of law except his innocence of high crimes or misdemeanors, as charged in the indictment, it proved impeachment to be "an impracticable thing" for partisan purposes, and it decided the permanence of those lines of Constitutional development which were a reflection of the common law. Henceforward, the legal profession had its own way of expanding the principles and expanding the powers of the central government through the Judiciary.[449]

After the failed impeachment of Justice Chase, Thomas Jefferson never again attempted impeachment. In a letter to Senator William Branch Giles during the Burr trial, he opined: "For impeachment is a farce which will not be tried again...." After he left the presidency, in several letters, he wrote critically about impeachment. For instance, to Judge Spencer Roane: "Impeachment is not ... even a scarecrow..." Later, he wrote Thomas Ritchie: "Having found, from experience, that impeachment is an impracticable thing, a mere scare-crow, they consider themselves secure for life...." In 1821, Jefferson wrote: "Impeachment therefore is a bugbear which they [judiciary] fear not at all..."[450]

---

448 *Memoirs of John Quincy Adams*, pp. 370-372.
449 Adams *History*, pp. 466-467.
450 Thomas Jefferson to William Branch Giles, April 20, 1807; Thomas Jefferson to Spencer Roane, September 6, 1819; Thomas Jefferson to Thomas Ritchie, December 25, 1820; Thomas Jefferson to James Pleasants, December 26, 1821. *Works* 10, pp. 383-388; *Works* 12, pp. 135-140; 175-179; 213-217.

15. JOHN MARSHALL'S OPINION

The testimony had concluded and counsel presented their arguments to the Court. It now fell upon Chief Justice Marshall to not only define and clarify the law of treason, but to address the province of the court and the jury as to the law and facts. Should the Court be a mere figurehead in the jury trial or was it for the judge to determine and define the law and the jury to then determine the facts and apply the law as charged by the court?

On August 31, 1807, Chief Justice Marshall delivered his opinion, consisting of more than 2,500 words. In this opinion, he cited more legal authority than he did in most of his opinions. This was one of Marshall's greatest opinions. Not only did it set the standard for the law of treason for years to come, but was delivered with great courage. The opinion took more than four hours to read.

Marshall was confronted with multiple problems. If he found that an "overt act" had not been committed by the defendant, the loose wording employed in the earlier Supreme Court decision of *United States v. Bollman and Swartwout* must be addressed and clarified. Just as importantly, an opinion adverse to the government would subject Chief Justice Marshall and the judiciary to the wrath of President Jefferson and his supporters, perhaps provoking the Administration and its followers to seek impeachment. The less controversial course, of course, would be for the Court to allow the case and testimony to proceed, permit the prosecution to present all its evidence, and charge the jury with the responsibility to determine Burr's guilt or innocence. To so rule, however, would not have been the proper decision. Chief Justice Marshall was never afraid to make a controversial ruling; he never shirked from his responsibility by taking the easy way—Chief Justice Marshall attempted to do right as he saw it.[451]

Typical of the Chief Justice, he commenced his opinion by graciously praising counsel: "The question now to be decided has been argued in a manner worthy of its importance, and with an earnestness evincing the strong conviction felt by the counsel on each side that the law is with them. A degree of eloquence seldom displayed on any occasion has embellished a solidity of argument and depth of research by which the Court has been greatly aided in forming the opinion it is about to deliver."

Marshall first identified the question before the Court; must the defendant be present at the time the alleged conspiracy was committed:

> The testimony adduced on the part of the United States, to prove the overt act laid in the indictment, having shown, and the attorney for the United States having admitted, that the prisoner was not present when that act, whatever may be its character, was committed, and there being no reason to doubt but that he was at a great distance and in a different state, it is objected to the testimony offered on the part of the United States, to connect him with those who committed the overt act, that such testimony is totally irrelevant and must therefore be rejected.

The Court made two points:

> "1st. That conformably to the Constitution of the United States, no man can be convicted of treason who was not present when the war was levied. 2nd. That if this construction be erroneous, no testimony can be received to charge one man with the overt acts of others, until those overt acts as laid in the indictment be proved to the satisfaction of the court."

Chief Justice Marshall then proceeded to review English legal authority that defined the term "levying of war", although the Court was not persuaded that English law was binding when applied to the crime of treason defined by the Constitution of the United States. Marshall reviewed the Constitutional definition of treason at length and found that the indictment brought against Burr was faulty. Marshall opined that Burr had not been given proper notice of facts as required by the Sixth Amendment, since the government fictionally placed Burr on Blennerhassett's Island, the scene of the alleged conspiracy. During trial, the prosecution admitted that Burr was

---

451 Newmyer, pp. 199-202.

not present on Blennerhassett's Island at the time alleged in the Indictment. Therefore, the indictment did not adequately permit Burr to defend himself.

The Chief Justice then addressed the earlier Supreme Court decision in *United States v. Bollman and Swartwout*, attempting to clarify that decision:

> It may now be proper to notice the opinion of the Supreme Court in the case of the *United States against Bollman and Swartwout*. It is said that this opinion in declaring that those who do not bear arms may yet be guilty of treason, is contrary to law, and is not obligatory, because it is extrajudicial, and was delivered on a point not argued. This Court is therefore required to depart from the principle there laid down...

> The Court had employed some reasoning to show that without the actual embodying of men war could not be levied. It might have been inferred from this, that those only who were so embodied could be guilty of treason. Not only to exclude this inference, but also to affirm the contrary, the Court proceeded to observe, "It is not the intention of the Court to say that no individual can be guilty of this crime who has not appeared in arms against his country. On the contrary, if war be actually levied, that is, if a body of men be actually assembled for the purpose of effecting by force a treasonable object, all those who perform any part, however minute, or however remote from the scene of action, and who are actually leagued in the general conspiracy, are to be considered as traitors."

> This Court is told that if this opinion be incorrect it ought not to be obeyed, because it was extrajudicial. For myself, I can say that I could not lightly be prevailed on to disobey it, were I even convinced that it was erroneous; but I would certainly use any means which the law placed in my power to carry the question again before the Supreme Court for reconsideration, in a case in which it would directly occur and be fully argued.

Chief Justice Marshall explained how the earlier opinion had been formulated by the Court:

> The Court which gave this opinion was composed of four judges. At the time I thought them unanimous, but I have since had reason to suspect that one of them, whose opinion is entitled to great respect, and whose indisposition prevented his entering into the discussions, on some of those points which were not essential to the decision of the very case under consideration, did not concur in this particular point with his brethren. Had the opinion been unanimous, it would have been given by a majority of the judges. But should the three who were absent concur with that the judge who was present and who perhaps dissents from what was then the opinion of the Court, a majority of the judges may overrule this decision. I should therefore feel no objection, although I then thought, and still think

the opinion perfectly correct, to carry the point if possible again be-fore the Supreme Court, if the case should depend upon it.

In saying that I still think the opinion perfectly correct, I do not consider myself as going further than the preceding reasoning goes. Some gentlemen have argued as if the Supreme Court had adopted the whole doctrine of the English books on the subject of accesso-ries to treason. But certainly such is not the fact. Those only who perform a part, and who are leagued in the conspiracy are declared to be traitors. To complete the definition both circumstances must concur. They must "perform a part," which will furnish the overt act, and they must be "leagued in the conspiracy." The person who comes within this description, in the opinion of the court levies war. The present motion, however, does not rest upon this point; for, if under this indictment, the United States might be let in to prove the part performed by the prisoner, if he did perform any part, the court could not stop the testimony in its present stage.

Marshall explained how the evidence presented by the prosecution did not meet the requirements for treason as defined by the Constitution. Under English law, Aaron Burr's actions may have been treason; not so under United States law.

After distinguishing *United States v. Bollman and Swartwout*, Chief Justice Marshall referred to his first Burr opinion (April 1, 1807):

[T]he same testimony was offered with that which had been ex-hibited before the Supreme Court, and was required to give an opin-ion in almost the same case. Upon this occasion he said, "War can only be levied by the employment of actual force. Troops must be embodied; men must be assembled in order to levy war." Again he observed, "... the fact to be proved in this case is an act of public notoriety. It must exist in the view of the world or it cannot exist at all. The assembling of forces to levy war is a visible transaction, and numbers must witness it".

It is not easy to doubt what kind of assemblage was in the mind of the judge who used these expressions, and it is to be recollected that he had just returned from the Supreme Court and was speaking on the very facts on which the opinion of that Court was delivered.

The same judge in this charge to the Grand Jury who found this bill, observed, "to constitute the fact of levying war, it is not nec-essary that hostilities shall have actually commenced by engaging the military force of the U.S. or that measures of violence against the government shall have been carried into execution. But levying war is a fact in the Constitution of which force is an indispensable ingredient. Any combination to subvert by force the government of the U.S. violently to dismember the union, to compel a change in the administration, to coerce the repeal or adoption of a general law, is a conspiracy to levy war, and if the conspiracy be carried into effect by the actual employment of force, by the embodying and assembling of men for the purpose of executing the treasonable design which was previously conceived, it amounts to levying of war. It has been held that arms are not essential to levying war provided the force assembled be sufficient to attain, or perhaps to justify attempting the object without them." This paragraph is immediately followed by a reference to the opinion of the Supreme Court.

The Chief Justice explained that in order for a participant to be charged with treason, that person must have been part of the conspiracy and war must actually have been levied in order for conspirators not present to be indicted. He further stated that although these conspirators could be indicted, it was not settled law that they are guilty of treason.

Marshall addressed evidence presented by the Prosecution against Aaron Burr:

> It is then the opinion of the Court that this indictment can be supported only by testimony which proves the accused to have been actually or constructively present when the assemblage took place on Blennerhassett's Island, or by the admission of the doctrine that he who procures an act may be indicted as having performed that act.

> It is further the opinion of the Court that there is no testimony whatever which tends to prove that the accused was actually or constructively present when that assemblage did take place. Indeed the contrary is most apparent. With respect to admitting proof of procurement to establish a charge of actual presence, the Court is of opinion that if this be admissible in England on an indictment for levying war, which is far from being conceded, it is admissible only by virtue of the operation of the common law upon the statute, and therefore, is not admissible in this country unless by virtue of a similar operation; a point far from being established, but on which, for the present, no opinion is given. If, however this point be established, still the procurement must be proved in the same manner and by the same kind of testimony which would be required to prove actual presence.

In the most famous passage in his opinion, Chief Justice Marshall directly addressed Prosecutor Hay's threat of impeachment. Although anticipating that his opinion would be criticized, Chief Justice Marshall professed that he had done his duty:

> Much has been said in the course of the argument on points, on which the Court feels no inclination to comment particularly, but which may, perhaps not improperly, receive some notice.

> That this Court dares not usurp power is most true.

That this Court dares not shrink from its duty is not less true.

No man is desirous of placing himself in a disagreeable situation. No man is desirous of becoming the peculiar subject of calumny. No man, might he let the bitter cup pass from him without self-reproach, would drain it to the bottom. But if he has no choice in the case; if there is no alternative presented to him but a dereliction of duty or the opprobrium of those who are denominated the world, he merits the contempt as well as the indignation of his country who can hesitate which to embrace.

That gentlemen, in a case the utmost interesting, in the zeal with which they advocate particular opinions, & under the conviction in some measure produced by that zeal, should on each side press their arguments too far, should be impatient at any deliberation in the Court, and should suspect or fear the operation of motives to which alone they can ascribe that deliberation, is perhaps a frailty incident to human nature; but if any conduct on the part of the Court could warrant a sentiment that they would deviate to the one side or the other from that line prescribed by duty and by law, that conduct would be viewed by the judges themselves with an eye of extreme severity, and would long be recollected with deep and serious regret.

Chief Justice Marshall concluded:

The arguments on both sides have been intently and deliberately considered. Those which could not be noticed, since to notice every argument and authority would swell this opinion to a volume, have not been disregarded. The result of the whole is a conviction as complete as the mind of the court is capable of receiving on a complex subject, that the motion must prevail.

No testimony relative to the conduct or deliberations of the prisoner elsewhere or subsequent to the transaction on Blennerhassett's Island can be admitted, because such testimony, being in its nature merely corroborative, and incompetent to prove the overt act itself, is irrelevant, until there is proof of the overt act by two witnesses.

This opinion does not comprehend the proof of two witnesses that the meeting on Blennerhassett's Island was procured by the prisoner. On that point the Court, for the present, withholds its opinion for reasons which have already been assigned; and as it is understood from the statements made on the part of the prosecution that no such testimony exists. If there be such let it be offered and the Court will decide upon it.

The Court had decided the motion in favor of the defense. The prosecution could not present additional witnesses unless it offered competent evidence to establish an overt act of treason. Chief Justice Marshall charged the jury:

> The jury have now heard the opinion of the Court on the law of the case. They will apply the law to the facts, and will find a verdict of guilty or not guilty as their own consciences may direct.
>
> It is true, that although no further testimony be offered, yet, it is in the power of the Jury to find its verdict of *guilty* or *not guilty*. The Court have given its opinion; it has said, that yet, if the Jury can satisfy themselves of the guilt of the prisoner, by the evidence of two witnesses, they have the right to find a verdict of *guilty*. The Court have done its duty; and it is for the Jury to do theirs.[452]

ACQUITTAL

After Chief Justice Marshall concluded, Prosecutor Hay requested additional time to review the Court's ruling. The next day, Hay informed the Court that the prosecution had no further evidence to present. Marshall then sent the case to the jury. The jury deliberated for a brief time and returned a verdict of not guilty, although the form of the verdict was irregular: "We of the jury say that Aaron Burr is not proved to be guilty under the indictment by any evidence submitted to us. We therefore find him not guilty." Although Burr objected to the form of the verdict, Marshall permitted the verdict to stand, considering this a "not guilty" verdict.[453]

On the same day the jury returned it's "not guilty" verdict, United States Attorney Hay wrote President Jefferson:

> The papers, I presume, have already informed you of the motion to stop the examination of the witnesses against Burr. The Court yesterday pronounced its opinion, and has decided that no further evidence shall be received. They expressly declared that the transactions and assemblage at Blennerhassett's Island, did not amount to an overt act of levying war. This decision protects the whole party from a prosecution for treason in the State of Virginia. What course we shall now pursue is the subject of our deliberations: the question is whether we shall proceed to the trial of the misdemeanor, or move for his commitment for treason at the mouth of Cumberland, and his transmission to Kentucky for trial.–We must decide in an hour if the latter course is adopted, the prosecution for the misdemeanor must be abandoned.

---

452 *PJM* VII, pp. 74-116. The preceding paragraphs of Chief Justice Marshall's opinion may be found at these pages.

453 *PJM* VII, pp. 118-119, n. 68; Robertson II, pp. 495-552.

The opinion of the Chief Justice is too voluminous to be generally read, and on the great question about the overt act of levying war was too obscure and perplexed to be understood. The explanation of the opinion of the Supreme Court in the case of *Bollman and Swartwout*, renders it very difficult to comprehend what was before perfectly intelligible.–If I can find time, I will lay before the public, an exposition of the principle, relied on in opposition to the motion, which every man who can read shall understand.

Wirt is sick, my strength and flesh are declining, and every body almost complains except Luther Martin. His speech lasted 14 hours, and does not appear to have had the slightest effect even in his voice.–I believe that the Judge by cutting off all the trials for treason has saved my life.[454]

After the jury's verdict, defense attorney William Wirt was reportedly asked: "Why did you not tell Judge Marshall that the people of America demanded a conviction?" "Tell *him* that!" replied Wirt. "I would as soon have gone to Herschel and told him that the people of America insisted that the moon had horns as a reason why he should draw her with them." William Wirt later opined that Chief Justice Marshall "stepped in between Burr and death."[455]

ANALYSIS OF CHIEF JUSTICE MARSHALL'S OPINION

The Burr trial has often been portrayed as a battle between President Jefferson and Chief Justice Marshall. From a legal perspective, the Chief Justice strictly construed the criminal law and protected the Constitutional rights of the accused. There is little question that Marshall's opinion on the law of treason was consistent with the intent of the Constitution. A loose definition of treason was never intended by the Framers of the Constitution and would not be permitted in John Marshall's courtroom.

Historian Edward S. Corwin years ago suggested that Chief Justice Marshall's opinion was an example of how Marshall delighted in embarrassing President Jefferson. Corwin believed that Marshall permitted political bias rather than legal principle to decide the Burr case:

Marshall's conduct of Burr's trial for treason is the one serious blemish in his judicial record, but for all that it was not without a measure of extenuation. The President, too, had behaved deplorably and, feeling himself on the defensive, had pressed matters with

---

454 George Hay to Thomas Jefferson, September 1, 1807. *The Thomas Jefferson Papers*, Library of Congress digital. American Memory.
455 Beveridge III, p. 517.

unseemly zeal, so that the charge of political persecution raised by Burr's attorneys was, to say the least, not groundless. Furthermore, in opposing the President in this matter, Marshall had shown his usual political sagacity. Had Burr been convicted, the advantage must have all gone to the Administration. The only possible credit the Chief Justice could extract from the case would be from assuming that lofty tone of calm, unmoved impartiality of which Marshall was such a master—and never more than on this occasion—and from setting himself sternly against popular hysteria....[456]

Interestingly, Professor Corwin never suggested that Burr was guilty or should have been found guilty.

Since 1919, after Corwin criticized this opinion and suggested it was the low point of Marshall's judicial career, many historians and Constitutional law authorities followed Corwin's lead. More recently, however, scholars have taken issue with Professor Corwin's opinion. Professor Robert K. Faulkner wrote convincingly that Marshall's opinion was governed by the necessity for strict construction of the treason clause in the Constitution. Strict construction of treason, the only crime defined in the Constitution, is exactly what the Framers intended. Faulkner submitted that if Marshall intended to embarrass Jefferson, this was hardly the case for him to do so. The public was opposed to Burr; Marshall himself had no use for traitors; and, immediately after trial, it was Marshall, not Jefferson, who received criticism.[457]

Historian Henry Adams offered this insight into Marshall's ruling:

> [T]his paper seemed, in the imagination of Marshall's enemies, to betray a painful effort to reconcile the dictum in Bollman's case with the exclusion of further evidence in the case of Burr. To laymen, who knew only the uncertainties of law; who thought that the assemblage on Blennerhassett's Island was such an overt act as might, without violent impropriety, be held by a jury to be an act of levying war; and who conceived that Burr, although absent from the spot, was as principal present in a legal sense such as would excuse a jury in finding him guilty,—an uneasy doubt could not fail to suggest itself that the chief justice, with an equal effort of ingenuity, might have produced equal conviction in a directly opposite result. On the other hand, the intent of the Constitution was clear. The men who framed that instrument remembered the crimes that had been perpetrated under the pretense of justice; for the most part they

---

456 Edward S. Corwin. *John Marshall and the Constitution: The Chronicle of the Supreme Court*, pp. 111-112.

457 Robert Kenneth Faulkner. *The Jurisprudence of John Marshall*; see also, Bradley Chapin. *The American Law of Treason: Revolutionary and Early National Origins*, pp. 109-113; James Willard Hurst. *The Law of Treason in the United States.*.

had been traitors themselves; and having risked their necks under the law they feared despotism and arbitrary power more than they feared treason. No one could doubt that their sympathies, at least in 1788, when the Constitution was framed, would have been on the side of Marshall's decision. If Jefferson, since 1788, had changed his point of view, the chief justice was not under obligations to imitate him.[458]

458 Henry Adams. *History of the United States During the Administrations of Thomas Jefferson*, p. 925.

16. FURTHER PROCEEDINGS

Everyone was exhausted, particularly the prosecution. The day after Burr's acquittal, Hay requested the Court to conduct a hearing to determine whether Burr and his co-defendants committed an act of treason outside the jurisdiction of the Court and if so, to commit them for trial in the appropriate jurisdiction. Even though Burr had been acquitted in Virginia, the prosecution was considering whether to bring treason charges in another Federal Court. Since Burr was still under indictment for violation of the Neutrality Act, the Court ruled that the misdemeanor charge must first be resolved. The Court reduced Burr's bond from $10,000 to $5,000.[459]

Burr renewed his request for documents in possession of the government. Among other things, Burr again requested a letter from General Wilkinson to the President that had not yet been provided. Prosecutor Hay acknowledged possession of the letter and invoked executive privilege. The Court ordered a subpoena *duces tecum* served on Hay to produce the letter. Hay advised that he would produce only that portion of the letter he deemed relevant. The defense moved for postponement of the misdemeanor trial until the letter was produced. After argument, the Court ruled that although executive privilege may be a valid reason to withhold a document, the President must invoke the privilege, not the District Attorney. Further, when a claim of executive privilege is asserted, the President must specify the exact parts of the document that he deems privileged and provide ex-

---

459 *PJM* VII, pp. 119-23.

planation for its exclusion. The Court was reluctant to refuse production of any relevant document to the defendant. Marshall ordered the defendant and his attorneys, upon receipt of the letter, to not make it public; at the appropriate time the Court would consider and rule on the claim of executive privilege.[460]

On September 4, President Jefferson provided new instructions to the prosecution:

> Yours of the 1st came to hand yesterday. The event has been what was evidently intended from the beginning of the trial, that is to say, not only to clear Burr, but to prevent the evidence from ever going before the world. But this latter must not take place. It is now, therefore, more than ever indispensable, that not a single witness be paid or permitted to depart until his testimony has been committed to writing, either as delivered in Court, or as taken by yourself in the presence of any of Burr's counsel, who may choose to attend to cross-examination. *These whole proceedings will be laid before Congress, so that they may decide, whether the defect has been in the evidence of guilt, or in the law, or in the application of the law, and that they may provide the proper remedy for the past and the future.* I must pray you also to have an authentic copy made out (without saying for what) and to send it to me; if the Judge's opinions make out a part of it, then I must ask a copy of them, either under his hand, if he delivers one signed, or duly proved by affidavit.
>
> The criminal is preserved to become the rallying point of all the disaffected and the worthless of the United States, and to be the pivot on which all the intrigues and the conspiracies which foreign governments may wish to disturb us with, are to turn. If he is convicted of the misdemeanor, the Judge must in decency give us respite by some short confinement of him; but we must expect it to be short. Be assured yourself, and communicate the same assurance to your colleagues, that your and their zeal and abilities have been displayed in this affair to my entire satisfaction and your honor.[461] [Emphasis added.]

The next day, Hay wrote to President Jefferson about the most recent subpoena *duces tecum*, among other matters:

> Enclosed you will receive a subpoena *duces tecum*, and the letter of 12 Nov. 1806 which it requires. A subpoena was served on me yesterday, upon which I made the return stated in the 3rd Col: of the 3rd page of the enclosed gazette. I amended that return this day, by stating that there were other passages in the letter, exclusively of a public nature, which I did not think ought to be disclosed, and which I conceived you would not disclose. The parts with a black

---

460 *PJM* VII, pp. 123-28.
461 Thomas Jefferson to George Hay, September 4, 1807. *Works* X, pp. 360-361.

line under them are the parts omitted in the copy accompanying the return but not yet filed.

I sent Bob up expressly for the purpose of procuring your return to the subpoena, with such parts of the letter, as you may think proper to communicate.–The newspaper does not give a correct idea of the Judges opinion. He stated very distinctly that whatever rights the President of the United States might have to withhold parts of the letter that right could not be delegated, and seemed to think that any return from the President himself would be sufficient. But upon this point he was far from being explicit, and it is impossible to foresee what will be the state of his nerves. Wirt, who has hitherto advocated the integrity of the Chief Justice, now abandons him. This last opinion has opened his eyes, and he speaks in the strongest terms of reprobation.

I acknowledge to you Sir that I am very decidedly of the opinion that these prosecutions will terminate in nothing. Burr is discharged from the treason, Dayton is also released, and Blennerhassett and Smith must under the opinion of the Court be acquitted of the treason charge in the present indictment. I shall therefore enter a *Nolle Prosequi* [voluntary dismissal without prejudice] as to them and move for their commitment and transmission to Kentucky, or Tennessee, or the Western territory as the case may be. But the misdemeanor must be first disposed of. I have no doubt from intimations dropped by the Court, that we shall be defeated there too. I am of opinion therefore that I would be well to dismiss these indictments, and move for the commitment of Burr, Blennerhassett, and Smith. Will you be pleased to instruct me especially on this point.–I write in great haste, because I wish to dispatch the Express as soon as possible, and because the oppression which continued labor has produced is greatly aggravated by an increasing influenza.[462]

Two days later, Hay again wrote Jefferson:

By the northern mail of this afternoon I received your letter of the 4th inst. Your directions with respect to the evidence shall be obeyed. If the testimony is not delivered in Court, I will do whatever is practicable to obtain the affidavits of the witnesses. There are some who will not, I am persuaded, communicate what they know except in Court...This however is not much to be regretted: men who are base enough to unite in so vile a confederacy will not speak truth.—

A printed copy of the opinion of the Chief Justice, will, I presume be sufficient, if accompanied by an affidavit from the Editor that it was taken from the original manuscript furnished by the Chief Justice himself, and that the proof sheets were corrected by him.

---

462 George Hay to Thomas Jefferson, September 5, 1807. *The Thomas Jefferson Papers,* Library of Congress digital. American Memory.

Your acknowledgment that my colleagues and myself have done our duty is highly grateful to my feelings: to theirs, when communicated, it will be equally acceptable. But my duty is not yet ended. The late decision presents to the United States, several subjects, entitled to the most serious consideration. It is time that we should know whether the Common Law of England is in force under the Government of the United States or not. Upon this point the Chief Justice expressly declares that he gives no opinion, and then very deliberately proceeds to resort to the common law, as the substratum (to use his own word) of his argument and decision. When this discussion is terminated, the regularity of the motion to amend the evidence may be effectually controverted, and his opinions, especially on the three last points stated by himself, clearly refuted. If my health will permit, and time can be *taken* (from business almost ruined by the preposterous length of this prosecution), I will endeavor to make a few remarks on these topics, in language, which every man, who can read, shall understand.–What I shall say will be intended for the people. Men of information will fully comprehend the subject, (perhaps) from the arguments which preceded the decision.[463]

Jefferson wrote two letters to Hay on September 7:

I received, late last night, your favor of the day before, and now re-enclose the subpoena. As I do not believe that the district courts have a power of commanding the executive government to abandon superior duties & attend on them, at whatever distance, I am unwilling, by any notice of the subpoena, to set a precedent which might sanction a proceeding so preposterous. I enclose you, therefore, a letter, public & for the court, covering substantially all they ought to desire. If the papers which were enclosed in Wilkinson's letter may, in your judgment be communicated without injury, you will be pleased to communicate them. I return your original letter.

I am happy in having the benefit of Mr. Madison's counsel on this occasion, he happening to be now with me. We are both strongly of opinion that the prosecution against Burr for misdemeanor should proceed at Richmond. If defeated, it will heap coals of fire on the head of the Judge; if convicted, it will give time to see whether a prosecution for treason against him can be instituted in any, and what other court. But we incline to think, it may be best to send Blennerhassett & Smith (Israel) to Kentucky, to be tried for the treason & misdemeanor. The trial of Dayton for misdemeanor may as well go on in Richmond.[464]

---

463 George Hay to Thomas Jefferson, September 7, 1807. *The Thomas Jefferson Papers*, Library of Congress digital. American Memory.
464 Thomas Jefferson to George Hay, September 7, 1807. *Works* X, pp. 408-409.

In his second letter, Jefferson wrote: "Understanding that it is thought important that a letter of Nov. 12, 1806, from General Wilkinson to myself, should be produced in evidence on the charges against Aaron Burr, depending in the District Court now sitting in Richmond, I send you a copy of it, omitting only certain passages, the nature of which is explained in the certificate subjoined to this letter. As the attorney for the United States, be pleased to submit the copy & certificate to the uses of the Court..." The enclosed certificate read:

> On re-examination of the letter of Nov. 12, 1806, from General Wilkinson to myself, (which having been for a considerable time out of my possession, and now returned to me) I find in it some passages entirely confidential, given for my information in the discharge of my executive functions, and which my duties & the public interest forbid me to make public. I have therefore given above a correct copy of those parts which I ought to permit to be made public. Those not communicated are in nowise material for the purposes of justice on the charges of treason or misdemeanor depending against Aaron Burr; they are on subjects irrelevant to any issues which can arise out of those charges & could contribute nothing towards his acquittal or conviction. The papers mentioned in the 1st & 3rd paragraphs, as enclosed in the letters, being separated there from & not in my possession, I am unable, from memory, to say what they were, I presume they are in the hands of the attorney for the U.S....[465]

Misdemeanor Trial

Burr's trial for violation of the Neutrality Act commenced in Chief Justice Marshall's Court on September 9, 1807. The Neutrality Act provided, in pertinent part:

> That if any person shall within the territory or jurisdiction of the United States begin or set foot or provide or prepare the means for any military expedition or enterprise to be carried on from thence against the territory or dominions of any foreign prince or state with whom the United States is at peace, every such person so offending shall upon conviction be adjudged guilty of a high misdemeanor and shall suffer fine and imprisonment at the discretion of the court in which the conviction shall be had, so as that such fine shall not exceed three thousand dollars nor the term of imprisonment be more than three years.[466]

When the prosecution called its first witness, Richard Niel, Burr's attorneys immediately objected. The objection centered on a conversation

465 Thomas Jefferson to George Hay, September 7, 1807. *Works* X, p.409.
466 United States Statutes at Large, Volume I, Third Congress, Session I, p. 384.

between Niel and Blennerhassett which the defense argued was hearsay. Chief Justice Marshall declared that Niel's testimony was hearsay, finding that declarations of third persons not part of the transaction or made in the presence of the accused are inadmissible. Although the law of conspiracy provided an exception to the hearsay rule, the Indictment did not charge conspiracy. The Court opined:

> That the acts of accomplices, except so far as they prove the character or object of the expedition, cannot be given into evidence.

> That the acts of the accused in a different district which constitute in themselves substantive causes for a prosecution cannot be given in evidence unless they go directly to prove the charges laid in the indictment.

> That any legal testimony which shows the expedition to be military or to have been designed against the dominions of Spain may be received.[467]

The prosecution next called James McDowell. Burr objected to his testimony and Chief Justice Marshall clarified his earlier opinion on proof necessary to establish the crime of treason:

> The question then is, whether the means were *provided* or not on Blennerhassett's Island. If there be any testimony that will go to prove this, I certainly am not at liberty to refuse it. But gentlemen will consider whether they are not wasting the time and money of the United States, and of all those persons who are forced to attend here, whilst they are producing such a mass of testimony which does not bear upon the cause....

> Any arguments on the principle which was stated, that the testimony respecting means provided elsewhere, supporting this charge, I am willing to hear. If the opinion of the Court before given can be proved to be erroneous, I shall be happy to hear it pointed out, because I wish to be as correct as possible: but if these principles are not erroneous why do gentlemen bring witnesses forward in direct opposition to them? I can ascribe no other reason to it, than because the law does not give definite ideas on the subject of its own provisions.

> The truth is, the words of the law must be taken to retrospect to the origination of the plan. For instance, General Eaton states that in Washington the accused laid before him a certain plan, when he said that he had sufficient means, &c. Now, if those means could be discovered, it certainly shows that the beginning of the expedition

467 *PJM* VII, pp. 128-39.

was in Washington, but the indictment states that it be on Blennerhassett's Island.

Now, unless the fact itself shall be proved, how can there be evidence given of motives, yet undiscovered?[468]

Following this Court's clarification, Hay understood the futility of proceeding with trial and moved to enter a *Nolle Prosequi* (a prosecution motion
to dismiss the case without prejudice—charges could be reinstated at a future time—"we will no longer prosecute"). Burr's attorneys opposed Hay's
motion, since they wanted the case to be decided by a jury verdict; if Burr
was acquitted, as expected, jeopardy would attach and Burr could not then
be recharged for this crime. After Hay presented two additional witnesses,
the case was submitted to the jury. Hay was at his wits' end. He renewed his
request to enter a *Nolle Prosequi*, which was again denied by the Court. After
the case was submitted to the jury, it returned a not guilty verdict within
twenty minutes of submission.[469]

COMMITMENT FOR TREASON IN OTHER JURISDICTIONS

There were no additional charges pending against Burr. The prosecution moved for Burr's commitment for treason for overt acts committed in
other jurisdictions. Burr's attorneys opposed the motion on two grounds:
the Court had no authority to send Burr to another jurisdiction to stand
trial and most importantly, the acquittal of Burr on the two charges served
as a double jeopardy bar to further prosecution. Although Chief Justice
Marshall opined that he was without authority to commit Burr to another
jurisdiction for trial, he was uncertain whether the jury acquittals served as
bars to further proceedings.[470]

The prosecution requested that the Court hear additional testimony
and determine whether there was a jurisdiction within the United States
that may be an appropriate venue to bring further proceedings against Burr.
The prosecution attempted to establish an overt act of treason committed
against the United States, most likely in Kentucky. The defense objected to
relevancy of the testimony. Chief Justice Marshall ruled:

... to attack New Orleans, for the purpose of subverting the government of the United States is *treason*. Also, that a body of men, assembled, and in a condition to execute it, although they have not

468 *PJM* VII, pp. 140-41.
469 *PJM* VII, pp. 141-42.
470 *PJM* VII, pp. 142-47.

executed it actually, is *treason.* The gentlemen in the defense say it is not; the Court says it is treason....

The charge is that this body met together with a design to take New Orleans, and to subvert the government of the United States there. Now it certainly is a proper subject of enquiry, whether this body was adequate to its object or not? To find this, gentlemen must undoubtedly prove the situation in New Orleans. This is certainly a proper step to the enquiry, although this enquiry would prove the particular allegation.[471]

The Chief Justice reluctantly permitted the prosecution to call its witnesses. The prosecution called more than fifty witnesses over the next month in support of its motion to commit. Witnesses not called to testify in the earlier trials for treason and violation of the Neutrality Act now testified in support of the motion. By calling these witnesses to testify under oath, Hay was able to satisfy President Jefferson's request to have the testimony of all assembled witnesses so that he could submit their testimony to Congress.

During these protracted hearings, General Wilkinson finally testified. Wilkinson's testimony commenced on September 26, 1807 and continued intermittently through October 3, 1807. After Wilkinson's poor performance before the Grand Jury together with numerous questions about Wilkinson's credibility and loyalty, the prosecution chose not to call Wilkinson as a witness in the earlier trials.[472] Throughout his testimony, Wilkinson repeatedly contradicted himself and frequently requested permission to retract or amend statements previously made. Upon cross-examination, Wilkinson admitted that he altered parts of the cipher letter in order to protect himself.[473] During Wilkinson's testimony, it was obvious why the prosecution had not called him as a witness in the treason trial. Not only was Wilkinson a poor witness; he could not tell the truth. Wilkinson was as guilty as any of the alleged co-conspirators, including Burr. Wilkinson simply could not to be believed.

After Wilkinson's testimony, Prosecutor Hay wrote President Jefferson:

Gen. Wilkinson said to me the other day, that as soon as he got to Washington, he should solicit an inquiry before a court martial into his conduct. I hope he will do so, and whether he does or not, I hope

---

471 *PJM* VII, pp. 148-49.
472 T. Carpenter. *The Trial of Col. Aaron Burr.* (Short hand of Carpenter), pp. 512-556.
473 Library of Congress digital, American State Papers, Miscellaneous, Volume 1, pp.539-555; 10th Congress, 1st Session.

the inquiry will be initiated. The declaration which I made in Court in his favor some time ago was precipitate: and though I have not retracted it, every body sees that I have not attempted the task which I, in fact, promised to perform. My confidence in him is shaken, if not destroyed. I am sorry for it, on his own account, in the public account, and because you have expressed opinions in his favor. But you did not know then what you will soon know, and what I did not learn until after, long after my declaration above mentioned.

I confess to you, sir, that I cannot entirely conquer the apprehension that you may deem me somewhat presumptuous in making this communication. But it is obvious that I cannot be influenced by any unworthy motive and you will excuse me for saying what I know and facts to be true, that what I have said has been produced by a real regard for the public good, for the national honor, and for your reputation as far as it can depend on the fidelity and truth of those who are honored by an appointment from you.

I certainly do not wish that the fact of my having made this communication should be publicly known, but I am perfectly content that you should state it according to your discretion, and particularly to General Wilkinson himself, if any circumstance shall render it in your judgment proper.[474]

President Jefferson offered his opinion on the Burr trial and Chief Justice Marshall:

Your favor of July 10 came safely to hand and with that the first 72 pages of your view of Burr's trial. I have read this with great satisfaction, and shall be happy to see the whole subject as well digested....

The scenes which have been acting in Richmond are sufficient to fill us with alarm. We had supposed we possessed fixed laws to guard us equally against treason & oppression. But it now appears we have no law but the will of the judge. Never will chicanery have a more difficult task than has now accomplished to warp the text of law to the will of him who is to construe it. Our case is more desperate as to attempt to make the law plainer by amendment is only throwing out new materials for sophistry....[475]

William Thomson, recipient of this letter, later wrote a number of articles in Republican newspapers. The articles served as a frontal attack upon Chief Justice Marshall. Although Jefferson was not directly involved with publication of the "Letters to John Marshall" written by Lucius (Thomson),

---

474 George Hay to Thomas Jefferson, October 15, 1807. *The Thomas Jefferson Papers*, Library of Congress digital. American Memory.
475 Thomas Jefferson to William Thomson, September 26, 1807. *Works X*, pp. 501-502.

Jefferson surely was pleased with their publication. Jefferson was delighted to have Marshall "condemned in the court of public opinion."[476]

Although President Jefferson and his supporters were unhappy with the judiciary and Chief Justice Marshall, there was some support for the Court's actions in the Burr prosecution. The Virginia Gazette, on September 30, 1807, reprinted an article from an earlier edition of the United States Gazette (Philadelphia):

> The prevailing fashion in this country is now to run down the judicial authority and attempt to merge it in that of the executive. If the executive declares that a man is guilty of treason, and afterwards puts him upon his trial before a court and jury, the democrats will not allow that court and jury to do any thing more or less than to confirm the sentence of the executive and the executive the offender. This they consider as maintaining the rights of the people.
>
> While the democratic faction is thus feelingly alive to what they affect to consider as usurpation on the part of the Judiciary, they are perfectly unconcerned at the most enormous and unexampled usurpations on the part of the executive. History will hardly furnish an example of such oppressive tyranny as has been practiced under the administration of Mr. Jefferson towards a number of men who were supposed to be concerned in the schemes of Col. Burr. In England damages have been given to the amount of ten thousand pounds for arresting and detaining a man for a few hours, under a general warrant, issuing from the cabinet of the king. In the United States, and under the administration of Mr. Jefferson, several men have been arrested without any warrant at all; hurried away from their friends under circumstances of the aggravated cruelty and barbarity; forced on board of crazy vessels, and in the winter season transported to the distance of several thousand miles; and after being landed, sent under military escort from one post to another to avoid the process of laws of the country; all this in a time of profound tranquility—and for what? Why, for nothing at all, except for not having the good fortune to be agreeable to Mr. Jefferson and his officers; for upon examination it was found that against some of them the government had not even an accusation to bring, and against none of them were they able to substantiate any charge whatever.
>
> Yet such monstrous usurpation, so destructive of every principle of civil liberty, is not thought worthy of even a comment by those who profess to be the exclusive champions of the rights and liberties of the people.[477]

476 Malone 5, pp. 354-355; *Aurora*, November 21, 25, 28 and December 1, 1807; *Richmond Enquirer*; Beveridge III, pp. 525-26, 533-35.
477 *Virginia Gazette*, September 30, 1807.

Attorney General Rodney wrote Jefferson on October 1, 1807, after the treason and misdemeanor charges had been dismissed against Burr: "The judiciary have been so much elevated above every other department of the government, by the fashion & I may add the folly of the times, that it seems dangerous to question their omnipotence. But the period has arrived when this colossal power, which bestrides the Legislative & Executive authorities, should be reduced to its proper limits...Our counsel at Richmond have acted like men & have acquitted themselves with honor. But it is in vain to struggle against wind & tide. The current on the beach was irresistible... "[478] In this letter Rodney opined that the entire country was convinced of Burr's guilt. On October 8, 1807, Jefferson wrote Rodney and advised him that he looked forward to Rodney's earliest return to Washington since his assistance was needed. In particular, Jefferson required Rodney's assistance for: "The selection & digestion of the documents respecting Burr's treason, which must be laid before Congress in two copies (or perhaps printed, which would take 10 days)."[479]

President Jefferson wrote Prosecutor Hay on October 11, 1807: "As I understand by the newspapers that the examination of the witnesses in Burr's case & that of the other persons accused is closing, I/we must collect as early a communication as possible of the proceedings & evidence. Congress being so near meeting, and a copy being to be made out so that each House may have one, it is evident we shall have no time to spare. If your copy for us is not wholly ready, perhaps you could send it by peace-meal as it is ready, which would enable us to be forwarding it, in the same way...."[480] President Jefferson urgently desired to carry his battle against the judiciary and Chief Justice John Marshall to the Republican controlled Congress.

Hay responded:

> Your letter of the 11th inst. did not reach me until yesterday morning after the departure of the mail.
>
> A copy of the proceedings accompanied by the Judges opinions will be forwarded in a few days. The latter taken from the Gazette in which they were published by the Editor, who received the original manuscript from the hands of the Judge, may be, I presume, sufficiently authenticated by the Printer himself. Mr. Henning whom I

---

478 Caesar Rodney to Thomas Jefferson, October 1, 1807. *The Thomas Jefferson Papers*, Library of Congress digital. American Memory.

479 Thomas Jefferson to Caesar Rodney, October 8, 1807. *Works X*, pp. 502-503.

480 Thomas Jefferson to George Hay, October 11, 1807, *The Thomas Jefferson Papers*, Library of Congress digital. American Memory.

employed to take down the evidence is busily and constantly employed in transcribing it, and says that he expects to finish his task early next week. I shall urge him, and have already urged him to lose no time in its completion....

Will you pardon me for asking you, whether the island at the Mouth of Cumberland River lies within the ancient limits of Virginia, before the separation of Kentucky, or whether it belonged to North Carolina? I am afraid, if the Judge should commit, the trial may be embarrassed by some plea to the jurisdiction of the Court.—

A correct and perspicuous legal history of this trial would be a valuable document in the hands of intelligent legislators. Among others it might perhaps do mischief. It might produce a sentiment towards all judicial systems and law itself, the operation of which might perhaps be fatal to the tranquility and good order of society...[481]

George Hay again wrote President Jefferson on October 21, 1807:

I have forwarded by the mail which comes this letter, Bollman's communications and letters. They are under a cover addressed to yourself.

I have sent to the Attorney General all the evidence that has been exhibited in the prosecutions with perhaps two or three exceptions. The deficiency will be supplied as soon as the notes can be corrected, transcribed, and printed. I also expect to send printed copies of the several opinions delivered by the Chief Justice, the last case that will be soon forwarded.

The Chief Justice on the final motion to commit, again decided, that there has been no overt act of levying war: but, he committed Burr and Blennerhassett for misdemeanors to be tried in Ohio. Burr was disappointed, and exasperated. He was rude and insulting to the Judge.

I am inclined to believe, after these repeated expositions of the law of treason, by the Chief Justice, that the conviction of Burr and his associates of that offence cannot be expected—...

I think it no more than justice to inform you that the Chief Justice, who has been an eye witness of the incessant labor and fatigue which the Counsel for the U.S. have undergone and who knows the sacrifice which they have made for so many months of all their business in the other courts and even in their offices, and who could have no sentiment towards me either personal or political, which could mislead his judgment, has under the Act of Congress allowed me a fee of $2000—This will probably seem a large sum to you; but I

---

481 George Hay to Thomas Jefferson, October 15, 1807, *The Thomas Jefferson Papers*, Library of Congress digital. American Memory.

assure you most solemnly, that I would not again undergo the same labor, fatigue, and anxiety, for twice the amount; and I do conscientiously believe that if Wirt should receive the same sum, his compensation will be trivial indeed, after deducting what he would have made in the regular course of his business. Mr. MacRae's sacrifices probably have not been too great, but his zeal has been sincere and his attention without remission.—To leave the admission of this letter by the mail tomorrow, I must conclude it here—I shall again have occasion to trouble you—[482]

On October 21, 1807, Chief Justice Marshall delivered his final opinion in the Burr case. The Court committed Burr and Blennerhassett for violation of the Neutrality Act. Both were later indicted in Ohio in January, 1808; however, the government never proceeded with these cases. Marshall concluded his final opinion with this observation: "If those whose province and duty it is to prosecute offenders against the laws of the United States shall be of the opinion that a crime of deeper dye has been committed, it is at their choice to act in conformity with that opinion..."[483]

---

482 George Hay to Thomas Jefferson, October 21, 1807, *The Thomas Jefferson Papers*, Library of Congress digital. American Memory.
483 *PJM* VII, pp. 151-64.

17. CONCLUSION: AFTERMATH OF THE TRIALS

After the Burr trial concluded, Chief Justice Marshall was hung in effigy in Baltimore together with Burr, Blennerhassett, and Martin. President Jefferson and Congress proposed changes to the Judiciary; none were adopted. The authority of the Court was never again challenged by the Jefferson Administration. The Judicial Branch was now a co-equal partner with the Executive and Legislative Branches.[484]

Marshall wrote a colleague after the Burr trial:

> Among the very few agreeable occurrences of the last nine months was your letter....
>
> I have as yet been able only to peep into the book, not to read many of the cases. I received it while fatigued & occupied with the most unpleasant case which has ever been brought before a Judge in this or perhaps in any other country affected to be governed by laws, since the decision of which I have been entirely from home. The day after the commitment of Colonel Burr for a misdemeanor I galloped to the mountains whence I only returned in time to perform my North Carolina circuit which terminates just soon enough to enable me to be here to open the court for the antient dominion. Thus you perceive I have sufficient bodily employment to prevent my mind from perplexing itself about the attentions paid me in Baltimore & elsewhere.
>
> I wish I could have had as fair an opportunity to let the business go off as a jest here as you seem to have had in Pennsylvania: but it was

---

484 Beveridge III, pp. 532-540.

a most deplorably serious & I could not give the subject a different aspect by treating it any manner which was in my power. I might perhaps have made it less serious to myself by obeying the public will instead of the public law & throwing a little more of the sombre upon others.[485]

Chief Justice Marshall was not the only target of criticism for the unsuccessful Burr prosecution; President Jefferson received his share of condemnation. Former United States Attorney Daveiss criticized Jefferson: "But he has long since made his judgment play the whore to his ambition; for I have no doubt he has been intriguing through the instrumentality of the vilest printers and tools for the place he now fills almost ever since the constitution was adopted; and that the character given me of him by the ever to be lamented Hamilton, is that which the historian of the next age will give him—'that he was a man as fond of place and power, and as great a hypocrite as ever lived.'"[486] Blennerhassett wrote: "This performance, together with Judge Marshall's last volume of the *Life of Washington*, exposing the origin and the views of the present Democratic party in power, have by this time, I have no doubt, inspired Jefferson with a more deadly hatred of the Marshall faction than he has ever conceived of all the Burrites that he ever heard of."[487]

In his Seventh Annual Message to Congress, President Jefferson reported:

> I informed Congress at their last session of the enterprises against the public peace, which were believed to be in preparation by Aaron Burr and his associates, of the measures taken to defeat them, and to bring the offenders to justice. Their enterprises were happily defeated by the patriotic exertions of the militia whatever called into action, by the fidelity of the army, and energy of the commander-in-chief in promptly arranging the difficulties presenting themselves on the Sabine, repairing to meet those arising on the Mississippi, and dissipating, before their explosion, plots engendering there. I shall think it my duty to lay before you the proceedings and the evidence publicly exhibited on the arraignment of the principal offenders before the circuit court in Virginia. You will be enabled to judge whether the defect was in the testimony, in the law, or in the administration of the law; and wherever it shall be found, the legislature alone can apply or originate the remedy. The framers of our Constitution certainly supposed they had guarded, as well their

---

485 John Marshall to Richard Peters, November 23, 1807. *PJM* VII, pp. 164-65.
486 J.H. Daveiss. *A View of the President's Conduct, Concerning the Conspiracy of 1806.* Frankfort, KY: Press of Joseph M. Street, 1808. p. 143; Malone 5, p. 356.
487 Blennerhassett Papers, October 27, 1807, pp. 464-466; Malone 5, pp. 355-356.

government against destruction by treason, as their citizens against oppression, under pretence of it: and if these ends are not attained, it is of importance to inquire by what means, more effectual, they may be secured?...[488]

President Jefferson presented Congress with extensive witness statements and testimony together with the opinions of Chief Justice Marshall during the Burr proceedings.[489] Congress was requested by the President to determine what, if anything should be done i.e.–impeachment or a Constitutional amendment restricting the authority and/or terms of federal judges. After President Jefferson submitted his report to Congress, Senator Tiffin of Ohio proposed that the Constitution be amended to limit judges to serve only a term of years and to permit removal of judges by the President upon a vote of two-thirds of the members of both houses of the Legislature. Later, Senator Giles proposed legislation to more precisely define and punish treason. Those who opposed his bill argued that such changes were unconstitutional; only a Constitutional Amendment could changes the Constitutional definition of treason. Neither bill passed Congress.[490]

Before his appointment to the Supreme Court, Representative Joseph Story, a Republican from Massachusetts, described Senator Giles actions in Congress after the Burr treason trial:

> I heard him a day or two since in support of a bill to define treason, reported by himself. Never did I hear such all un-hinging and terrible doctrines. He laid the axe at the root of judicial power, and every stroke might be distinctly felt. His argument was very specious and forensic, sustained with many plausible principles and adorned with various political axioms, designed *ad captandum*. One of its objects was to prove the right of the Legislature to *define* treason. My dear friend, look at the Constitution of the United States and see if any such construction can possibly be allowed! ... He attacked Chief Justice Marshall with insidious warmth. Among other things he said, "I have learned that judicial opinions on this subject are like changeable silks, which vary their colors as they are held up in political sunshine."[491]

In fall 1808, a treason trial was convened in Federal Court in Vermont. *United States v. Hoxie*[492] further restricted the law of treason. That Court held

---

488 Seventh Annual Message, October 27, 1807. Writings, Volume III, pp. 444-45.
489 Library of Congress digital, The Annals of Congress, Senate, 10th Congress, pp. 386-778.
490 17 *Annals of Congress* 21, 108-33; Smith, p. 641, n. 146.
491 Adams, pp. 1068-69, citing Story, *Life and Letters of Joseph Story*, I, 158-59.
492 26 F. Cas. 397 (C.C.D. Vt. 1808), Federal Case No. 15407.

that treason could not be employed as a weapon to enforce federal laws. Justice Livingston opined: "No single act in opposition to or in evasion of a law, however violent or flagrant, when the object is private gain, can be construed into levying war against the United States."[493]

JEFFERSON'S OPINION ABOUT THE TRIAL IN LATER YEARS

President Jefferson wrote a number of letters that explained events in the Burr prosecution from his perspective. In a letter to Doctor James Brown on October 27, 1808, President Jefferson expressed frustration that Burr and others had not received the punishment they deserved:

> I wish it were possible to extend my belief of innocence to a very different description of men on New Orleans; but I think there is sufficient evidence of there being a set of foreign adventurers, & native mal-contents, who would concur in any enterprise to separate that country from this. I did wish to see these people get what they deserved; and under the maxim of the law itself, that *inter silent leges* (in times of war, the laws are silent), that in an encampment expecting daily attack from a powerful enemy, self-preservation is paramount to all law, I expected that instead of invoking the forms of law to cover traitors, all good citizens would have concurred in securing them. Should we have ever gained our Revolution, if we had bound our hands by manacles of the law, not only in the beginning, but in any part of the revolutionary conflict? There are extreme cases where the laws become inadequate even to their own preservation, and where, the universal resource is a dictator, or martial law. Was New Orleans in that situation? Although we knew here that the force destined against it was suppressed on the Ohio, yet we supposed this unknown at New Orleans at the time that Burr's accomplices were calling in the aid of the law to enable them to penetrate its suppression, and that it was reasonable according to the state of information there, to act on the expectation of daily attack. Of this you are the best judge.

> Burr is in London, and is giving out to his friends that that government offers him 2 Millions of dollars the moment he can raise an ensign of rebellion as big as a handkerchief. Some of his partisans will believe this, because they wish it. But those who know him best will not believe he says it. For myself, even in his most flattering periods of the conspiracy, I never entertained one moment's fear. My long & intimate knowledge of my countrymen, satisfied & satisfies me, that let there ever be occasion to display the banners of the law, & the world will see how few & pitiful are those who shall array themselves in opposition....[494]

---

493 Ibid.; Smith, p. 374.
494 Thomas Jefferson to Doctor James Brown, October 27, 1808. *Works* XI, pp. 52-55.

In March 1809, President Jefferson purchased a copy the transcript of the Burr trial.[495] Jefferson later wrote Hay in 1810: "I hope our practice in this country relieves us from the special plea which Mr. Rodney speaks of. This would place everything under the grip of the judge, who in the cases of *Marbury* & of Burr has given us lessons of the plastic nature of law in his hands. To him nothing is to be ultimately submitted...."[496]

On September 20, 1810, former President Jefferson responded to a letter from John Colvin. Colvin requested that Jefferson respond to the following question: Are there not periods where, in free government, it is necessary for officers in responsible situations to exercise an authority beyond the law— and was not the tie of Burr's treason such a period? Jefferson responded:

> The question you propose, Whether circumstances do not some-times occur which make it a duty in officers of high trust to assume authorities beyond the law, is easy of solution in principle, but sometimes embarrassing in practice. A strict observance of the writ-ten laws is doubtless *one* of the high duties of a good citizen, but it is not the *highest*. The law of necessity, of self-preservation, of saving our country when in danger, are of higher obligation. To lose our country by a scrupulous adherence to written law, would be to lose the law itself, with life, liberty, property & all those who are enjoy-ing them with us; thus absurdly sacrificing the end to the means....
>
> ... To proceed to the conspiracy of Burr, & particularly to General Wilkinson's situation in New Orleans. In judging this case we are bound to consider the state of the information, correct and incor-rect, which he then possessed. He expected Burr and his band from above, a British fleet from below, and he knew there was a formi-dable conspiracy within the city. Under these circumstances, was he justifiable: 1. In seizing notorious conspirators? On this there can be but two opinions; one, of the guilty & their accomplices; and the other, that of all honest men. 2. In sending them to the seat of gov-ernment when the law gave them a right to trial in the territory? The danger of their rescue, of their continuing their machinations, the tardiness and weakness of the law, apathy of the judges, active patronage of the whole tribe of lawyers, unknown disposition of the juries, an hourly expectation of the enemy, salvation of the city, and of the Union itself, which would have been convulsed to its center, had that conspiracy succeeded, all these constituted a law of neces-sity & self-preservation, and rendered the *salus populi* supreme over the written law. The officer who is called to act on this superior ground, does indeed risk himself on the justice of the controlling powers of the Constitution, and his station makes it his duty to

---

495 Account with bookseller Joseph Milligan, March 8-10, 1809. *PTJ-Retirement* 1, pp. 35-38.
496 Thomas Jefferson to George Hay, June 18, 1810. *PTJ-Retirement* 2, pp. 473-474.

incur that risk. But those controlling powers and his fellow citizens generally, are bound to judge according to the circumstances under which he acted. They are not to transfer the information of this place or moment to the time & place of his action; but to put themselves in that situation. We knew here that there never was danger of a British fleet from below, & that Burr's band was crushed before it reached the Mississippi. But General Wilkinson's information was very different, and he could act on no other.[497]

Thomas Jefferson wrote Gideon Granger in 1814, describing the events that led him to distrust Burr:

"[T]hat in 1806, I communicated by the first mail after I had gained knowledge of the fact, the supposed plans of Burr in his Western expedition; upon which communication your council was first called together to take measures in relation to that subject."—not exactly in that single communication. On the 15th and 18th of September, I had received letters from Colonel George Morgan, and from Mr. Nicholson of New York, suggesting in a general way the maneuvers of Colonel Burr. Similar information came to the Secretary of State from a Mr. Williams of New York. The indications, however, were so vague that I only desired their increased attention to the subject, and further communications of what they should discover. Your letter of October 16, conveying the communications of General Eaton to yourself and to Mr. Ely gave a specific view of the objects of this new conspiracy, and corroborating our previous information. I called the Cabinet together, on the 22nd of October, when specific measures were adopted for meeting the dangers threatened in the various points in which they might occur....[498]

The earlier warnings from Daveiss, Truxton, and others were, once again, either ignored or made little or no impression upon President Jefferson.

In a letter to John Adams in 1814, Thomas Jefferson wrote:

And I dare say our cunning Chief Justice [Marshall] would swear to, and find as many sophisms to twist it out of the general terms of our Declarations of rights, and even the stricter text of the Virginia "act for freedom of religion" as he did to twist Burr's neck out of the halter of treason. May we not say then with him who was all candor and benevolence "woe unto you, ye lawyers, for ye lade men with burdens grievous to bear."[499]

On June 26, 1822, Thomas Jefferson wrote Mrs. Katherine Duane Morgan:

---

497 Thomas Jefferson to John Colvin, September 20, 1810. *PTJ-Retirement* 3, pp. 99-101.

498 Thomas Jefferson to Gideon Granger, March 9, 1814. *PTJ-Retirement* 7, pp. 234-238.

499 Thomas Jefferson to John Adams, January 24, 1814. *PTJ-Retirement* 7, pp. 146-151.

...Your connection too with the family of the late Colonel Morgan is an additional title to my grateful recollection. He first gave us notice of the mad project of that day, which if suffered to proceed, might have brought afflicting consequences on persons whose subsequent lives have proved their integrity and loyalty to their country...[500]

IMPACT OF THE BURR TRIAL

Historians have written about the Burr trial for years. Although most criticize President Jefferson and some criticize Chief Justice Marshall, virtually all agree there was insufficient evidence at trial to convict Burr. The prosecution was outmatched and outmaneuvered by the defense. The trial judge strictly construed evidence and insured that the rights of the accused were protected. In the end, a brave judge heard the Burr case and did not surrender to public sentiment or government demands.

It is legally certain, based upon trial evidence, that Burr did not commit treason. However, did Burr intend to commit treason? In the opinion of historian Milton Lomask, the answer is no.[501] We will never know for sure Burr's intent since there are so many gaps in the record. At the time of trial in 1807, much evidence was unknown or unavailable—i.e. Wilkinson's dealings with Spain, Burr's dealings with Ambassador Merry of Great Britain, and the origin of the cipher letter. Many of Burr's letters and records were lost at sea when his daughter tragically died in a shipwreck. Years later, Burr responded to his biographer's question about whether he intended to sever the Union. Burr stated: "Mo, I would as soon have thought of taking possession of the moon, and informing my friends that I intended to divide it among them." His objectives were to "*First*, the Revolutionizing of Mexico, and *Second*, a settlement on what was known as the Bastrop lands."[502]

The treason trial was not only a test of wills between two powerful men, President Thomas Jefferson and Chief Justice John Marshall. In the end, it was a Judge who strictly construed the law in a criminal prosecution in contradistinction to governmental officials who advocated a loose construction. A judge who took his oath of office seriously, believing it his responsibility to ensure that a criminal defendant, no matter how despicable

---

500 Thomas Jefferson to Katherine Duane Morgan, June 26, 1822. *Works* XII, pp. 291-292.
501 Lomask II, p. xiii.
502 Lomask II, 5.

and no matter the public sentiment, was protected from the government by rights guaranteed by the Constitution and the Bill of Rights.

In contrast, President Jefferson's actions in the Burr case—implicating Burr, declaring his guilt without benefit of trial and orchestrating the prosecution, were not those of one who sought justice. Rather, Jefferson's actions were those of someone who sought to ignore Constitutional protections at the cost of a citizen's life. Jefferson's betrayal of Bollman, his declaration of Burr's guilt without charge or trial, his attempt to charge defense attorney Luther Martin as a co-conspirator, and the numerous letters written to Prosecutor Hay and others displayed a vengeful intent; clearly Jefferson's actions were not those of an avowed and honored civil libertarian. Jefferson, throughout the proceedings, not only wanted Burr to be convicted but wanted to limit the authority of the Judiciary. In the Burr case, Jefferson never accepted the duty of the Court to insist upon proof beyond a reasonable doubt before pronouncing a defendant guilty. Most importantly, Thomas Jefferson failed to heed the adage: "facts are stubborn things."

Typical perceptions about Thomas Jefferson and John Marshall were reversed in the Burr trial. The Thomas Jefferson that history lauds as a champion of individual rights and liberties is the same man who publicly declared Burr guilty before he was arrested and indicted, let alone convicted. Thomas Jefferson ignored the fact that his commanding general denied *writs of habeas corpus* and other constitutional guarantees to United States citizens. He unleashed the full power and resources of the Federal government to convict Burr. A biographer of Andrew Jackson, Robert V. Remini, wrote: "During the entire conspiracy and the subsequent trial Jefferson acted badly. His spite and his desire for revenge—not fear for the safety of the Union—drove him to persecute Burr. He overreacted to the conspiracy: he claimed more in the way of a potential danger than actually existed. From start to finish his was a disgraceful performance."[503] Jefferson, as was his wont, never admitted mistakes and cast his lot with the greatest scoundrel in the case, General James Wilkinson. Without Jefferson's support of Wilkinson, there would have been no case against Burr. Jefferson discredited himself by blindly supporting this dishonorable man.

Chief Justice John Marshall has historically been portrayed as a protector of property rights and commercial interests and an advocate for a

---

503 Robert V. Remini. *Andrew Jackson and the Course of American Empire 1767-1821.* Volume 1. New York: Harper & Row, Publishers,1977, p. 157.

strong federal government. In the Burr case, Marshall showed himself as a civil libertarian who protected individual rights against an overzealous government. Marshall had no reason to protect Burr, other than in his capacity as judge. Not only did Burr kill Alexander Hamilton in a dual, a man admired by Marshall, but Burr was charged with treason, a crime that the Chief Justice despised. Chief Justice Marshall's contempt for traitors, particularly General Benedict Arnold and Major Andre, may be found in the biography he wrote, *The Life of Washington*, Volume III, where he commented about how Arnold betrayed the American cause and became a general in the British army:

> Yet it is impossible that rank could have rescued him from the contempt and detestation in which the generous, the honorable, and the brave, could not cease to hold him. It was impossible for men of this description to bury the recollection of his being a traitor, a sordid traitor, first the slave of his rage, then purchased with gold, and finally secured at the expense of the blood of one of the most accomplished officers in the British army.[504]

Irving Brant, biographer of James Madison and hardly a Marshall supporter, wrote:

> Although Marshall's political animus was evident, his fundamental rulings were sound. As treason is defined in the Constitution, a man may commit it by adhering to the country's wartime enemies, or, during war or peace, by "levying war" against the United States. Marshall held rigidly to this definition, and also to the requirement that the crime be proved either by confession in open court or by "the testimony of two witnesses to the same act".

> Combining the testimony in court with the contents of the British and Spanish archives, it is clear that Burr's purposes were treasonable. But his actions were not. Lack of support for the traitorous features of the conspiracy caused him to omit them before any overt act of treason was committed, and warranted the verdict of acquittal. In the long run, Marshall's rejection of "constructive treason" far outweighed the evil of letting a villain escape punishment.[505]

Chief Justice Marshall performed remarkably well in the Burr case. When he made a mistake, he corrected it immediately. He treated all who came before his Court with respect, including attorneys who surely must

---

504 John Marshall. *The Life of George Washington*. Volume III, pp. 264-66.
505 Irving Brant, *James Madison, Secretary of State 1801-1809*, Volume IV. New York: Bobbs-Merrill, 1953, p. 357.

have tested his patience. Marshall upheld the rule of law and ironically saved President Jefferson from himself.

Two former Supreme Court Justices, among others, have praised John Marshall's performance in the Burr trial. Chief Justice Earl Warren said: "[Marshall's] sense of duty is epitomized by the trial of Aaron Burr, which he conducted fearlessly in spite of the intense feeling of the public and the national Administration against the defendant."[506] Associate Justice Harold Burton praised Marshall's judicial courage and demeanor, his seriousness and evenhandedness in presiding over the Burr trial. He referred to Marshall as "the guardian of liberty."[507] There can be no greater tribute.

---

506 Address of Chief Justice Earl Warren. 78th Convention of the American Bar Association, August 24, 1955.
507 Harold H. Burton. "Justice the Guardian of Liberty: John Marshall and the Trial of Aaron Burr." *American Bar Association Journal*, Volume 37, p. 735 (1951).

ACKNOWLEDGEMENTS

I wish to thank many for their support and assistance with this project. The librarians at the Carrie Rich Library at Campbell University in Buies Creek, North Carolina, particularly Anita Brown, were extremely helpful. The staff of the Campbell University Norman A. Wiggins School of Law in Raleigh, North Carolina was of great assistance, particularly Vice Dean B. Keith Faulkner and Professor and Director of the Library Olivia L. Weeks. The librarians at Sandhills Community College Library (Boyd Library) in Pinehurst, North Carolina were always helpful and provided great assistance. Finally, I appreciate the time and information provided by Mark Greenough, historian at the Virginia State Capitol and portrayer of John Marshall, for his knowledge about John Marshall and the Aaron Burr trial.

Family members have encouraged this project. Thanks to my sister, Marilyn Sue (Mimi) Sturgell, and her husband Brian who have always been supportive. Thanks also to Mimi and Brian's wonderful daughters, Laurie Knowles and Stacey Iofredo and their husbands, Nathan and Matt. Finally, thanks to my wife's parents, Ed and Joann Cannon, and her sister, Vicki Bates and Vicki's husband Kim, for their support and encouragement throughout the years.

This book is dedicated to my parents Ruth and Don Zellar, my wife Conni, and my son Ryan. I am fortunate to have two such wonderful parents. They have always provided encouragement, from sports and education, through my career as a lawyer, and now for this project.

My son Ryan, a recent graduate of law school and now a practicing at-torney in North Carolina, is my soul mate in the love of history. His un-dergraduate research paper was the original inspiration for this book. Throughout this project, he has offered encouragement and provided help-ful thoughts and perspectives.

My wife Conni has not only been incredibly understanding throughout this project, but has served as chief proofreader, editor, computer expert and assisted me in processing my thoughts. She has persevered without complaint, not only during this project, but throughout our marriage.

Bibliographic Sketch

During the course of my research, I consulted numerous original and secondary sources. Rather than provide an exhaustive list of all works reviewed, a sketch of the most useful publications follows.

Thomas Jefferson

Primary Sources

Thomas Jefferson was a compulsive letter writer. He kept everything; it is thought that there are more than 19,000 letters extant. Jefferson believed that it was so important to retain his letters that he used an early device (known as a polygraph) to copy his letters.

The Papers of Thomas Jefferson (PTJ) has become the pre-eminent source for Jefferson's letters and documents. *The Papers* currently consist of thirty-seven volumes from 1760 to June 30, 1802. There are two problems. First, beyond the editors' control, many of Jefferson's earliest letters are unavailable due to a fire at Jefferson's Shadwell home. The other relates to the sheer volume and location of the Jefferson's papers. The Editors have been working on this project since at least 1950; *The Papers*, at present, take us through the early months of Jefferson's second year as President. As a result, important events such as the investigation and prosecution of Aaron Burr, the impeachments of Judge John Pickering and Justice Samuel Chase, and the *Marbury v. Madison* opinion are yet to be recorded in *The Papers*.

In 2004, *The Papers of Thomas Jefferson – Retirement Series (PTJ-RS)* were first published to expedite the process of collecting Jefferson's papers and writings. This series now has seven published volumes which cover Jefferson's post presidential years. This series begins in March 1809 and presently takes us through September 1814. Unfortunately, *The Papers of Thomas Jefferson* does not yet cover July 1, 1802 to March 4, 1809, and October 1814 to Thomas Jefferson's death on July 4, 1826.

The Papers of Thomas Jefferson. (Volumes 1–37). Julian Boyd, et al. Editors. Princeton: Princeton University Press, 1950—.

The Papers of Thomas Jefferson, Retirement Series. (Volumes 1–7). J. Jefferson Looney, Editor. Princeton: Princeton University Press, 2004–.

There are several sources available for missing Jefferson papers. The Thomas Jefferson Papers Collection at the Library of Congress is available online at: http://memory.loc.gov/ammem/collections/jefferson_papers/.

This site was of great assistance in locating letters written during the period of this book. In particular, letters written to President Jefferson by Prosecutor George Hay and William Branch Giles were located. Unfortunately, these letters were not transcribed. Therefore, I had to transcribe the letters from the handwriting of the letters.

Two older compilations of Jefferson writings were useful: *The Works of Thomas Jefferson.* Federal Edition. (Works) Paul Leicester Ford, Editor. New York: G.P. Putnam's Sons. 1904–05 (Twelve Volumes) and *The Writings of Thomas Jefferson Writings).* Albert Ellery Bergh and Andrew A. Lipscomb, Editors. Washington, D.C.: The Thomas Jefferson Foundation, 1905. I found Ford's work more useful and reliable. His work may be found online at: http://oll.libertyfund.org/?option=com_staticxt&staticfile=show. php%3Ftitle=1734.

There are several other collections of note: Correspondence between Thomas Jefferson and James Madison. James Morton Smith. Republic of Letters; The Correspondence between Thomas Jefferson and James Madison, 1776–1826 (3 volumes). New York: W. W. Norton & Company, 1995.

Correspondence between Thomas Jefferson and John and Abigail Adams. Lester J. Cappon. *The Adams–Jefferson Letters.* Chapel Hill: University of North Carolina Press, 1959.

General collection of Jefferson's papers. *Thomas Jefferson: Writings.* Peterson, Merrill D., Editor. New York: Literary Classics of the United States, Inc., 1984.

Finally, although Jefferson never wrote a complete autobiography, several of his writings are of particular note:

The Autobiography of Thomas Jefferson, 1743–1790. Paul Leicester Ford, Editor. Philadelphia: University of Pennsylvania Press, 2005.

The Complete Anas of Thomas Jefferson. Franklin B. Swivel, Editor. New York: The Round Table Press, 1903, pp. 237–241.

Notes on the State of Virginia. David Waldstreicher, Editor. New York: Bedford/ St. Martin's, 2002.

Secondary Sources

Books and articles about Thomas Jefferson are exhaustive. There are, however, several works I found particularly useful:

The premier biography of Thomas Jefferson is Dumas Malone's six volume *Jefferson and His Time.*

Jefferson and His Time: Jefferson the Virginian. Volume 1. Boston: Little, Brown and Company, 1948.

Jefferson and His Time: Jefferson and the Rights of Man. Volume 2. Boston: Little, Brown and Company, 1951.

Jefferson and His Time: Jefferson and the Order of Liberty. Volume 3. Boston: Little, Brown and Company, 1962.

Jefferson and His Time: Jefferson the President First Term 1801–1805. Volume 4. Boston: Little, Brown and Company, 1970.

Jefferson and His Time: Jefferson the President Second Term 1805–1809, Volume 5. Boston: Little, Brown and Company, 1974.

Jefferson and his Time: The Sage of Monticello. Volume 6. Boston: Little, Brown and Company, 1981.

Other works of note:

Joseph J. Ellis. *American Sphinx: The Character of Thomas Jefferson.* New York: Alfred A. Knopf, 1996. An excellent book. The author has a great ability to "turn a phrase."

Leonard W. Levy. *Jefferson and Civil Liberties: The Darker Side.* Chicago: Ivan R. Dee, Inc. 1989. A guide book for this book. This is a Jefferson with whom few are familiar.

David N. Mayer. *The Constitutional Thought of Thomas Jefferson.* Charlottesville:

University of Virginia Press, 1994. Excellent treatment of Jefferson's "different" ideas about the Constitution.

Forrest McDonald. *The Presidency of Thomas Jefferson*. Lawrence: University Press of Kansas, 1976.

Peter S. Onuf, editor. *Jeffersonian Legacies*. Charlottesville: University Press of Virginia, 1993.

Peter S. Onuf. *The Mind of Thomas Jefferson*. Charlottesville: University of Virginia Press, 2007.

Merrill D. Peterson *The Jeffersonian Image in the American Mind*. New York: Oxford University Press, 1960.

Merrill D. Peterson *Thomas Jefferson and the New nation: A Biography*. New York: Oxford University Press, 1970.

James F. Simon. *What Kind of Nation: Thomas Jefferson, John Marshall, and the Epic Struggle to Create a United States*. New York: Simon & Schuster, 2002. Another guidebook. This book is more of a survey of the Jefferson–Marshall battles, not only during Jefferson's eight year presidency, but during the entirety of their careers.

JOHN MARSHALL

Primary Sources

The writings of John Marshall are not nearly as extensive as those of Jefferson. Marshall's writings are compiled in twelve volumes. *The Papers of John Marshall (PJM)*, Volumes I–XII. Edited by Herbert A. Johnson, Charles F. Hobson, et al. Chapel Hill: The University of North Carolina Press, 1974–2006. This is an excellent series and includes a number of useful notes. Marshall was not as interested as Jefferson in retaining his writings and letters. We know that, late in life, he destroyed a number of documents. John Marshall to Joseph Story, April 24, 1833. *PJM* XII, pp. 272-273.

At the request of Justice Story, John Marshall prepared a brief autobiography that ends with his appointment to the Supreme Court by President John Adams. *"The Events of My Life": An Autobiographical Sketch of John Marshall*. Lee C. Bollinger and John C. Dann, Editors. Washington, D.C.: Supreme Court Historical Society, 2001.

Secondary Sources

There are far fewer biographies about Marshall than Jefferson. I found the following biographies useful:

Albert J. Beveridge. *The Life of John Marshall*. 4 volumes. Boston: Houghton Mifflin Company, 1916–1919. This is the pre-eminent Marshall biography. Although biased in Marshall's favor and clearly anti-Jefferson, it is well researched and stands the test of time.

Leonard Baker. *John Marshall: A Life in Law*. New York: Macmillan Publishing Co., Inc., 1974. Somewhat cumbersome, but a solid biography.

Charles F. Hobson. *The Great Chief Justice: John Marshall and the Rule of Law*. Lawrence: University Press of Kansas, 1996. An excellent insight into John Marshall by the primary editor of *The Papers of John Marshall.*

R. Kent Newmyer. *John Marshall and the Heroic Age of the Supreme Court.* Baton Rouge: Louisiana State University Press, 2001. A fine biography from a legal perspective by a law professor.

David Robarge. *A Chief Justice's Progress: John Marshall from Revolutionary Virginia to the Supreme Court.* Contributions in American History Series, Number 185. Westport: Greenwood Press, 2000. Good presentation of Marshall's early life.

James F Simon. *What Kind of Nation: Thomas Jefferson, John Marshall, and the Epic Struggle to Create a United States.* New York: Simon & Schuster, 2002. See, Jefferson.

Jean Edward Smith. *John Marshall: Definer of a Nation.* New York: H. Holt and Co., 1996. Perhaps the best Marshall biography since Beveridge's.

Melvin Urofsky. Thomas Jefferson and John Marshall: What Kind of Constitution Shall We Have? *Journal of Supreme Court History*, 31:2, (2006), pp. 109-125.

AARON BURR AND THE BURR CONSPIRACY

Primary Sources

Trial of Aaron Burr. New York: James Cockcroft & Company, 1875. (Transcription of the trial by David Robertson.) This transcription, in two volumes, may be found online at http://books.google.com/books?id=Y408AAAAIAAJ&pg=PA460&dq=Robertson+on+Burr+trial+Volume+I#v=onepage&q&f=false.

T. Carpenter. *The Trial of Col. Aaron Burr.* (Short hand of Carpenter). Washington City: Westcott & Co., 1808. Another transcription of the Burr trial.

The Library of Congress, in its Annals of Congress, houses numerous witness statements and other documents from the Burr trial. This information may found online at the Library of Congress website.

Secondary Sources

Numerous works are available that provide accounts of the Burr trial, together with biographies of Aaron Burr and General James Wilkinson:

Burr Trial

Thomas Perkins Abernathy. *The Burr Conspiracy.* New York: Oxford University Press, 1954.

Harmon Blennerhassett. *The Blennerhassett Papers.* William Safford, editor. Cincinnati: Moore, Wilstach & Baldwin, 1864.

Washington Irving. *The Life and Letters of Washington Irving.* Pierre M. Irving, Editor. London: Richard Bentley.Publisher, 1862.

Milton Lomask. *Aaron Burr: The Conspiracy and Years in Exile, 1805–1836.* Volume II. New York: Farrar, Straus, and Giroux, 1982. A two-volume biography of Burr. Good treatment of the Burr case.

Walter Flavius McCaleb. *The Aaron Burr Conspiracy and A New Light on Aaron Burr.* New York: Argosy-Antiquarian, LTD., 1966.

Buckner F Melton. *Aaron Burr: Conspiracy to Treason.* New York: John Wiley & Sons, 2002. Very helpful.

Joseph Wheelan. *Jefferson's Vendetta: The Pursuit of Aaron Burr and the Judiciary.* New York: Carroll & Graff, 2005. A good, recent treatment of the Burr trial.

Louis B. Wright and Julia H. MacLeod. "William Eaton's Relations with Aaron Burr." *The Mississippi Valley Historical Review,* Vol. 31, No. 4 (March, 1945), pp. 523-536.

Aaron Burr

Correspondence and Public Papers of Aaron Burr, Volume II. Mary-Jo Kline, Editor. Princeton: Princeton University Press, 1983. Ms. Kline has some excellent insights into the Burr prosecution.

Matthew L. Davis. *Memoirs of Aaron Burr, Volume II.* New York: Da Capo Press, 1971. (First published in 1836).

Nancy Isenberg. *Fallen Founder; The Life of Aaron Burr.* New York: Viking Penguin Group, 2007. An excellent, recent biography on Burr; paints him in a more favorable light.

Nathan Schachner. *Aaron Burr: A Biography.* New York: A. S. Barnes & Company, Inc., 1961.

James Wilkinson

Thomas Robson Hay and M.R. Werner. *The Admirable Trumpeter: A Biography of General James Wilkinson*. Garden City, NY: Doubleday, Doran & Company, Inc., 1941.

Andro Linklater. *An Artist in Treason: The Extraordinary Double Life of General James Wilkinson*. New York: Walker Publishing Company, 2009). Recent biography.

General James Wilkinson. *Memoirs of My Own Times*. Volume II. Philadelphia: Abraham Small, 1816.

LEGAL ISSUES

Adoption of Constitution/ Judiciary Prior to 1801

Richard Beeman. *Plain, Honest Men: The Making of the American Constitution*. New York: Random House, 2009.

William R. Casto. *The Supreme Court in the Early Republic: The Chief Justiceships of John Jay and Oliver Ellsworth*. Columbia, SC: University of South Carolina Press, 1995.

Richard Ellis. *The Jeffersonian Crisis: Courts and Politics in the Young Republic*. New York: Oxford University Press, 1971.

Stanley Elkins and Eric McKitrick. *The Age of Federalism: The Early American Republic, 1788–1800*. New York: Oxford University Press, 1993.

The Federalist Papers. Clinton Rossiter, editor. New York: The New American Library of World Literature, Inc., 1961.

Julius Goebel, Jr. *History of the Supreme Court of the United States: Antecedents and Beginnings to 1801*. The Oliver Wendell Holmes Devise, Volume I. New York: The Macmillan Company, 1971.

Pauline Maier. *Ratification: The People Debate the Constitution, 1787–1788*. New York: Simon & Schuster, 2010. An outstanding work on the Ratification debates utilizing the work of *The Documentary History of the Ratification of the Constitution* project.

Maeva Marcus, Editor. *The Documentary History of the Supreme Court of the United States, 1789–1800*. New York: Columbia University Press, 1992, Volumes 1–8. Excellent work supported by the Supreme Court Historical Society.

David O. Stewart. *The Summer of 1787: The Men Who Invented the Constitution*. New York: Simon and Schuster Paperbacks, 2007.

Impeachment

Trial of Samuel Chase. Taken in short-hand by Samuel H. Smith and Thomas Lloyd. Volumes I & II. Washington City: Printed for Samuel Smith, 1805. May be found online.

Peter Charles Hoffer, and N.E.H. Hull. *Impeachment in America, 1635–1805.* New Haven: Yale University Press, 1984.

Richard B. Lillach "The Chase Impeachment." *American Journal of Legal History*, Vol. 4, No. 1 (Jan.1960), pp.49-72.

Lynn W. Turner "The Impeachment of John Pickering." *The American Historical Review.* Vol. 54, No. 3 (April, 1949), pp. 485–507. This is the definitive account of this impeachment.

William H. Rehnquist. *Grand Inquests: The Historic Impeachments of Justice Samuel Chase and President Andrew Johnson.* New York: William Morrow and Company, Inc., 1992.

Judiciary Acts

Leonard Baker. "The Circuit Riding Justices." Yearbook 1977 Supreme Court Historical Society.

Joshua Glick. "Comment: On the Road: The Supreme Court and the History of Circuit Riding." Cardozo Law Review, Vol. 24, (April, 2003).

George Lee Haskins and Herbert A. Johnson. History of the Supreme Court of the United States: Foundations of Power: John Marshall, 1801–15. The Oliver Wendell Holmes Devise, Volume II. New York: Macmillan Publishing Co., Inc., 1981. This is a particularly useful account of the early Marshall Court and its conflicts with the Jefferson Administration.

Kathryn Turner. "Federalist Policy and the Judiciary Act of 1801." *The William and Mary Quarterly*, 3rd Series, Volume 22, Number 1 (January, 1965), pp. 3-32. The three articles written by Ms. Turner expertly explain events related to the Judiciary Act of 1801.

Kathryn Turner. "The Appointment of Chief Justice Marshall." *The William and Mary Quarterly*, 3rd Series Volume 17, Number 2 (April, 1960), pp. 143-163.

Kathryn Turner. "The Midnight Judges." *University of Pennsylvania Law Review*, Volume 109, Number 4 (Feb. 1961), pp. 494-523).

Charles Warren. *The Supreme Court in United States History, Volume I.* New York: Little, Brown, and Company, 1922. This volume excellently portrays challenges that confronted the Supreme Court in its early years.

MARBURY V. MADISON

Lawrence Goldstone. *The Activist: John Marshall, Marbury v. Madison, and the Myth of Judicial Review.* New York: Walker & Company, 2008.

Larry D. Kramer. *The People Themselves: Popular Constitutionalism and Judicial Review.* New York: Oxford University Press, 2004.

William E. Nelson *Marbury v. Madison: The Origins and Legacy of Judicial Review.* Lawrence: University Press of Kansas, 2000.

Cliff Sloan and David McKean. *The Great Decision: Jefferson, Adams, Marshall and the Battle for the Supreme Court.* New York: Public Affairs, 2009.

Louise Weinberg. "Our *Marbury.*" Marbury v. Madison: A Bicentennial Symposium. *Virginia Law Review,* Vol. 89, No. 6, (October 2003), pp. 1235-1412.

Gordon S. Wood. *Empire of Liberty: A History of the Early Republic, 1789-1815.* New York: Oxford University Press, 2009. This is an excellent survey of this period. Professor Wood does an excellent job explaining the background and importance of *Marbury v. Madison.* Professor Wood may be the pre-eminent authority for this period of our nation's history.

Gordon S. Wood *The Creation of the American Republic, 1776-1787.* Chapel Hill: University of North Carolina Press, 1998.

TREASON

Bradley Chapin. *The American Law of Treason: Revolutionary and Early National Origins.* Seattle: University of Washington Press, 1964. Very helpful.

L. M. Hill. "The Two-Witness Rule in English Treason Trials: Some Comments on the Emergence of Procedural Law". *The American Journal of Legal History,* Vol. 12, No. 2 (April, 1968), pp. 95-111.

Peter Charles Hoffer. *The Treason Trials of Aaron Burr.* Lawrence: University Press of Kansas, 2008. Well written and researched.

James Willard Hurst. *The Law of Treason in the United States.* Westport, CN: Greenwood Publishing Corporation, 1971.

Richard L. Perry and John C. Cooper, Editors. *Sources of Our Liberties: Documentary Origins of Individual Liberties in the United States Constitution and Bill of Rights.* Chicago: American Bar Foundation, 1978. A good resource for the sources of our rights and liberties.

John C. Yoo. "The First Claim: The Burr Trial, *United States v. Nixon,* and Presidential Power." 83 *Minnesota Law Review* (1999), pp. 1435-1474.

MISCELLANEOUS

Henry Adams. *History of the United States During the Administrations of Thomas Jefferson.* New York: Literary Classics of the United States, Inc., 1986. Adams has an interesting perspective on events.

The Diary of John Quincy Adams, 1794–1845. Allan Nevins, Editor. New York: Charles Scribner's Sons, 1951.

Memoirs of John Quincy Adams. Charles Francis Adams, Editor. Philadelphia: J.B. Lippincott & Co., 1874.

The Writings of John Quincy Adams: 1801–1810. Volume III. Worthington Chauncey Ford, Editor. New York: The Macmillan Company, 1914.

Paul. S. Clarkson and R. Samuel Jett. *Luther Martin of Maryland.* Baltimore: The Johns Hopkins Press, 1970.

Jane Shaffer Elsmere. *Justice Samuel Chase.* Muncie, Indiana: Janevar Publishing Co., 1980.

Robert Kenneth Faulkner. *The Jurisprudence of John Marshall.* Princeton: Princeton University Press, 1968,

Joanne B. Freeman. *Affairs of Honor: National Politics in the New Republic.* New Haven: Yale University Press, 2001. An excellent book. Discusses conflicts between Jefferson and Marshall, Burr and Hamilton.

William Plumer. *William Plumer's Memorandum of Proceedings in the United States Senate.* Everett Somerville Brown, Editor. New York: The MacMillan Company, 1923.

St. George Tucker. *Blackstone's Commentaries: With Notes of Reference to the Constitution of the United States; and the Commonwealth of Virginia.* Volume 5 (1803). Electronic Edition, Lonang Institute, 2003, 2005. www.Lonang.com

Lynn W. Turner. *William Plumer of New Hampshire, 1759–1850.* Chapel Hill: University of North Carolina Press, 1962.

William Wirt. *The Letters of a British Spy.* New York: Harper & Brothers, Publishers, 1875.

INDEX